MAY — 7 2009

Keep

S0-BZB-182

ADDRESS UNKNOWN

The Homeless in America

James D. Wright

With a new introduction
by the author

ALDINETRANSACTION
A Division of Transaction Publishers
New Brunswick (U.S.A.) and London (U.K.)

New material this edition copyright © 2009 by Transaction Publishers, New Brunswick, New Jersey. Original copyright 1989 by Walter de Gruyter., New York.

All rights reserved under International and Pan-American Copyright Conventions. No part of this book may be reproduced or transmitted in any form or by any means, electronic or mechanical, including photocopy, recording, or any information storage and retrieval system, without prior permission in writing from the publisher. All inquiries should be addressed to AldineTransaction, A Division of Transaction Publishers, Rutgers—The State University of New Jersey, 35 Berrue Circle, Piscataway, New Jersey 08854-8042. www.transactionpub.com

This book is printed on acid-free paper that meets the American National Standard for Permanence of Paper for Printed Library Materials.

Library of Congress Catalog Number: 2008055050
ISBN: 978-0-202-36257-1
Printed in the United States of America

Library of Congress Cataloging-in-Publication Data

Wright, James D.
  Address unknown : the homeless in America / James D. Wright.
          p. cm.
  Orginally published: New York : A. de Gruyter, c1989. (Social institutions
    and social change). With new introd.
  Includes bibliographical references and index.
  ISBN 978-0-202-36257-1
    1. Homelessness--United States. I. Title.

HV4505.W75 2009
362.50973--dc22

                                                    2008055050

Contents

3 0053 00858 5849

Introduction to the Transaction Edition[1]

Address Unknown: The Homeless in America was originally published in 1989, the second of three books I have written on homelessness. *Homelessness and Health* was published in 1987; *Beside the Golden Door* appeared in 1998. *Address Unknown* contained my thoughts on the problem of homelessness as of the mid-to-late 1980s; *Beside the Golden Door* updated the story through the middle 1990s, more or less the *Son of Address Unknown* ten years later. The present essay focuses mainly on what we've learned in the ten years since.

The critical reception afforded *Address Unknown* was generally positive and with a few exceptions it seems to me that most of the book has worn reasonably well. So I was generally pleased by the announcement that Transaction Books intended to issue a reprint. Still, an author's introduction to a new edition affords the opportunity to correct earlier misstatements and to refract the original themes and arguments through the lens of two decades of new research.

My first research grant to study homeless issues was awarded by the Robert Wood Johnson Foundation in 1984.[2] Lectures and professional presentations on the topic began showing up on my *vita* early in 1985 and my first published article dealing with homelessness appeared in 1986. So I have been in the homeless business for about 25 years. In that quarter-century, I have written on virtually every conceivable aspect of the problem: on physical and mental health issues; the low income housing supply; addictions and treatment; the number of the homeless; homelessness and race; homelessness and poverty; homeless children in the United States and in Honduras; homeless teens; homeless women; the elderly homeless; homeless veterans; the family backgrounds of homeless people; violence committed by and against the homeless; social service eligibility and utilization; methodological issues in researching the homeless; even the efficacy of ultraviolet air disinfection in reducing the transmission of tuberculosis in facilities for the homeless. Actually, as one of my graduate students recently pointed out, I've only written about a dozen papers on the homeless but I seem to have published each of them five or six times. The same could be said of the material contained in this essay, a fair amount of which has been pirated from my other writings.

THE NUMBER AND TYPES OF HOMELESS PEOPLE

When I was writing *Address Unknown*, the most pressing question people were raising about the homeless was just how many of them there were (an issue Rossi and I joined in our somewhat infamous efforts to count the homeless of Chicago in 1985 and 1986). An internal memo in the US Department of Housing and Urban Development (HUD) from 1984 had suggested, based on some evidence, that the homeless only numbered in the few hundreds of thousands. At the same time, homeless advocates were claiming numbers in the millions, and the war was on. Efforts by the US Census to resolve the issue, somewhat halfheartedly in 1980 and much more aggressively in 1990, did not produce a definitive count—if anything, the Census efforts only fueled the flames of contention.

The discussion of the "numbers" controversy in *Address Unknown* contained a few good guesses but is now otherwise *passé*, perhaps the most dated section of the book and therefore least useful to contemporary readers. The discussion in *Beside the Golden Door* is far more complete, with one entire chapter reviewing the Chicago efforts and the results from Census S-Night in 1990 and a second chapter explaining "Why the Homeless Can't be Counted." Quite contrary to what we assumed for decades, most homelessness is not a chronic condition; much is episodic and recurring, and even more is a one-shot transitional experience. (Studies that have nailed down the relative proportions are reviewed below.) The question, "How many homeless people are there anyhow?" assumes a constancy of condition that the data do not substantiate. The number fluctuates day-to-day, month-to-month, year-to-year.

One important aspect of this inconstancy of numbers, and a possible resolution of the disparities in the reported numbers (or so it seemed at the time), was the obvious difference between the number of homeless people *on any given night* (point prevalence) and the number destined to experience at least one episode of homelessness *in the course of a year* (period incidence). "Homelessness," I wrote, "is a heterogeneous mixture of transitory short term and chronic long-term housing problems" (p. 22). Clearly, one-night counts (such as S-Night was intended to be) will produce much lower numbers than annual counts of service utilizing homeless people (such as one gets when asking a homeless agency how many people they served last year), even when the latter are de-duplicated. The much-disputed HUD number was a compilation of one-night shelter counts in a number of large cities; advocates' counts were often based on annual compilations derived from service providers' records. *Of course,* the latter numbers would be larger and the former smaller.

Rossi and I had uncovered evidence in the Chicago study that showed homelessness to be a mixture of chronic and transitory or episodic housing difficulties. The 1986 survey of Chicago homeless showed that "the modal time homeless in these samples was one month (median, 7.6 months), indicating considerable turnover within the literally homeless population. *It therefore follows that many more people are homeless over a year than are homeless on any given evening.*"[3] Some additional calculations suggested that in Chicago, the ratio of annual to one-night homeless might be on the order of three to one, or possibly even higher.

Address Unknown reviewed the Chicago data and other 80's-era data on the ratio of annual to one night homeless counts, concluding that the ratio was at least 3:1 and possibly closer to 5:1. These ratios are still widely cited, for example, when local Continuum of Care agencies, who do annual "point-in-time" counts of the homeless in their service areas because it is required in funding applications to HUD, attempt to convert the one-night point prevalence data to an annual incidence figure.

Probably the definitive treatment of the "numbers" controversy was the series of studies by Martha Burt and her associates conducted between 1989 and 2001.[4] The final study in this series was based on the National Survey of Homeless Assistance Providers and Clients (NSHAPC), conducted in 1996 and still the closest thing we have to a true national sample of the homeless. Without belaboring the details, Burt's estimate was on the order of a million homeless people on any given night and some three times that number in a typical year. In other words, ~1% of the American population suffers at least one episode of homelessness annually, an astonishing conclusion when you think about it.

Clearly, we and other investigators had intuited by the mid-1980's that the difference between point-prevalence and period-incidence estimates of the number of the homeless was significant, both to understanding the condition of homelessness and formulating a policy response. But it fell to Dennis Culhane and his associates to put a sharp point on the implications and in the process to revolutionize how we looked at the problem and what would be required to solve it.

Culhane and his collaborators published four critically important studies between 1994 and 1999.[5] All four were based on essentially the same data from the same two cities, or on subsequent updates. Sharply in contrast to a long tradition of shelter studies, these studies were *not* one-night shelter surveys, or for that matter, surveys of any sort, but were based, rather, on analyses of administrative data bases focused on patterns of shelter utilization (or admission rates) over time, specifically, over a year. The basic idea behind the research was to follow specific persons over time in the shelter data bases, i.e., to determine how many people of which description were in the shelter every night of the year, most nights of the year, just a few nights or indeed only one night of the year, etc.

All these studies came to the same essential conclusion, namely, *that a relatively small fraction of chronically homeless people—people who tend to remain homeless for long periods of time—consume a relatively large fraction of the total shelter capacity, or "shelter nights."* Most homeless people, that is, are irregular or infrequent shelter utilizers, people whose shelter consumption amounts to a night here, a night there. But some are "frequent flyers," i.e., people who are in the shelters night after night after night.

Culhane and his associates thus came to distinguish among three different kinds of homeless people: the transitionally homeless, the episodically homeless, and the chronically homeless (Kuhn & Culhane, 1998). The *transitionally homeless* are comprised of persons who enter the shelter system due to some calamitous incident, such as job loss, fire, eviction, divorce, or abandonment, etc. These people, by definition, are only homeless for a short time before they "transition" back into a stable housing situation, perhaps never to be homeless again. Remarkably, in studies where this group of homeless people can be identified, they account for the *substantial majority* of the homeless population. In the New York and Philadelphia shelter data specifically, the transitionally homeless accounted for 81% and 78% of the total, respectively, of the homeless studied. The transitionally homeless are generally younger than other groups and have the smallest percentage of non-whites. They are also the least likely to suffer from mental illness and substance abuse.

The *episodically homeless* consist of people who pop in and out of homeless episodes, typically on short time scales. They have many episodes of shelter use that vary in length. The episodically homeless represented 9.1% of the New York clients and 11.7% of the Philadelphia clients in the Kuhn & Culhane study. Illustrating the disordered housing dynamics of episodically homeless people, a study by Sosin and associates of homeless adults in Minneapolis[6] found that 60% went from being homeless to being housed and back to being homeless again in a *single six-month period.* The episodically homeless, like the transitionally homeless, are younger than the chronically homeless but similar to the chronically homeless in terms of substance abuse and mental illness.

Lastly, the *chronically homeless* are people who become homeless and stay in that condition for extended periods of time, often years. They are more likely to be enveloped in the shelter system and to use the shelters as long-term housing rather than emergency shelter. The chronically homeless comprised roughly a tenth of the Kuhn and Culhane samples and yet they consumed about half of the total shelter days. They tend to be older, non-white, and, consistent with HUD's definition of "chronically homeless," they suffer high rates of mental illness and substance abuse.

An essential point, one central to the policy implications that were drawn from this line of research, is that there is a very large disparity between the percentage of homeless people in each of these three groups and the percentage of shelter days consumed by each group. Transitionally homeless people comprise the very large majority of homeless people but because they are homeless only rarely, and then only for short periods, they consume a very small fraction of the total shelter days. The chronically homeless, in contrast, are but a tenth or so of the total but because they are homeless for long periods of time, they consume far more than a tenth of the total shelter days, indeed, about half in the Culhane studies.

The policy implication of these results—implicit in a lot of the research that I and many others did in the 1980's but never made explicit—is that since a small fraction of the homeless consumes a large fraction of the emergency shelter capacity, if permanent housing could be found for that small fraction, the total demand for emergency shelter would drop sharply. And this proved to be the key insight behind what has evolved into a national effort to "end chronic homelessness in ten years," an effort based on an intervention principle known as Housing First!

The Culhane studies and subsequent replications suggest that most adult homeless (on the order of 80%) experience short-term, temporary homelessness and would therefore appear to be candidates for prevention or rapid relocation (rehousing) programs. For them, "Housing First" means finding ways to keep them from entering the shelter system in the first place, or if they happen to enter, getting them out as quickly as possible. Most of them appear to exit homelessness without formal rental assistance anyway or, for that matter, without much in the way of "services" of any kind. Importantly, most do not have significant behavioral health treatment histories or other disabling conditions to complicate their housing search.

As for the chronically homeless, those who have historically lingered in the shelter system for years or even decades, the question must be raised whether emergency shelters are in fact appropriate as long-term housing solutions and even more fundamentally whether time spent in the emergency shelters is the least bit therapeutic in any way. Most people appear to degenerate the longer they linger in the shelters so rather than promoting self-sufficiency, the shelters foster dependence. Here, the evident implication is to build supportive housing, i.e., housing options with critical health and social services attached, then place the chronically homeless in that housing so they might enjoy some modicum of dignified, independent living.

As one Housing First advocate explained the model to me, "We've realized there is very little we can do to make the homeless unpoor, or uncrazy, or unaddicted. So now we focus all our efforts on making them unhomeless. And that seems to be working."

Housing First is very different from the traditional model of providing assistance to homeless people, a model that might be called Treatment First. The traditional approach avoids placing homeless people in housing prematurely, before they are "ready" to assume the responsibilities that housing placement entails. Often, this means extensive psycho-social assessments, individualized treatment plans, then months and months of addiction treatment, mental health counseling, adult education, job readiness and skills training, financial management workshops, housing readiness workshops, and on through a long list. The CEO of a large homeless facility in Florida explained it this way. "Here, we assume that homelessness *per se* is never the problem. Homelessness is the result of other problems. And until we identify and address what those other problems are, we cannot effectively address homelessness."

The ideas behind Housing First—housing homeless people rather than warehousing them in shelters, matching housing resources to individual and family needs, preventing homelessness as much as possible—all seem sensible. At the same time, it is hard to escape the feeling that the model is being oversold by advocates as an all-purpose panacea that will solve all our problems. So it is appropriate to close this discussion by raising some precautions, some obvious and some not.

(1) The Culhane finding (replicated in many studies, including work my group has done in Orlando) is that the long-term homeless make up only 10% of the population, yet consume half the shelter capacity. It has been assumed but not yet demonstrated that they therefore probably consume half of all the resources we spend on homeless people: half the feeding resources, half the addiction and mental health treatment, half the Health Care for the Homeless resources, half of *everything*. And that may or may not be true. Many chronically homeless people who show up each night for shelter are almost pathological in their avoidance of any other service or treatment. So it is not clear that housing the 10% who are chronically homeless will generate a 50% savings in homeless expenditures across the board.

(2) Addressing the housing needs of chronically homeless people is an expensive proposition and is therefore most cost-effective in cities that are already spending a lot to deal with their homeless problem. The classic case in point is New York City, which allegedly spends somewhere around $50,000 per homeless person per year to provide emergency shelter and related support services. In this cost environment, an annual subsidy of $15,000 or even $20,000 to place and keep a homeless person in permanent housing is extremely cost efficient. In a city such as Orlando, and presumably many others, whose annual public expenditure is much less than $1000 per homeless person per year, a subsidy sufficiently large to keep the homeless population permanently housed would represent a very significant *increase* in expenditures on the homeless. And that is often politically problematic.

(3) A focus on housing the *chronically* homeless requires a public commitment to the least attractive, least sympathetic element within the homeless

population—the chronically homeless, addicted, disabled single homeless individual. Many homeless advocacy organizations speak continually about "The Changing Face of Homelessness," emphasizing that the homeless are not just the filthy broken-down alcoholics panhandling on the street corner, that an increasing number are women, children, teens, and families. Public sympathy for women, children, and families is pretty easy to generate. Not so the chronically homeless addiction-disabled single adult male, exactly the group whose homelessness Housing First intends to address.

(4) Many Housing First advocates have become vociferous critics of the shelter system, in many cases to the point of accusing the shelters of *creating*, or helping to create, the homeless problem in the first place. In the sense that many shelters have allowed themselves to evolve into permanent housing for the chronically homeless, the concern is not without foundation. At the same time, all those hundreds of thousands, or millions, of transitionally homeless people who pop in and out of homelessness each year obviously need some port where they can weather the storm, and perhaps even a helping hand to point the way back to shore, and these important functions surely require some sort of emergency overnight shelter system for the days, weeks, or months when transitionally homeless people otherwise have no place to live.

(5) We have known for some time what is required to make homeless prevention programs successful. At the head of the list are housing vouchers to underwrite the housing costs of low income families.[7] In the Burt evaluation, housing subsidies for extremely low income people consistently showed the strongest effects of the five strategies tested. More recent research[8] shows that housing vouchers "are successful in helping families exit homelessness and can protect poor families from becoming homeless" (p. 1). Unfortunately, the Federal government has been backing out of the Housing Choice Voucher (Section 8) program for more than a decade, with the result that voucher waiting lists are now years long in virtually every major market. Absent a renewed federal commitment to deep housing subsidies for low and extremely low income families, homeless prevention devolves into a cruel charade.

(6) Finally, the differences between chronically, episodically, and transitionally homeless people are matters of degree, not of kind. HUD has a definition of "chronically homeless" that has been the subject of much controversy and has recently been modified. Given a sufficiently lousy economy, many episodically homeless people will see the intervals between episodes shortening, and soon enough, the episodes may blur into chronic homelessness. And likewise, given a sufficiently lousy economy, many transitionally homeless people will soon enough find themselves transitioning back and forth often enough to qualify as episodic (and then episodic long enough to qualify as chronic). In the end, these are terribly interesting but also largely

arbitrary distinctions—maybe too arbitrary to provide a firm footing for social policy.

What is clear, in short, is that whatever the distribution across chronic, episodic, and transitional categories today, a poor economy and continuing deterioration of the low income housing supply is perpetually creating new homeless people. No matter how rapidly we can get people to exit the homeless condition, there are legions waiting in the wings of economic uncertainty to take their place.

HOMELESS ETHNOGRAPHY

Address Unknown opened with a chapter on "The Human Faces of Homelessness," a series of short vignettes describing the lives and circumstances of a half dozen homeless people with whom I had become familiar. The express purpose of these vignettes was to "illustrate the diversity of homelessness in contemporary America and show some of the human faces behind the numbers presented later."

Since the book was published, quite a number of accomplished ethnographers have produced (in Kim Hopper's words) "arias of heartbreaking tragedy and quiet heroism." I am speaking, of course, of Jonathon Kozol's *Rachel and Her Children: Homeless Families in America*,[9] a gut-wrenching portrayal of homeless families housed in the Martinique Hotel in New York City (ironically, also the home of Yvette Diaz, the "Child's Face" in my own series of small vignettes); Elliot Liebow's *Tell Them Who I Am: The Lives of Homeless Women*,[10] a study of women living in large "emergency" shelters in Washington, some of them literally for decades (the book is also notable as Liebow's last before his death from cancer in 1994 at age 69); and Hopper's own *Reckoning with Homelessness*,[11] which I regard as the all-time champion of the genre, a *tour de force* that demands (and amply repays) attentive reading, a stunning piece of reflection and self-examination, and as good a book on the subject as has ever been written.

When I set out in 2003 to review Hopper's ethnography, I did a bit of Googling and discovered that there were more than 700 books on homelessness then in print. What more was possibly left to say? *Reckoning with Homelessness* made it plain that there was plenty left to say, that the last chapter in this sad, sorry history of homelessness in America had not yet been written.

As everyone in the homeless business knows, Hopper is an anthropologist whose writings on this "random, visible suffering" date back to the late 70's. (His 1981 report with Ellen Baxter, *Private Lives/Public Spaces*, good bits of which make their way into *Reckoning*, is the first piece of research on the homeless I ever read.) Few who have written on the topic can claim a longer tenure in the field. *Reckoning* is less a research report than a retrospective, a taking stock of the products of a long, compassionate, accomplished career. In the process, Hopper also takes stock of applied anthropology as a discipline, of the history of advocacy in behalf of the homeless, of policies tried and found wanting.

Readers unfamiliar with the terrain will find Hopper a more than capable guide who calls attention to all the usual landmarks: madness and dislocation, housing shortages, hostile communities, a distorted labor economy, how people come to survive on next to nothing, how a life, or a passing semblance of one, can be knitted together from the waste spaces and products of the modern post-industrial city. Those for whom all this is old hat will learn a different but no less important set of lessons: how science and advocacy can co-exist in a single *corpus*, neither subordinate to the other; how an inquisitive mind can spend three decades in the trenches yet remain lucid in its moral purpose; above all, how the grittiest material imaginable can be expressed in a prose style that is lyrical only when not downright poetic. The book has to be among the best-written, most elegantly expressed works of urban anthropology ever.

Hopper's gratifying meander starts as autobiography, spends most of the journey revisiting his prior ethnographic works, and ends with an abrupt "So what?" For all the splendid description that homeless ethnographies have produced, all the fine detail, all the painstaking accounts of toils and troubles, there is, Hopper admits, the dread possibility that none of it has anything to do with solving the problem. What, he asks, are the "practical implications of our parasitic texts?" He argues that "ethnographic work is essentially unfinished if it pulls up short at description and commentary. Engagement must be the complement to witnessing" (p. 205).

No idle chatter, that. In addition to his accomplished scholarly career, Hopper is also a co-founder of both the New York and National Coalitions for the Homeless and has proven a tireless advocate for the disenfranchised and the oppressed. And there have been victories along the way, "some noteworthy—if limited—accomplishments" (p. 207). But Hopper asks whether the small victories even repay the compromise required to achieve them or the effort required to sustain them and has the courage to consider that the answer may well be no. "We gave them names, showed you their faces, ransacked our field notes for arias of heartbreaking tragedy and quiet heroism" and yet in the process "homelessness became domesticated, routine, an all-but-expected feature of the urban landscape" (p. 193). One failure is of special note: "advocacy's neglect to build the broader alliances that could have moved the enlarged agenda" (p. 194). "We manage," Hopper laments, "high-handedly and with great regularity, to annoy our friends and exasperate our constituency" (p. 198). The wonder, then, is not how little has been accomplished, but how much.

Hopper's ethnographic ramble through the makeshift haunts of the world's richest city is inevitably ironic, bitterly painful, unfailingly informative. "Emma's Story" (pp. 12-13) is an elegant recounting of the "but fors" that keep marginal people housed. "For the eight years I knew her, Emma lived a hair's breadth away from homelessness. But for the kindness of our building super...; but for the solicitousness of the neighbors who would look in from time to time...; but for the rent-controlled apartment she had inherited from her mother; but for the sure sanctuary she found in that ramshackle tenement – she could have wound up one of the city's rag-wrapped street dwellers" (p. 13). More than most, Hopper recognizes that homelessness is ultimately not about mental illness or drug addiction or hopelessly inadequate supplies of low-income housing, although all these are important contributing factors. For most people most of the time, it is kith and kin that "ease the bite of misfortune," and only when these "support networks" fail is homelessness the result. Not individual pathology but social dislocation lies at the heart of the problem.

Bums, tramps, hobos, beggars, bag ladies, gutter punks—these are the modern stereotypes, the customary bigotries, of the homelessness "discussion." Useful correctives are to be found on nearly every page of Hopper's text. My personal favorite is a quotation from a homeless woman: "You have to understand that this is a condition, this homelessness. It's not who we are" (p. 142).

Remarkably, "for a substantial portion of shelter users in cities for which figures are available, the institution [emergency shelter] appears to work.... For these users, that is, either through their own efforts or those of officials charged with relocation, it adequately serves as a way-station en route to stable rehousing" (p. 184). This is one of the great secrets of the homeless assistance system, namely, that for most homeless people, the system somehow works.

Quite contrary to widespread opinion, for most homeless people, as I stressed earlier in this essay, homelessness is a brief, transient bout between the last stable housing situation and the next, not a chronic, year-in, year-out descent into abjection. Why isn't this hopeful fact better known? "Once people manage to escape from the streets and shelters, they typically prefer to pick up their new lives as 'neighbors,' 'workers' and 'citizens'—and not as tagged specimens of the 'formerly homeless'" (p. 184). Thus, "the evidence of successfully resolved homelessness—although all around us—is bound to be difficult to detect." Undetected, it is not cited as evidence of the value of our collective investment.

HOMELESSNESS IN AMERICAN HISTORY

When I first started lecturing on homeless topics in the mid-80s, many of the people I talked to seemed to think that homelessness was somehow a "new problem," something never before witnessed in American history. So in *Address Unknown* I took pains to point out that "homeless people have always existed in American society (and for that matter, in most other societies as well" (p. 27). At the time, I was unable to find much historical material on homelessness (I was evidently looking in the wrong places) and simply pieced together the few fragments that I had come across up to that point (see pp. 27-31). In the years since, a number of very capable and revealing histories have appeared, of which two bear extended mention: Todd DePastino's *Citizen Hobo* and Kenneth Kusmer's *Down and Out, On the Road.*[12]

Citizen Hobo created quite a stir when it first appeared, partly because of its discussion of hobo culture ("hobohemia") and the early twentieth century relationship of that culture to the Wobblies (members of the IWW, the Industrial Workers of the World) but in greater measure because the book depicts hobohemia, "with its job-shirking, binge-drinking, anti-family ways," as a direct assault on the ethos of industrial capitalism and therefore as a major influence on FDR's response to the Great Depression and the development of his thinking about the New Deal. If a man could be well-fed with no job, adequately sheltered from the elements with no home and sexually fulfilled with no wife, then what purpose was served by enslavement to a machine?

In the immediate aftermath of the Civil War, "great armies of tramps" wandered across the American landscape, often searching for work but always "conjuring up widespread fears of gender disorder, class warfare, and a masculine regression to 'savagery'" (p. xxii). In the process, the idealized "open road" came to challenge "hearth and home" as essential for independent manhood. Hoboes soon emerged in the popular culture as the symbols of "virile manhood," as the new frontiersmen of the late nineteenth and early twentieth centuries. (An entire generation of pulp fiction aided in this definition.) The implicit challenge of hobohemia to the culture of industrial capitalism was made much more explicit by the radical left wing of the American labor movement, the Wobblies, who promoted hobo life as "the most authentic bearer of proletarian consciousness." The Wobblies transformed the symbolism of the hobo from "a despised shiftless creature to a powerful useful man" (p. 104).

Never mind that "job-shirking, binge drinking, sexually promiscuous family deserters" (p. 96) were exceedingly poor candidates for a revolutionary vanguard. The Wobblies took pains to depict hobohemia as "a viable alternative to the norms of homes and family that prevailed virtually the world over" (p. 112), norms that supported industrial capitalism by chaining men to the wage economy, by lashing them to their machines.

Romancing the hoboes continued in various forms until the end of the Second World War, after which the "virile manhood" of tramps and hoboes was transformed in the popular mind into the degeneracy and dependence of "homelessness." As with many other contemporary writers, DePastino reminds us that "those we call homeless differ very little, if at all, from the laboring poor in general. As a symptom of poverty, the dramatic loss of home is rarely permanent, and the resort to the streets largely episodic" (p. xxiv). Then and now, here, there, and everywhere, "poor people who reject or are rejected by the nuclear family face a gruesome existence where the protections and immunities of citizenship do not include housing" (p. 271). From at least the nineteenth century through to the twenty-first, homelessness however labeled or reviled has "sparked successive crises of home and nationhood that fundamentally challenged the narrow domestic visions upon which the privileges of American citizenship have historically been based" (p. 271).

Kusmer's fine history covers much of the same material as DePastino and was reviewed for the *New York Times* by Barbara Ehrenreich, who remarked, "It is a pleasure to announce that the homeless, who have so little else, have at least gained a history of their own."[13] As in *Address Unknown* (see pp. 29-30), Kusmer's account begins in Colonial times, when jurisdictions up and down the seaboard enacted laws and ordinances to regulate vagrants, the "wandering poor," beggars, transients, and all the other social misfits who would today be classified as homeless. Freed slaves, former indentured servants, transient seamen, immigrants, and— always—the casualties of war comprised the bulk of the Colonial homeless. Periodic downturns in the Colonial business cycle "added another important factor influencing the growth of homelessness" (p. 14). Strategies of control included institutionalization in prisons, workhouses, and almshouses, "warning out" (being told to leave town), public whipping, "binding out" (indentured to local families needing servants or laborers), and in the extreme case, being sold into slavery. The occasional benevolence of private charities towards the homeless of the era was amply offset by "the tendency toward harsh, moralistic positions in dealing with the poor" that characterized public policy (p. 27).

The homelessness of the Colonial era and that of the early Republic, however, were as nothing compared to the vast outpouring of vagrancy that accompanied the end of the Civil War. If nothing else, the Civil War taught two large armies of men the skills of "riding in trains, camping out and foraging for food" (in Ehrenreich's words)—in short, how to be hobos. Kusmer reminds us that "tramping" originally referred to a military foraging expedition, common to both Northern and Southern armies. "Bum" was derived from "bummer," a word originally applied to soldiers who were "keen on the scent of rebels, or bacon, or silver spoons, or corn, or anything valuable" (p. 37), or in other words, an overly enthusiastic forager. Even the term "hobo" might have originated as an elision of "hoe boy," a reference to the simple piece of farm equipment carried over the shoulders of legions of migratory farm workers in the decades following the Civil War. Thus, the Civil War enriched the vocabulary of homelessness as much as it swelled their numbers.

A century later, the "fickle, irresolute, characterless" and probably criminal homeless man of the post-Civil War era had evolved in the public consciousness into "the drunk, addicted, just plain shiftless" and probably criminal homeless man that Stuart Bykofsky reviles in the *Newsweek* essay discussed in the Preface to *Address Unknown.* Kusmer gets high marks for his insistence that in all historical eras, the homeless are more the victims of economic downturn and the living casualties of war than they are hereditarily dissolute or voluntarily unhoused. It is hard to read the book and not be reminded that this nation was *founded* by homeless people, people who set off across the Atlantic to escape religious persecution and populate the new continent. These days, we rarely think of the homeless as builders of nations, but this thought was very much in the mind of Emma Lazarus, who in 1883 penned her sonnet, "The New Colossus," a well-known passage from which adorns the base of our Statue of Liberty (and that provided the title to my sequel to *Address Unknown*):

Give me your tired, your poor,
Your huddled masses yearning to breathe free.
The wretched refuse of your teeming shore,
Send these, *the homeless*, tempest-tost, to me.
I lift my lamp beside the golden door.

HOMELESSNESS IN COMPARATIVE PERSPECTIVE

Address Unknown said virtually nothing about homelessness outside the United States; indeed, the title of Chapter Two ("Homeless in America: The New American Nightmare") might lead one to think that in modern times, homelessness is a uniquely American problem. Of course, it is not! Partly as a reaction to increasingly shrill advocacy claims in the 1980's (and since) that "only in America would something like this be allowed to happen," the sequel, *Beside the Golden Door*, contained two chapters of comparative material: "Outside American Cities: Rural and European Homelessness"

(Chapter 9) and "Street Children in North and Latin America" (Chapter 10), the latter resulting from a "street kids" health education project in Teguci-galpa, Honduras, with which I was involved for many years.

Even in acknowledging that homelessness was a significant social problem elsewhere in the advanced industrial societies, the material in *Beside the Golden Door* on European homelessness was largely a *pastiche* cobbled together from materials I had come across in some reports issued in the early 1990's by the European Observatory on Homelessness and the Council of Europe's Study Group on Homelessness.[14] At the time, my co-authors and I were struck by the similarities between the European and American cases: the struggle over issues of definition and numbers; the preponderance of men but the growing number of homeless women and children; the surprisingly young average age; extreme poverty and low levels of educational attainment; high rates of physical and mental illness; and the relative paucity of low-income housing as a root cause. The principal difference we saw between the US and European cases was in the policy response. Although some of the European states had clearly failed "to become directly involved in this domain of social provision" (p. 192), in many cases (France, Finland, Denmark, Belgium, and others), social policy with respect to the homeless was remarkably progressive and far-sighted, often based on an explicit recognition that, as one European author put it, "each single homeless person is a reminder to European governments and peoples of just how much is yet to be done before we can call ourselves civilized nations..." (p. 184)

By far the best and most comprehensive piece to have appeared since is Marybeth Shinn's "International Homelessness: Policy, Socio-Cultural and Individual Perspectives," an introduction to and overview of the several papers comprising a special issue of *Journal of Social Issues* on homelessness in comparative perspective.[15]

One paper Shinn discusses in depth is Paul Toro's essay on lifetime prevalence rates of homelessness in various national populations.[16] Building on telephone survey methodology pioneered in an early 90's survey by Bruce Link, Toro and associates showed that lifetime prevalence rates (percentage of the population literally homeless at least once in a lifetime) varied from highs of 6.2% and 7.7% in the U.S. and United Kingdom respectively, to much lower values of 4.0% (Italy), 3.4% (Belgium) and 2.4% (Germany). Given the sample sizes, constant definitions and identical data-gathering methodologies employed, these differences are both statistically and substantively significant. There is discernibly more homelessness *per capita* in the U.S. and U.K. than elsewhere in Europe.

Why? Numerous lines of explanation are explored, of which the most promising are, first, much more inequality in the income distributions of the U.S. and U.K. than elsewhere; secondly, many fewer dollars spent on transfer programs in the U.S. and U.K. than on the continent, especially on housing subsidies for the low income population; and third, stigmatization and social exclusion of oppressed racial and ethnic minorities.

Both GINI coefficients and the share of national income going to the poorest tenth of the population show that the U.S. has the greatest degree of income inequality of any of the nations in the study, followed in both cases by the U.K. So it is not just the size of the poverty population but the gap in income (and wealth) between rich and poor that apparently generates homelessness.

Why would this be the case? In most of the advanced democracies, inequalities in income are mitigated by steeply progressive income tax policies, the revenues from which are used to fund social services and income transfer programs that, in essence, establish a living-standards "floor" below which no citizen is allowed to fall. When expenditures on social programs are expressed as a percentage of GNP, it is obvious that the U.S. spends far less than continental Europe, with the U.K. in between. So if the question is why there are proportionally more homeless people in the U.S. than in many of the advanced European societies, the answer is that the U.S. spends proportionally less to prevent it.

A key indicator of the national commitment to homelessness prevention is the degree of housing subsidy for poor people. In France, about 16% of all dwellings are public (or "social") housing; the same is true for about 20% of the housing in England and Wales and 30% of the housing in Scotland. Housing subsidies are also widely available in Germany. But in the U.S., public housing comprises less than 2% of the housing stock and less than 6% of the rental housing stock. There is also a stigma associated with public housing in the United States that is missing in most of Europe.

U.S. social spending on families is especially deficient; as a percentage of GNP, we spend about a fifth of what the Western Europeans spend to support families. "Because the United States spends so much less than Europe on families, we might expect homelessness among families to be more severe in the United States, and this appears to be the case" (Shinn, p. 663). Indeed, the proportion of homeless people who are members of homeless families averages about 17% in the Western European countries studied and about *twice* that in the U.S.

The U.S. spends less to prevent homelessness than most European nations, has more homeless people, and also embraces less compassionate attitudes towards the homeless. For example, Americans are less likely than Europeans to believe that "poverty is society's fault" and are in general less likely to endorse social or environmental explanations of poverty and homelessness and more likely to look to individual deficiencies as causally responsible. Precise causal connections among cultural beliefs, political decisions, and social policy are notoriously difficult to pin down, but it is hard to believe that all this coalesces randomly.

Finally, there is racism, stigma, and social exclusion and these too contribute to homelessness, not just in the U.S. but everywhere. "Every paper in this issue that reports on minority groups finds higher rates of homelessness among them" (Shinn, p. 666). In the U.S., African-Americans and Native Americans are grossly over-represented among the homeless. In France, it is people from overseas departments and Africa; in Japan, the Ainu, Koreans, Okinawans, and Hinin; in Australia, the aborigines; in Canada, First Nations people; etc. Racism is linked to homelessness through four well-known and related mechanisms: employment, wealth, housing, and incarceration. Here's the recipe for disproportionate rates of homelessness among racial and ethnic minorities: Deny them jobs, prevent them from accumulating wealth, severely restrict their housing options, and lock them up at rates tens or hundreds of times higher than the rates for the majority population. Homelessness is the inevitable result.

The comparative evidence on homelessness in the Western democracies reminds me of a quotation, possibly apocryphal, attributed to Gandhi. When asked by a reporter what he thought of Western civilization, the Mahatma is said to have replied, "I think it would be a good idea."

THE POLITICAL ECONOMY OF HOMELESSNESS: HOUSING AND POVERTY

It says a great deal about the state of our understanding of homelessness in the 1980's that the proposition advanced in *Address Unknown*—that homelessness was at least partly a *housing* problem—was considered both insightful and controversial. People had become accustomed to thinking of homelessness as a mental health problem, particularly a problem caused by the widespread deinstitutionalization of the mentally ill, or as an alcohol or drug addiction problem, or in some cases as a problem resulting from family breakdown and estrangement. In the 1980's, in short, we had come to "understand" homelessness as the result of individual failings. It fell to people like me, Rossi, Joel Blau, Marty Burt, and a number of others to frame homelessness as a problem rooted in the political economy of the cities.[17]

The basic argument was straightforward. "The past ten years have witnessed a virtual decimation of the low income housing supply in most large American cities. During the same period, the poverty population of the cities has increased. Less low-income housing for more low-income people predestines an increase in the numbers without housing. The coming of the new homeless, in short, has been "'in the cards' for years..." (p. 37). The economics of urban housing, I argued, had created a housing "game" that some were destined to lose. And it is scarcely surprising that the "losers" turned out to be the most marginal and most vulnerable sectors of the urban poverty population: the extremely poor, the drunk and addicted, those hobbled by physical and psychiatric illness, those without support networks to sustain them through times of crisis. But just as there is every difference between the rules of blackjack and the characteristics of those who perpetually lose their shirts at the blackjack tables, so too is there every difference between the "rules" of the urban housing game and the characteristics of homeless people who were (and are) unable to compete in that game successfully.

This general line of reasoning about homelessness was dismissed as misguided, if not pernicious and to that extent reprehensible, by Alice Baum and Donald Burnes in one of the most controversial books written about the homeless in the 1990's, *A Nation in Denial.*[18] In their account, vast majorities of the homeless, upwards of four in five, are mentally ill, substance abusive, or people with criminal records, and moreover, these disabilities explain *why* they are homeless as well. Baum and Burnes argue that people become homeless because they are disaffiliated, that is, because they are cut off from social networks of family, friendship, and work that provide the social "glue" in most people's lives; and that people become disaffiliated (in this sense) because of the corrosive effects of psychiatric illness, substance abuse, or legal troubles on social networks. Absent from their analysis is any recognition of social-structural factors such as poverty, unemployment, or housing, which (they argue) were at the time being stridently but wrongly emphasized by zealous advocates and fuzzy-headed researchers who were ideologically motivated to deny some simple but important truths. *Address Unknown* is specifically cited as an example of the sort of "denial" they are talking about.

Making matters worse, this collective act of denial obstructed the development of policies that would truly help the homeless. The insistence of advocates and researchers such as me that homelessness is fundamentally a *housing* problem, they argued, was especially wrong-headed. More low-income housing is *not* the solution because the lack of affordable housing is *not* the cause. Only mental health and substance abuse treatment programs will make a substantial dent in the problem. My arguments about housing were not only flat wrong but making it difficult for policy makers to do things that would actually help. This is as close as I have ever come in a thirty-five-year career to being described in print as both stupid and morally bankrupt.

Accordingly, we took up the Baum and Burnes charges in detail in *Beside the Golden Door*. We were quick to acknowledge that the pertinent evidence, then and now, *overwhelmingly* supports the conclusion that most of the homeless suffer from physical, mental, chemical dependency, or other disorders and that these personal deficiencies must therefore play some important role in the process by which people become homeless. Indeed, if one expands the concept of "disability" to include such "deficits" as criminal records, inadequate personal hygiene, sub-average intelligence, estrangement from family, lack of supportive networks, and on through a very long list, essentially *all* homeless people qualify as "deficient" in one or another important respect.

The essential descriptive *facts*, in short, were not in serious dispute. The issue is whether these descriptive facts constitute an adequate *explanation* for the rise of homelessness over the past couple of decades. And it is ridiculously simple to show that they do not.

Burt, for example, had pointed out that if mental illness and substance abuse were going to *explain* the large increase in the number of homeless people that her research clearly documented, then a minimum requirement would be evidence showing that mental illness and substance abuse were more common today than in the past, and there is no real evidence to this effect. "Population rates of chronic or severe mental illness are very stable across time and place, including non-Western and less developed countries and cultures" (Burt, *Over the Edge,* p. 108). Ditto substance abuse: "The proportion of alcohol abusers and alcoholics in the US population has remained relatively constant at least since the late 1960s" (p. 109). As a matter of fact, aggregate consumption of alcohol had been *declining* in the U.S. population as a whole since the late 1970's; the trend in illicit drug consumption was also *downward* throughout the 1980's.[19] It is therefore difficult to ascribe increasing homelessness to increasing mental illness or increasing alcohol and drug use because mental illness and substance abuse had apparently not been increasing. This alone is decisive evidence that there must be more to the homelessness story than Baum and Burnes allow.

Burt also pointed out that if mental illness and substance abuse were indeed causally responsible for the rise of the "new homeless" (i.e., today's homeless), then we would expect to find more mental illness and substance abuse among the homeless of today than was found among the homeless of earlier eras, and this too is not consistent with the available evidence. To the contrary, "the presence of the mentally ill among skid row and homeless populations may have increased somewhat during the 1980s, but it is by no means a new phenomenon" (p. 109). Concerning substance abuse, "Stark summarizes twenty-three studies, conducted in every decade from the 1890s through the 1970s. Their findings are very similar to more recent studies...Not too much has changed, it seems, with regard to the prevalence of alcohol problems among homeless populations in the United States" (p. 111).

The argument pursued in *Beside the Golden Door* is that the Baum and Burnes' emphasis on personal defects as an explanation of homelessness diverts attention from more basic issues of housing, poverty, welfare, and public policy, issues that I have been addressing for nearly twenty-five years. To achieve a proper understanding of homelessness in contemporary American society, one must consider the problem in its larger social, political, and economic context. Ascribing the causes of homelessness to the personal deficiencies of homeless people is an unwarranted case of "blaming the victim" and should be avoided not because it is mean-spirited but because it is misleading. It tells part, but not the whole, of the story. As indicated above, analyses in the style of Baum and Burnes mistake the characteristics of people who have lost the housing game for the rules of the game itself, and these are definitely not the same things. It mistakes the needs that homeless people have, which indisputably include mental health and substance abuse treatment, with the reasons why they are homeless, which has more to do with poverty, housing, and related structural conditions than with personal disabilities and dysfunctions.

Another problem with Baum and Burnes' emphasis is that treatment programs for alcohol, drug, and mental disorders are demonstrably not very effective. They often function as revolving doors that produce short-term remission while clients remain in treatment but precious little in the way of long-lasting improvement. One important reason *why* ADM treatment is not especially effective with homeless clients is that treatment rarely addresses the more fundamental social-structural issues of poverty, housing, welfare, and employment that lie at the heart of the matter.

These considerations let us put an even sharper point on a line of thinking described earlier. Treatment, it seems, does relatively little to make the homeless lucid, clean, or sober, but affordable housing unquestionably makes them un-homeless, and that, after all, is the point. Our recent update on the low income housing situation shows that the trends first noted in *Address Unknown* have continued largely unabated.[20] Many government policies enacted over the last fifty years have resulted in the destruction of what was once affordable housing. Other polices have restricted the construction of multi-family units, which typically provide most affordable housing options. The result is almost certainly less housing for the nation's poor population than at any previous time in American history.

HUD agrees that the affordable housing crisis is worsening. HUD defines income categories for households based on the area median income (AMI):[21]

- Extremely low income: households earning no more than 30% of AMI
- Very low income: households earning between 30-50% of AMI
- Low income: households between 50% and 80% of AMI.

HUD's 2007 report to Congress[22] says that households in all three of these income categories are having a more difficult time securing affordable housing than they did in the recent past. Often this is because rental units are being occupied by households that have higher incomes. In 2005, there were 77 affordable units available for rent for every 100 very low-income renter households. In 2003, the ratio was 81 per hundred. The situation is even worse for extremely low-income renter households. In 2005, there were 40 affordable units available per 100 households, while in 2003 the ratio was 43 per 100.

Overall, renters are disproportionately low income. However, since 1995, both housing prices and rents have risen rapidly. Inflation adjusted rents have been at their highest levels since the housing "boom year" of 1995. At the same time, inflation adjusted income has fallen for the average renter by 8.4%. Although the vacancy rate has been ~10% since 2003, a higher vacancy rate than at any time since the 1960's, rents have still increased because the alternative to renting—purchasing a home of one's own—is simply not feasible for many low income families.[23] Therefore, even though rents are higher, incomes are lower so renting remains the only housing option for many low and even moderate income families. Further evidence for the low income housing crisis is found in the increasing housing burdens borne by low-income families. "Housing cost burden" is defined as the proportion of income persons or households pay each month for their housing. By tradition, a "reasonable" housing cost burden is ~30% of monthly income, but the housing burden for those that do manage to obtain housing has also been increasing. These days, many people are paying much more than 30% of their income on housing, and this is especially true of those with the lowest incomes. For example, as of 2000, 79% of low income households spent more than 30% of their income on housing, an increase of 12 percentage points from 1970.[24] Overall, the percentage of households that spend 35% or more of their income for rent has risen from one-fifth to over one-third of all renter households.

As indicated, housing cost burden is based on the percentage of income a household must pay for housing costs, with 30% typically considered acceptable. When a household spends between 31% and 50% of its income on housing, the household is considered to have a "high" housing cost burden, and if the cost of housing exceeds 50% of income, the housing cost burden is considered "severe." According to data from the 2001 American Housing Survey, 58% of extremely low income people have a severe housing cost burden while an additional 16% have a moderate cost burden; in short, about three-quarters have sufficiently high rent burdens that they must be considered at least "at risk" for homelessness. In more affluent income categories, people can afford to "over-spend" on housing because the remaining income is sufficient, or in the most affluent categories, more than sufficient, to cover other basic needs. Extremely low income people do not have the luxury of "over-spending" on housing unless they avail themselves of community feeding programs for free food, thrift shops for free or reduced-price clothing, free community health clinics and other services to cover their basic needs. Those who are able to do this can remain housed; those who cannot become homeless.

Housing that was once erected specifically to house low income individuals and families has been torn down in various efforts at "urban renewal" and (more recently) "downtown redevelopment" or "revitalization." Construction of affordable replacement units has failed to keep pace with the need. Particularly pertinent here is the widespread destruction of Single Room Occupancy (SRO) hotels. During the 1970s, when urban renewal was occurring in nearly all major metropolitan areas, virtually the entire SRO stock was wiped out along with the rooming and boarding houses that had traditionally served as the "housing of last resort" for low income single men.[25] Add to this the growing loss of low-income housing through the processes of gentrification and condo conversions and the destruction of hundreds of thousands of public housing units through HOPE VI redevelopment projects[26] and the result is a serious and worsening low income housing crisis that most certainly lies at the heart of the contemporary problem of homelessness.

HOMELESSNESS AND PUBLIC POLICY

Through the guidance of the Inter-Agency Council on the Homeless and the National Alliance to End Homelessness, and with the assistance of bucket-loads of fresh federal money to underwrite the effort, some 250 American cities have formulated and have begun to implement ten-year plans to end chronic homelessness (and in more than a few cases, to end homelessness altogether). Cities from Seattle to Denver to Atlanta to Miami have been reporting impressive declines in their homeless counts as these cities and many others move towards the Housing First intervention models discussed in an earlier section of this essay. For the first time in a quarter century, there is a palpable resolve to fight the root causes of homelessness rather than resign ourselves to its inevitability.

For every city that has resolved to end homelessness through prevention and through the provision of truly affordable housing options, however, there is another seemingly hell-bent on dealing with the homeless by criminalizing the status of being without housing and by making the survival behaviors of homeless people illegal. More and more cities, it seems, have either enacted new legislation or called for more aggressive enforcement of existing legislation to prohibit such things as panhandling, loitering, camping in public places, and public intoxication. The use of "greyhound therapy" has also been employed in many smaller communities where the homeless are simply supplied a bus ticket to elsewhere, a policy starkly reminiscent of the Colonial-era strategy of "warning out." Some local initiatives have targeted those who want to assist the homeless as opposed to targeting the homeless themselves. For example, Orlando and Las Vegas have enacted ordinances restricting the feeding of homeless people in public places.

A 2006 joint report by the National Coalition for the Homeless and the National Law Center on Homelessness and Poverty reports that criminalization initiatives are on the rise.[27] Comparing the most recent report with a similar one conducted in 2002, the report noted a 3% increase in laws that prohibit loitering, loafing, or vagrancy; a 14% increase in laws that prohibit sitting or lying down in specific public spaces; and an 18% increase in laws prohibiting aggressive panhandling. As the NCH report, *Illegal to be Homeless: the Criminalization of Homelessness in the United States*, puts it, "The underlying assumption behind these actions is that homelessness is a 'public safety' issue. Therefore, cities attempt to eliminate visible homelessness through enforcing 'quality of life' ordinances, which seek to improve the 'quality of life' of housed and higher-income individuals by removing from sight those people who look poor and homeless. Arrest and incarceration have become an expedited way of removing individuals from sight. Unfortunately, many people justify criminalization as a 'benevolent' means of coercing individuals into treatment and other services that are not voluntarily available."

Panhandling. Of all the behaviors associated with homelessness in the public mind, beggary is evidently the most offensive; thus, panhandling and the criminalization of begging behaviors are at the forefront of efforts to "clean up the streets." Never mind that empirical studies of the phenomenon report with great consistency that "contrary to common belief, panhandlers and homeless people are not necessarily one and the same. Many studies have found that only a small percentage of homeless people panhandle, and only a small percentage of panhandlers are homeless."[28] Although exact numbers are unavailable, estimates of the percentage of homeless people that engage in panhandling range from 5-40%, i.e., a definite and perhaps rather small minority of the total homeless population.[29]

Ordinances attempting to ban or regulate panhandling are often viewed as a way of removing the homeless from public view. The idea that panhandlers are not "really" needy, that beggary is some sort of scam, and that aggressive panhandlers rake in improbably large sums of money, only to drive home at the end of the day in shiny Cadillacs, is so widespread in contemporary American society that it has attained the status of an urban myth.

Empirical studies of panhandlers do not depict the activity as highly profitable. Scott says (see note 27), "Most evidence confirms that panhandling is not lucrative, although some panhandlers clearly are able to subsist on a combination of panhandling money, government benefits, private charity, and money from odd jobs such as selling scavenged materials or plasma. How much money a panhandler can make varies depending on his or her skill and personal appeal, as well as on the area in which he or she solicits. Estimates vary from a couple of dollars (U.S.) a day on the low end, to $20 to $50 a day in the mid-range, to about $300 a day on the high end." The high end estimates of hundreds of dollars a day or more are almost certainly exaggerated. Realistically, panhandling when combined with other income-generating activities would normally provide a subsistence income at best.

Panhandling has been ruled by the US Supreme Court to be legally protected behavior under the First Amendment, which guarantees free speech and freedom of religion. One can no more ban people from asking for spare change than one can ban people from asking for the time of day (free speech), and likewise, the asking for and giving of alms is constitutionally protected religious behavior. Thus, numerous efforts simply to ban panhandling have been stricken down as unconstitutional. But the Court has also ruled that regulations concerning the "place and manner" of panhandling are not unconstitutional, and this has led to a number of anti-panhandling ordinances that the Courts have allowed to remain in place.

Of these, the most common are laws prohibiting "aggressive panhandling." Most panhandling is in fact passive, not aggressive, and the definition of what constitutes "aggressive" panhandling remains unclear. But these points have not deterred cities from targeting this specific form of panhandling or prevented "no aggressive panhandling" ordinances from being enacted all across the country.

Necessarily, every jurisdiction wishing to ban "aggressive" panhandling has to develop some definition of what aggressive panhandling entails. In Cleveland, for example, the definition of aggressive solicitation prohibits panhandling in certain specific *places* (e.g., within twenty feet of a bus stop, rapid-transit shelter, or bus shelter, within fifteen feet of any pay telephone or the entrance or exit of any public toilet facility, etc.). Other cities, such as Seattle, attempt to define prohibited panhandling methods and behaviors (e.g., confronting someone in a way that would cause a reasonable person to fear bodily harm; touching someone without his or her consent; using obscene or abusive language toward someone; etc).

In 2004, the city of Orlando, Florida, passed an ordinance requiring panhandlers to obtain a permit from the municipal police department; this too is not an uncommon strategy. The Orlando ordinance further makes it a crime to panhandle in the commercial core of downtown Orlando, as well as within fifty feet of any bank or automated teller machine, except in specially designated "blue boxes" which have been painted onto downtown Orlando sidewalks. Thus, downtown Orlando panhandlers must have a police permit and stay inside the designated blue boxes. (In fact, hardly any do.) It is also considered a crime in Orlando for panhandlers to make false statements, to disguise themselves, or to use money obtained with a claim of a specific purpose (e.g. food) for anything else (e.g. alcohol). So in Orlando, if you tell someone you are hungry if in fact you are not, then take the money you are given and use it for a pack of smokes, you are in technical violation of the panhandling ordinance.

As might be anticipated, these anti-panhandling ordinances have often evolved into enforcement nightmares. As Scott notes, "Enforcing aggressive-panhandling laws can be difficult, partly because few panhandlers behave aggressively, and partly because many victims of aggressive panhandling do not report the offense to police or are unwilling to file a complaint." Many of these laws require police discretion (who's to say, for example, that someone has been confronted "in a way that would cause a reasonable person to fear bodily harm"?) and therefore invite selective enforcement, which then leads to citizen and business owners' complaints that the police are letting panhandlers get away with too much.

Because of dissatisfaction with the results obtained in efforts to ban aggressive panhandling, many cities (literally from Savannah to Evanston to San Diego) have begun to experiment with solutions that attempt to control the behavior of the *givers*, not the behavior of panhandlers themselves. The implementation of such measures entails public education to discourage giving money directly to individuals and instead encouraging people to donate their spare change to area service providers. In Baltimore, the "Make a Change" campaign provides collection boxes inside area hotels and businesses for people to deposit money that would have otherwise gone to panhandlers. Similarly, in Athens, Georgia among other places, parking meters have been converted into donation kiosks, where people can deposit spare change that is then given to local homeless service providers.

In almost all cases, these Do Not Give campaigns have stirred up some resentment among local homeless advocates and no city has managed to eliminate nuisance panhandling by any of these means. But most cities report some modest successes in reducing the most abusive cases. In Evanston, for example, there was a documented reduction in the number of panhandlers working the streets, a reduction in the number of citizen complaints, *and* survey results documenting an upturn in citizen perception of the downtown area as a safe place to shop and work.

Loitering. Idleness is apparently second only to beggary on the list of offensive homeless behaviors and loitering is therefore another behavior of which municipalities often find it necessary to legally disapprove. These ordinances come in the form of "anti-sitting" laws or laws regulating where a person can lie down, sleep, etc.

The National Coalition for the Homeless and the National Law Center on Homelessness & Poverty annually rank U.S. cities in terms of their "meanness" towards the homeless, based upon many factors including the number and enforcement of anti-homeless laws, the severity of penalties for violating those laws, and the existence of pending or recently enacted criminalization measures in the city. In 2005, Sarasota, Florida, was named the meanest city in America mainly due to the Sarasota ordinance that banned, among other things, sleeping "without permission on city or private property, either in a tent or makeshift shelter, or while atop or covered by materials."

In *Illegal to be Homeless*, 28% of the 224 surveyed cities prohibit "camping" in certain public places and 16% had citywide bans on "camping." Twenty-seven percent of the surveyed cities prohibit sitting or lying down in some public places. Thirty-nine percent prohibit loitering in specific public areas and 16% prohibit loitering anywhere in the city. Although having laws against loitering is not new, it is the selective enforcement of such laws that portend criminalization. If the law against sleeping on park benches is ignored when affluent businessmen catch a few winks after their luncheon martini but enforced aggressively against raggedy, broken down homeless people, that selectivity implies that the simple fact of being homeless has been operationally defined as a criminal act.

By definition, people without housing have nowhere to go during the day so if they are to seek respite from their daily activities, practically anything they do can be seen as loitering. Most emergency shelters for homeless people are only open at night. Some initiatives have been undertaken to assist homeless people during the day and to give them an alternative to being on the streets. In Glendale, California, the police department created a "day labor center" which offers such classes as computers and English for non-native speakers. And many cities either have created or are in the process of creating "drop-in" shelters open during the day where homeless people can get off the streets, perhaps shower or do their laundry, take a meal, watch TV, or see a social worker or case manager.

Street Sweeps. Street sweeps consist of targeting and removing homeless people who are living or loitering out of doors in public locations. A "sweep" entails law enforcement officers coming through an area, rousting homeless people, making them "move on," and often confiscating or destroying their things (usually on the bogus grounds that the "stuff" of homeless people is trash or litter). Often times the police work with other local government employees to clear an area of homeless, or apparently homeless people, often in conjunction with major local political or sporting events, appearances by visiting dignitaries, or other occasions that bring tourists and media attention to a particular area of a city.

In New York City, Mayor Bloomberg announced in July 2006 that the city would erect barriers blocking access to makeshift camps as well as disallowing homeless people from sleeping under highways and near train trestles as a way to help homeless people gain shelter. According to NCH, this occurred at the same time there was a 44% increase among sheltered homeless New Yorkers while rents in the city continued to rise. Sweeps of homeless people and encampments have become common across the nation, with recent documented sweeps in Honolulu, Cleveland, Orlando, and elsewhere.

The Fourth Amendment protects people from unreasonable search and seizure and street sweeps are often challenged on the grounds that they are violations of homeless peoples' Fourth Amendment rights. Sometimes these challenges are successful and some sort of redress or restitution is ordered. In the extreme case, the courts have used police violations of court orders against sweeps to order massive increases in local services for the homeless, as in Miami in the aftermath of the *Pottinger* decision. Pottinger was one among a number of homeless people living under Miami's highway overpasses whose belongings had been confiscated and destroyed over and over by the Miami police, despite repeated Court orders to desist in the behavior. The Court ruled that homeless people were *not* homeless by choice, that homelessness was an involuntarily-assumed status, and, as such, that laws against survival behavior by this group (loitering, public urination, sleeping in public, etc.) were unconstitutional. When the city lost its challenge against the Court ruling, it was forced to enact a special food and beverage tax to pay for the expanded shelter capacity and homeless services that the Court ordered into existence.

Dumping. "Dumping" is the elegantly simple strategy of putting trouble-some people on a bus to somewhere else with the hope that they don't find their way back. The dumping of "troublesome persons" by police officers has been documented throughout American history.[30] Homeless people are not the only "troublesome" element that municipalities will try to dump, but certainly they have experienced their share, and more, of dumping. In some cases, dumping has been practiced so egregiously that neighboring cities or concerned advocacy groups have sued the "dumping" city for their behavior.

The police agencies are not the only ones that engage in dumping. In 2006 in Los Angeles, city prosecutors charged area hospitals with dump-ing homeless patients in the infamous skid row area. There is no hospital in any American city of appreciable size that has not seen its emergency room utilization figures jump up with cases of "uncompensated care" (read: people without health insurance or a fee source to pay for their hospitalization). And while the hospitals are required by law to offer emergency care to anyone in need regardless of their ability to pay, the sooner the poor and homeless can be stabilized and released, the less they cost the hospital. At the Coalition for the Homeless facility in Orlando, taxi cabs have pulled up and discharged homeless people who were still in hospital gowns and had IV lines attached to their arms. So common is "dumping" by hospitals that the behavior has been given a name: GOMER (as in: "What happened to the broken leg in 3-B?" "He was GOMERed.") GOMER stands for Get Out of My Emergency Room!

While dumping is probably not a very common reaction to homeless individuals, the use of "greyhound therapy" appears to be more widespread. Greyhound therapy refers to the issuing of bus tickets to homeless individuals so they can leave town. Although these "relocation" programs have been widely criticized, as recently as January, 2007, the mayor of Daytona Beach announced that his city was instituting a program where homeless individuals would be given bus tickets so they could, in the mayor's belief, be "reunited with friends and family." Local homeless advocates pointed out that many of the Daytona Beach homeless are originally from the Daytona area and many more have no family or friends who would provide them with shelter.

Some programs take this concept a step further. In Reno, Nevada, the Homeless Evaluation Liaison Program (HELP) is a program run by the local police force. Homeless individuals may apply once per lifetime for a bus ticket to reunite with friends and family. The officers call the person that will be receiving the homeless individual in the other location to make sure that someone will in fact be taking them in. However, the homeless individual is not provided any services, only a bus ticket.

Many advocates contend that programs such as these do nothing but move homeless individuals around, never addressing the root problems. To be sure, every city will have some homeless people who are homeless because they got stranded, ran out of money, and have no way to get back to wherever it is they came from, and for these unfortunate few, a bus ticket may indeed be all their homelessness requires. This cannot possibly describe more than a percent or two of the homeless population in most cities. Nevertheless, the popularity of these "relocation" programs is growing in many cities.

Restrictions on Feeding. If you remove their food source, rats will move elsewhere, and numerous cities have employed a similar logic to rid themselves of the homeless through restrictions on the feeding of homeless people. These initiatives are unique because they focus on those that are supplying the food, not the homeless clients who receive it. In Las Vegas, Nevada, a federal judge blocked a law that banned serving food to the poor in city parks. However, similar laws still exist in other cities. In Dallas, Texas, feedings are limited to certain designated areas and providers must obtain a permit and attend food safety training.

The most recently enacted restrictions on feeding homeless people are in Orlando and are some of the most stringent in the country. Under Orlando's new law (currently being challenged by several organizations including the ACLU), a person or group cannot feed more than twenty-five people at a time without obtaining a permit. This permit can only be obtained twice a year. At first, the Orlando police simply ignored the ordinance as unenforceable, then tried to work with local organizations to assure that homeless people were being fed in lots of twenty-four or less. But in March, 2007, bowing to pressure from downtown residents and business interests, the Orlando police arrested an activist from the organization Food Not Bombs after he was filmed violating the feeding ordinance by undercover officers. His arrest was the first effort to enforce this controversial ordinance, which is supported by the majority of the local business community, particularly those located near the park where the feedings and this arrest took place. Feedings continue weekly despite the arrest (the case was thrown out by a local judge).

Victimization of the Homeless. As we have seen, cities all over the country are enacting measures to "clean up the streets" by driving away or locking up the visible homeless of the area. While these measures are rarely effective, are often found to be unconstitutional, and generally do nothing to address the real problems of homeless people, their popularity grows as the urban areas try to attract shoppers, tourists, and residents, none of whom seem comfortable having homeless people around. Michael Stoops, director of the National Coalition for the Homeless, argues that one notable consequence of the effort to criminalize homeless people and their behaviors has been to foster a generalized disregard for the civil rights of the homeless and that, Stoops argue, has had a direct effect on their victimization and on the stunning increase in what can only be described as hate crimes perpetrated against them.

Hate crimes against homeless people have burgeoned in recent years and have become a nationwide problem. Since 1999, the National Coalition for the Homeless has issued an annual report on these trends. The most recent in the series is *Hate, Violence, and Death on Main Street USA*, covering the years through 2006, available at the NCH home page (http://www. nationalhomeless.org). According to the 2006 report, "over the past seven years (1999-2005), advocates and homeless shelter workers from around the country have seen an alarming, nationwide epidemic in reports of homeless men, women and even children being killed, beaten, and harassed." The NCH data only include incidents from newspaper stories where victims are identified as homeless people and their assailants are known. Thus, the vast majority of these crimes must escape attention.

Still, between 1999 and 2005, 472 violent hate-crime attacks against the homeless were documented, resulting in 169 deaths. Incidents have been recorded in 165 cities in 42 states and Puerto Rico. In 2006, Florida experienced the greatest number of attacks with forty-seven incidents, with Arizona second with sixteen. Often it is assumed that Florida simply has more homeless people, which accounts for the higher number of attacks. However, this is not the case. California has nearly three times the number of homeless persons as compared to Florida and nowhere near as many assaults. Victims range from four-month-old babies to elderly people in their seventies. Most perpetrators are young males age fourteen to nineteen.

Although no one knows for sure why these attacks are increasing, advocates for the homeless believe that as a society, America is sending the message that homeless people simply do not matter. The NCH report notes, "The term 'hate crime' generally conjures up images of cross burnings and lynchings, swastikas on Jewish synagogues, and horrific murders of gays and lesbians." Interestingly, homelessness is not included in the federal definition of a hate crime. Attacks on people because of their religion, race, ethnicity, beliefs, or sexual orientation can be prosecuted as hate crimes and the penalties are more severe. Homelessness does not enjoy the same legal protection, although several states, including Massachusetts, California, Maryland, and Florida, are proposing legislation that would include housing status in the hate crime definition.

Rays of Light. American cities are not unanimous in their efforts to criminalize the behaviors of people experiencing homelessness and not all of them post signs at the city limits that read, in effect, "Homeless people not welcome. No sitting, lying, leaning, panhandling, loitering, camping, obstructing the sidewalk, sleeping in public or storing your stuff in public places. Poor people should register with the local police." The National Coalition for the Homeless has identified three "model cities"—Minneapolis, Philadelphia, and Ft. Lauderdale—that have made serious efforts to buck the criminalization trend.

In Minneapolis, a number of anti-homeless ordinances have been repealed, the police have been trained in how to link homeless people to the services they need rather than just roust them or toss them in jail, a Decriminalization Task Force was created to review all the local laws and practices whose effect, if not intent, was to criminalize homelessness, and an aggressive long-term effort to address the housing needs of homeless people was undertaken. In Philadelphia, police officers who encounter homeless people are required to contact social workers who respond within twenty minutes and homeless people who are sleeping outside (in violation of local ordinances) are referred to local shelters and transitional housing services rather than being fined or arrested. In Ft. Lauderdale, police and city officials have created outreach teams comprised of police officers and formerly homeless people to encounter and assess individuals on the street and make appropriate referrals.

These and other examples suffice to make the important point that there are creative and humane ways of addressing local homelessness problems that do not necessarily require oppressive, discriminatory, and unconstitutional measures. I conclude with a point made in the title of a book by the Rumanian author, Dmitry Sokolov: *You cannot drive tramps off the street with a club!* Evidence shows that many homeless people will respond positively to services, outreach, health care, or anything else that seems to represent an alternative way of living. But there is practically no evidence anywhere to suggest that they respond positively to threats, intimidation, or enforcement of laws that attempt to prohibit or criminalize their behaviors.

James D. Wright
Department of Sociology
University of Central Florida

NOTES

1. My thanks to Amy Donley for her assistance in preparing this essay.
2. My co-conspirator on that first homeless research project and on most everything else I was involved with in the 1980s was Peter H. Rossi, who died on October 7, 2006. Pete was a close friend whose passing was a grievous personal and professional loss.
3. Peter H. Rossi, James D. Wright, Gene Fisher, and Georgia Willis. "The Urban Homeless: Estimating Composition and Size." *Science* 235: 4794 (13 March 1987), pp. 1336 - 1341. The quotation is from p. 1339.
4. Martha Burt and Barbara Cohen, *America's Homeless: Numbers, Characteristics, and Programs that Serve Them.* Washington: The Urban Institute, 1989; Martha Burt, *Over the Edge: The Growth of Homelessness in the 1980s.* New York: Russell Sage, 1992; Martha Burt, Laudan Aron and Edgar Lee, *Helping America's Homeless: Emergency Shelter or Affordable Housing?* Washington: The Urban Institute Press, 2001.
5. Culhane, D.P., Dejowski, E.F., Ibanez, J., Needham, E., & Macchia, I. (1994). Public shelter admission rates in Philadelphia and New York City: The implications of turnover for sheltered population counts. *Housing Policy Debate*, 5(2), 107-139; Culhane, D.P. & Kuhn, R. (1997). Patterns and determinants of shelter

utilization among single homeless adults in New York City and Philadelphia: A longitudinal analysis of homelessness. *Journal of Policy Analysis and Management*, 17(1), 23-43; Kuhn, R. & Culhane, D.P. (1998). Applying cluster analysis to test a typology of homelessness by pattern of shelter utilization: Results from the analysis of administrative data. *American Journal of Community Psychology*, 26(2), 207-232; and Culhane, D.P. & Metraux, S. (1999). One-year prevalence rates of public shelter utilization by race, sex, age and poverty status for New York City (1990, 1995) and Philadelphia (1995). *Population Research and Policy Review*, 18(3), 219-236.

6. Sosin, M., I. Piliavin, H. Westerfelt, 1990. "Toward a longitudinal analysis of homelessness." *Journal of Social Issues* 46:4: 157-174.
7. See, e.g., Martha Burt, Carol Pearson, and Ann Elizabeth Montgomery, *Strategies for Preventing Homelessness*. Washington, DC: Office of Policy Development and Research, US Department of Housing and Urban Development, May, 2005.
8. Jill Khadduri, "Housing vouchers are critical for ending family homelessness." Washington, DC: National Allowance to End Homelessness, *Research Matters*, January 2008.
9. Three Rivers Press, 2006.
10. New York: The Free Press, 1993.
11. Ithaca: Cornell University Press, 2003.
12. Todd DePastino, *Citizen Hobo: How a Century of Homelessness Shaped America*. Chicago: University of Chicago Press, 2003. Kenneth Kusmer, *Down and Out, On the Road: The Homeless in American History*. Oxford Press, 2002.
13. Barbara Ehrenreich, "Hobo Heaven." *The New York Times* 20 January 2002.
14. M. Daly, *European Homelessness: The Rising Tide*. Brussels: European Federation of National Organizations Working with the Homeless, 1992; *Abandoned: Profiles of Europe's Homeless People*. Brussels: European Federation of National Organizations Working with the Homeless, 1993; *Homelessness: Social Cooperation in Europe*. Strasbourg, Germany: Council of Europe, Publication and Documentation Service, 1993.
15. *Journal of Social Issues* 63:3 (2007). Shinn's essay appears on pp. 657-677.
16. Paul Toro and co-authors, "Homelessness in Europe and the United States: A Comparison of Prevalence and Public Opinion," *Journal of Social Issues* 63:3 (2007), pp. 505-524.
17. See, e.g., Peter H. Rossi, *Down and Out in America: The Origins of Homelessness*. Chicago: University of Chicago Press, 1989; Joel Blau, *The Visible Poor: Homelessness in the United States*. Oxford University Press, 1993; Martha Burt, *Over The Edge, op. cit.*
18. Baum and Burnes, *A Nation in Denial: The Truth About Homelessness*. Boulder, CO: Westview Press, 1993.
19. See James D. Wright and Joel Devine, *Drugs as a Social Problem*. New York: Harper Collins, 1994.
20. James D. Wright, Amy M. Donley, and Kevin F. Gotham, "Housing Policy, the Low Income Housing Crisis, and the Problem of Homelessness." Chapter 3 in Robert McNamara (ed.), *Homelessness in America,* Volume 2. New York: Greenwood Publishing, 2008.
21. HUD and other government agencies have begun using these income categories in part because they recognize how hopelessly antiquated and useless the

official federal poverty definition has become for demarcating individuals and families that are truly in need.

22. US Department of Housing and Urban Development, 2007. *Affordable Housing Needs, 2005: Report to Congress* (*http://www.huduser.org/Publications/pdf/Af-fHsgNeeds.pdf*).

23. Nathaniel Loewentheil and Christian Weller, "The renter squeeze: Minority and low income renters feel pressures from housing boom and weak labor market." *Review of Policy Research*, 22: 6 (2005), pp. 755-769.

24. Quigley, J. & Raphael, S., "The economics of homelessness: The evidence from North America." *European Journal of Housing Policy* 1(3) (2004), pp. 323–336.

25. See among many others Hopper, *Reckoning with Homelessness, op. cit.* On the loss of SRO housing specifically during the era of "urban renewal," see "No Room in the Inn: The Disappearance of SRO Housing in the United States." Ch. 6 in Sharon Keigher (ed). *Housing Risks and Homelessness among the Urban Elderly.* Binghamton, NY: Haworth Press, 1991.

26. See Lawrence J. Vale, *Reclaiming Public Housing: A Half Century of Struggle in Three Public Neighborhoods.* Cambridge, MA: Harvard University Press, 2002.

27. The National Coalition for the Homeless and National Law Center on Homeless-ness & Poverty. *Dream Denied: The Criminalization of Homelessness in U.S. Cities.* Washington: NCH and NLCHP, 2006.

28. Michael S. Scott. *Panhandling.* Washington, DC: US Department of Justice, Office of Community-Oriented Policing Services, 2002.

29. Barrett Lee and Chad Farrell. "Buddy, Can You Spare a Dime? Homelessness, Panhandling, and the Public." *Urban Affairs Review*wentyrkers who respond within 2aotic vious chapter, 38 (January, 2003): 299-324.

30. King, William R., and Thomas M. Dunn. "Dumping: Police-Initiated Transjuris-dictional Transport of Troublesome Persons." *Police Quarterly* 7:3 (2004), pp. 339-358.

Preface

In the last decade alone, homelessness in America has grown from a minor problem in isolated areas of a few big cities into a near-epidemic that is sweeping across the face of urban America. Today, there is scarcely an American city of any appreciable size that does not have homeless people. Shelters for such persons and related facilities and programs have become an inescapable part of city services, as essential and as commonplace as police protection or water and sewage treatment. What to do for, with, or about the homeless has become a nagging and complex social policy issue that is being debated at all levels of government.

Who *are* the homeless? How many of them are there? How did they get to be homeless? Why here? Why now? What happened in American society in the decade of the 1980's to create this problem? And now that the problem exists, what, if anything, can be done to solve it? These are the questions I wish to take up in this book.

The principal villains of the piece are the myths, stereotypes, and scapegoats that have sprung up around the issue of homelessness in the past decade, like fetid toadstools in rotting stumps after a heavy rain. Chief among these is a viewpoint that many homeless people are, in President Reagan's words, "Well, we might say, homeless by choice." This is an extremely romanticized view of the problem, which derives ultimately from the belief that here in the land of boundless opportunity, people can make of themselves whatever they choose. If people are found to be sleeping in gutters and scavenging food from restaurant dumpsters, then it is because they have chosen to do so. At least there are no bills to worry about and no phone to answer. And the solution to the problem is equally straightforward: Sober up, take a shower, get a job.

In contrast to this voluntaristic view, I stress throughout the volume the large-scale social and economic forces that have operated over the past decade to price an increasingly large segment of the urban poor completely out of the housing market. Seen in this light, the problem of homelessness is that there are too many extremely poor people competing for too few affordable housing units. In Chapter 3 the point is made that the nation would now be facing a formidable homelessness problem even if there were no alcoholics, no drug addicts, no deinstitutionalized mentally ill people—no personal pathologies of any kind. Homelessness is, rather than a choice, the result of extreme poverty in housing markets that have very little to offer to extremely poor people.

A second viewpoint against which I argue is the notion that homelessness is somehow all "of a piece," that it makes sense to speak of "the" homeless as though they were a single, undifferentiated group whose problems result from one factor common to all. Though such a view is widely recognized as unrealistic by scholars, many lay people and certainly many policymakers subscribe to it.

Perhaps the most widespread viewpoint in this genre is the idea that the problem of homelessness was created by the movement, still ongoing, to deinstitutionalize the mentally ill. This is, at best, a half-truth. It suggests, first of all, that most or all homeless people are psychiatrically impaired and would not be homeless except that they have been kicked out of state mental institutions. In fact, as noted in Chapter 6, not more than about a third of the homeless are mentally ill by any meaningful clinical standard, which means that two-thirds are not, and thus the homelessness of the large majority must result from other factors.

A variation on the above theme is that the homeless are just old, broken-down alcoholics who would spend their nights in drunk tanks and jails except that we have relaxed the laws against public inebriation and vagrancy. As with the deinstitutionalization theme, there is some truth to this viewpoint. The police no longer sweep the drunks from the street every night, and to be sure, there are many drunks among the homeless. At the same time, the best available evidence suggests that among homeless men, only about half are alcohol-abusive, and this leaves another half who are not. (Among homeless women, only about one in six are alcohol abusers.) So while alcohol abuse is certainly a part of the homelessness story, it is far from the whole story.

Many of the misconceptions that surround homelessness involve the social welfare system in one or another way. There is, first, the viewpoint that most or all of the homeless are just "welfare bums," content to live on the dole, often defrauding the public tax coffers in the process. The more serious problem, of course, is the *under*-utilization of existing social and human service programs by the homeless population. There are no doubt many more homeless people who are eligible to participate in these programs but for whatever reason do not than there are ineligible homeless persons who nonetheless receive benefits and thereby cheat the system.

A contrasting but equally erroneous view is that if we could just "plug" homeless people into all the programs, benefits, and services that are available to them, their problems would be solved. In fact, as I discuss in Chapter 7, the eligibility criteria for many welfare programs are such as to virtually preclude homeless people from participating in them. Perhaps more to the point, the purchasing power of the welfare dollar has eroded so badly over the last twenty years that it is now impossible for many people to sustain themselves in a stable housing situation on the average welfare payment. Even if all homeless people participated in every benefit program available to them, the net benefit they would receive would, in many cases, still not keep them off the streets.

My depiction of the complexity of homelessness in contemporary America begins in Chapter 1, with a series of vignettes—case histories—of several homeless people that I have met or come to know about. My point is that there are as many different kinds of homeless people as there are kinds of people. We meet Radar, a homeless alcoholic; the McMullans, a homeless family; Yvette Diaz, a homeless 12-year-old girl, whose life and future are being destroyed by forces over which possibly no one, certainly not Yvette herself, has any control. A second purpose of these case studies is to impart some sense of the material and existential conditions of a homeless existence, to say something of what it means, day to day, to be homeless in this society.

Chapter 2 addresses the twin issues of definition and numbers. What, exactly, do we mean by homeless, and how many homeless people are there? The numbers issue has been very controversial. Informed guesses by advocacy organizations have run as high as three or four million. Official government estimates (for example, by the Department of Housing and Urban Development) put the figure in the low hundreds of thousands. My review of the pertinent studies suggests that the correct numbers are somewhere around half a million literally homeless people on any given day, perhaps a million and a half homeless at some point in the course of a year, and untold tens of millions at high risk for homelessness at any one time.

Many people seem to think that today's homelessness problem is something unique in the American experience, that it has never before existed on this scale. In fact, homelessness has arisen as a significant social problem many times in our history, most recently during the Great Depression. Historical studies reviewed in Chapter 2 show that homelessness was a problem even before the American Revolution. Still, there is unquestionably something different about the homelessness of today. Much of the rest of the book is an attempt to state just what that "something different" is.

My principal themes are few and simple. The homeless are *not* a homogeneous group, a point I stress throughout, especially in chapters 1 and 4. To the contrary, there are many different kinds of homeless people, they are homeless for very different reasons, and they need very different things. Likewise, homelessness is *not* a simple problem, although, as argued in the concluding chapter, it may have a simple (albeit very costly) solution—a renewed federal commitment to the public construction of low-income housing. Like many of my fellow scholars, I have come increasingly to look on homelessness as fundamentally a *housing* problem, an obvious point perhaps, but one that is too often lost in discussions of mental illness, alcohol abuse, cutbacks in social welfare spending, and the like.

Still, many other factors are often discussed in connection with homelessness, such as employment and unemployment, social disaffiliation, extreme poverty, and the like—and each of them plays some role in the problem of homelessness as we experience it today. The loss of low-income housing is only the background against which these many causal agents unfold. My intent throughout the book, and especially in chapters 5 through 7, is thus to assess the relative importance of the many contributing factors, in the hopes that some solutions are thereby made obvious. My thoughts about a solution are summarized in Chapter 8.

The most important fact about homeless people is that they are, indeed, *people*—each with their own biographies, their own problems, and their own resources. The next most important fact is that they are *poor* people, the poorest of the poor, who live as they do largely because they lack the means to live any other way.

Americans have always found it necessary to distinguish between the deserving and undeserving poor—the former, victims of circumstance who merit compassion; the latter, shiftless bums who could do better if they wanted to and who therefore merit contempt. Recent poll data suggest that most people, at least so far, consider the homeless to be among the deserving poor. More than two thirds of the respondents in a recent Gallup poll, for example, thought that we should be spending more money to "care for the homeless."

Still, there are some, perhaps many, who look on the homeless less as poor people deserving of sympathy and help than as detritus to be swept out of sight. One such person is Stuart Bykofsky, a reporter for the Philadelphia *Daily News* and the author of a recent "My Turn" column in *Newsweek* entitled, "No Heart for the Homeless."

Mr. Bykofsky's complaint is an increasingly common one: The streets are littered with "tattered human bundles." The bundles are offensive to the senses. They panhandle. They annoy. "I am fed up with the trash they bring into my neighborhood. The pools of urine . . . disgust me. I am fed up with picking my way down side-walks blocked by plastic milk crates, stepping over human forms sprawled on steam gratings. . . . They have got to go. . . . My tax money keeps the street—their home—paved and clean. That makes me their landlord. I want to evict them."

Evidently exasperated, Bykofsky muses early in his diatribe, "I don't know, exactly, when they got the *right* to live on the street. I don't know exactly when I *lost* the right to walk through town without being pestered by panhandlers. I do know I want them off my sidewalk."

There is a quaint theory embedded in this passage: homeless-ness is the result of more and more people exercising some newly won right to "live on the street." Does Bykofsky actually think that people sleep in the streets because they *want* to and because they think they have a *right* to do so if they wish? Does it not occur to him that the people who sleep in his gutters do so because they have nowhere else to go? Quite to the contrary. "The drunk, the addicted, and the just plain shiftless present an entirely different problem. They say they are on the streets because they have nowhere else to go. We must take that excuse away from them."

In Chapter 3 I review some recent data on housing trends in Bykofsky's city, Philadelphia. Between 1978 and 1982, the number of low-income rental units in that city fell by 26%, from about 211 thousand units to about 157 thousand. During that same period, the size of Philadelphia's poverty population rose from 516,000 to 708,000, an increase of 37%. Simple division thus shows that in the late 1970's, there were 2.4 poor people in Philadelphia for each available low-income unit. Four years later, there were 4.5 poor people per available unit. The housing squeeze being faced by Philadelphia's poor is unmistakable. That there is nowhere else to go is not an excuse. It has become an inescapable fact of the political economy of Philadelphia and many other cities.

"Tell me why," Bykofsky demands, "they are allowed to make the street their home—day and night, hot and cold—when I can't park a car at the curb for an hour without paying a meter. How is that possible?" Imagine: poor people get to spend their nights—even cold nights—sleeping on the street for free, and we still expect writers for the *Daily News* to put quarters in the parking meters. There is, I grant, a very disturbing lesson in this, but I do not think it is the lesson Bykofsky would have us learn.

Bykofsky groups the homeless into three rough categories: "(1) the economically distressed, who would work if they could find work; (2) the mentally ill, who can't work; (3) the alcoholic, the drug-addicted, and others who won't work."

As to the first, he recommends welfare or a "workfare" program. Clearly, those who "would work if they could find work" fit his sense of the deserving poor, and for them welfare is apparently acceptable. But does Bykofsky have any idea just how miserly welfare benefits are these days? Does he think we would actually reduce the number of "tattered human bundles" if everyone who "would work" were put on welfare? If so, he is mistaken.

The case I know best is Chicago. Perhaps Philadelphia is dramatically different, but I doubt it. In any case, the average monthly general assistance (welfare) payment to a single individual in Chicago is $151, and the average monthly rent for a room in the city's few remaining flophouse hotels is $195. In Chicago, at least, the average welfare payment will not quite allow one to rent the *cheapest* housing available in the city. One is thankful for Bykofsky's generosity to those whom he considers worthy, but he should be aware that even if we follow his advice, many of those "tattered human bundles" will still have to sleep on his street.

As for the second group, the mentally ill, Bykofsky's suggestions have more merit. "The mentally incompetent who now have the 'freedom' to die on cold streets must be steered to decent tax-supported homes or institutions that will care for them." Not everyone will agree with this viewpoint—the idea of reopening the large state mental institutions is anathema to many advocates for the homeless—but it is at least a policy option that very much needs to be considered.

This leaves the third group, "the drunk, the addicted, and the just plain shiftless." Bykofsky says nothing about their proportion relative to the total, but by the general tenor of the essay, one infers that he thinks they are in the majority. These are the ones whose "excuse"—that they have nowhere else to go—must be taken away. "New facilities do not have to be built. Every community has factories and warehouses that have closed down. Nearly every community has abandoned houses. These can be converted at minimal cost into a shelter that provides light, heat, and plumbing . . ."

Bykofsky is either unaware of building, health, and safety codes or grossly misinformed about their implications. A coat of paint on an abandoned warehouse will not make it fit for human habitation, not even by the drunk and shiftless. Many of those abandoned houses to which he refers were shut down in the first place because they were declared unfit by local departments of public health.

Bringing abandoned and unused buildings up to code is not a cheap proposition by any means. Building codes in most cities specify a certain amount of window and floor space per intended inhabitant. There are strict standards as to sanitation, ventilation, and lighting. There are fire, wind, and seismic safety codes to worry about as well. The experience in New York City is that the rehabilitation costs for a single apartment unit are often on the order of $50,000 or $60,000—this, mind you, not to create elegant apartments, but just to bring an existing abandoned unit up to the minimum building standards.

Providing more cheap housing to low-income people is a laudable goal; indeed, I think it is the only genuine solution to the homelessness problem. But anyone who thinks that the cost of doing so will be minimal is a fool.

One can readily understand, even share, Bykofsky's obvious exasperation. No one in their right mind actually likes picking their way through bodies huddled by heating grates. As Bykofsky correctly observes, "People sleeping on the streets depress property values, decrease tourism, tarnish a city's reputation and inhibit customers from entering shops. In subtle ways, we already are paying the price for homelessness." Beyond all question, homelessness degrades the quality of urban life.

I do not think, however, that the solution will be found in simplistic and mean-spirited scapegoating. It is convenient to believe that many of the homeless are responsible for their own plight, and that a few cheap, easy measures will solve the problem. This, alas, is not the case. Nor will homelessness go away if we offer welfare to the worthy, reopen the state mental hospitals, and warehouse the remainder in abandoned factories. It is not just the dignity of homeless people—as people and as fellow citizens—that we have to worry about. We should also be concerned about our collective dignity as a compassionate and just nation.

James D. Wright

Acknowledgments

The writing of this book was in many ways a family enterprise. I am indebted to my mother, Helen Wright, for many things and particularly for her frequent suggestion over the years that I write books like this one. I am also indebted to my wife, Christine Stewart, to my son, Matthew Wright, and to my sister, Nancy Wright, for having read earlier drafts and for having made many useful and interesting suggestions that have been incorporated in what follows. And I must also thank my family for their patience with the endless hours of supper-time conversation where many of the themes of this volume were first laid out and tested. Paraphrasing Camus and one of the principal lessons to be learned from this book, "without family, all life goes rotten."

My interest in the problems of the homeless grew out of a research project on the National Health Care for the Homeless Program, findings from which are strewn here and there throughout the volume. This research was funded mainly by a grant from the Robert Wood Johnson Foundation, whose support I gratefully acknowledge.

My ideas about homelessness, and what could be done to eliminate it, have evolved over a 5-year stretch of active research on the topic. During this period, I have had the opportunity to attend several dozen meetings, symposia, conferences, and the like, and to discuss my views and findings with scores of other scholars, homelessness advocates, policy makers, and others. The list of people to whom I am therefore indebted for the ideas contained in this book would run to many pages. At the risk of seeming invidious, I want to thank three of these people in particular: Peter Rossi, Dee Weber, and Steve Wobido. None of these three will agree with everything I have written, but they are directly responsible for more of it than any of them probably realizes.

CHAPTER ONE

The Human Faces of Homelessness

To many people, homelessness is little more than an abstraction, a convenient term that refers to a distant and ill-understood problem. To others, like Stuart Bykofsky, it has become an annoyance, less distant although in many cases no better understood. To the homeless themselves, however, homelessness is a fact, a way of life that is relentless and nearly unfathomable in its humiliation of flesh and spirit.

As stated in the preface, the most important fact about homeless people is that they are people, not abstractions, not "tattered human bundles," but flesh and blood human beings, some representative biographies of whom are recounted here. They illustrate the diversity of homelessness in contemporary America, and show some of the human faces behind the numbers presented later.

AN OLD FACE

Radar[1] is a chronic alcoholic, born in a New England mill town to a military family. He took his first drink on the night of his high school graduation, and has not stopped drinking since. His father got him a job just after his graduation but six years later, he quit the job because he was about to be fired—for drinking. From then on, his life has been a long downward spiral: "First you sell your car, then your clothes, then you're on the streets."

Radar has never had a home or even a stable living situation, nor has he held a steady job, since his early twenties. He has spent the last two decades as a street bum in a middle-sized New England community, admittedly having moved there because he had heard that welfare would be easier to get.

Here is the pattern of his life in his own words:

> You learn how to get along. In the summer you sleep out, mostly in the cemetery. You lay some cardboard down on the ground, 'cause it gets damp, you know. When you get up, you "rough up" the grass so nobody knows you been there.
>
> Sometimes you find a shiny tombstone and you use it like a mirror, to see yourself. You keep a toothbrush and some after-shave on you. You take the salt from a fast-food restaurant to brush your teeth, and splash on some after-shave to cover up, you know. Unless you have to drink it.

1

> You always keep a little liquor for the morning. Wild Irish Rose wine is the best, 'cause you can keep it down in the morning. You got to keep that first drink down, then you're all right to get the day going.
>
> During the day you find some buddies and you party. A favorite place is behind a super-convenience store, where there is a small wooded area and abandoned cars. It's easy to get liquor. Somebody is always getting a check, vets or Social Security. You share when you've got it and they share when they do.
>
> Easier to get a drink than a hamburger. You can always hit up a friend or a stranger for a little money. Charge the liquor at the "packy." Got to pay the money back though, or it dries up. Always pay the liquor bill first. Money doesn't mean anything, as long as you have a drink in front of you. Sometimes you go to the nice bars just to watch the local bigshots come in for a morning drink. They're no better.
>
> In winter, you get some buddies and rent a room. Then you put as many people in as possible. You can do that for a few nights and then you get thrown out because of the noise and fighting. If you got to stay out in winter, you try not to sleep. You get enough liquor to drink all night, then get inside in the day. Sometimes you get thirty or forty people together in the woods and "party" for two or three days. Then you have a fire and a big time.

Of course, there are times when no money comes or Radar is too sick to continue with the party. When this happens, he checks into the alcohol detoxification unit. By his own (possibly inflated) count, Radar has been "in detox" more than 400 times in the last nine years, not counting the times when he tried to get in but was turned away.

His stays in the unit vary from 1 night to 5 days. He was first detoxified when he was 31 years old, 11 years after his first drink. On one occasion, he failed to eat for a month and was sent to a 6-week inpatient alcohol rehabilitation program. He resumed drinking the day he was discharged.

Radar has evidently learned quite a bit from his frequent visits to the detox unit. For example, he knows the exact ethanol content of virtually everything you can drink, including Listerine (26%). He is also very knowledgeable about what chronic alcohol abuse does to a person's body, and he discusses his health matter-of-factly, in medical terminology. He says that he does not have "peripheral neuropathy," unlike some of his friends. He does have a "seizure disorder" that occurs when he stops drinking and for which he takes medication. His liver swells up when he drinks (probably "alcoholic hepatitis," since this also disappears when he stops drinking). He vomits every morning until he keeps his first drink down. He has very few teeth left and he needs glasses. Although Radar is not as sick as he might be given his addiction and his life-style, he is, likewise, not a well man.

His major health problems are the many injuries he suffers while he is drunk. He was once hit by a car in front of a package store and his leg was broken. He has had multiple scrapes and bruises from fighting on the streets. When the injuries are serious, the police take him to the emergency room of the local hospital. The hospital, he says, will not keep a homeless alcoholic who has no insurance. Radar is very bitter toward the health care system, except for the people in the detoxification unit that he sees as friends.

His attitude toward the police is cautious but respectful. He has been arrested four times for drunk driving, the last resulting in a 2-month sentence in the county jail, and he has been picked up for public intoxication more times than he can remember. He once spent 6 months in jail for assaulting his girlfriend. He reports that jail was not "too bad" since he could smoke pot all day and occasionally get liquor. He says, "If you are polite to the police and keep fairly well hidden, they won't bother you."

Radar's family or support network consists of the bottle gangs to which he belongs, small groups of fellow alcoholics who share liquor, companionship, and a sense of belonging. Although they are mostly men, there are some women in these groups, women that Radar initially meets in the detox unit. He says that the "regulars" protect the women when they are together. "If we are partying together, we'll give them our coats. Nobody hits on them while we are together." Apparently he chooses his sexual partners for other reasons, for example, if they have an apartment and will let him and one or two others sleep there in bad weather. He believes that street life is easier for women since "they can always pick up a man and go to his place for the night." This behavior is not considered prostitution, merely a matter of survival.

Radar lives for the here and now. There is no long-range planning, no goals for tomorrow or next week or next month. "If I have a drink in front of me and you offered me ten dollars to carry a package across the street, I wouldn't do it." He spends all his money on alcohol. Basics such as food and shelter are lesser concerns left to take care of themselves. And yet, despite the obvious depravity of his existence, he is (at least to all appearances) carefree and happy enough with who he is. As he puts it, "The streets are an adventure—you never know where you will go!"

I have described Radar as an old face not because of his age—the man was just 39 years old when interviewed—but because of the nature of his homelessness. His story conforms almost perfectly to a common stereotype of homelessness. He is a prime example of Bykofksy's "drunk, addicted and just plain shiftless," a hopeless alco holic with no real desire to change, who survives only through the generosity of friends and society. It is, I admit, hard to muster much sympathy for his situation or for tens of thousands of other homeless drunks just like him.

But many other faces also peer out at us from the homeless population. Let's look at another.

A New Face

In February 1987, I was given an opportunity to testify at hearings before the House Select Committee on Children, Youth, and Families, having been asked to speak about the effects of homelessness on the physical health of children. Also present at the hearings were Lisa and Guy McMullan and their four children: Jamie, Ryan, Morgan, and Ryder. Their fifth child, an infant, had recently died, a victim of Sudden Infant Death Syndrome.

The McMullans, adults and children alike, were clean and neatly dressed, although Mr. McMullan was the only man in the room not in a suit and tie. The three older children sat quietly and respectfully, apparently well coached in how they were supposed to behave in such grand surroundings. The youngest child, only a toddler, squirmed constantly and was handed back and forth between Mrs. McMullan and her oldest daughter throughout their testimony. Mrs. McMullan spoke at length about her family, their homelessness, and their troubles. Her prepared statement to the committee follows.[2]

> My name is Lisa McMullan. I am here with my husband, Guy, and my four children, Jamie, Ryan, Morgan and Ryder. The story of my family's experience with homelessness began in Mile City, Montana, early in 1986. My husband and I owned a house there, but when my husband's job was phased out due to the farm crisis, we could no longer make the mortgage payments so we gave the house back to the bank, sold everything and came East in the spring.
>
> We first stayed with my mother-in-law, but that didn't work out because there wasn't enough room for all of us. There were seven of us living in the basement. After a few months we moved to Baltimore, and my husband and I both held a number of jobs. In November or December 1986, we began to have problems paying the rent on our apartment. [Lack of construction work; day care too expensive.] After several eviction notices, we found ourselves without a place to live and with no place to go.
>
> I called around, with the help of Social Services, to several shelters

in Baltimore, but no one would take us as a whole family. Finally, the Salvation Army offered us a room to stay in. The room was very small with six people in it. The conditions at the shelter were very stressful for me and my family and the children particularly became much more difficult to manage. The food was not that good as you can probably imagine.

It was very crowded, and there's a weird feeling that goes along with being there. You feel like you're nothing because you suddenly don't have a home. You know you've done all you can do and it isn't your fault, but the whole situation makes you feel like you must have done something wrong.

My family and I tried very hard to overcome these feelings. Especially because it really hurts the children. Children need to know and feel who has control over their lives. And suddenly they are living in a situation where they see their parents needing outside help, and they are all suddenly living with many other people they don't know and who frighten them.

To combat all this, and to keep our family life in order, we tried very hard to maintain a schedule. We made sure we went on walks with the children, we kept them in school, and did all we could do to make them feel we still had control over our lives and were still there for them.

But this was a real struggle for us. We were up every morning at 6 a.m. to get my husband to work on time and to take the two older children to school. In doing this, we missed breakfast at the shelter every day until they began giving us boxes of cereal to bring along to eat later. We were fortunate in still having a car to be able to keep that schedule. Not everybody does.

We were at the shelter between three and four weeks. Many of our experiences there were frightening and added a lot to the stress in our family. There was no door on the women's shower and one night I caught a man peeking into the women's bathroom watching my 10-year-old daughter. The man also lived in the shelter and I reported him, but nothing was done about it. Another time, a woman accused my daughter of trying to push her down the stairs. As it turned out, we learned that the woman was mentally disturbed and hated to be touched, so if you got too close to her, she got very upset.

These were the kind of things—overcrowding, hunger, lack of privacy and insecurity about the future—that really put stress on our children and our family. It was very hard on us all. My two oldest children, 10 and 7 years old, were in counseling, originally to help them deal with the loss of their younger sister to crib death when we were at my mother-in-law's house. But then I kept them in counseling all throughout this period because I knew that not having the security of a home and living in a shelter would be hard on them.

We recently found a small apartment, but it turns out that our crisis was not over yet. A week after we moved in, my husband was laid off from his job at Bethlehem Steel. We are now both looking for jobs and are trying to get stability back in our children's lives. It is very, very difficult to maintain a family in this kind of insecure environment. I know that if it weren't for each other, we probably couldn't keep struggling to improve things.

Unfortunately, I know what great damage and harm that homelessness can do to a family, even when they're all trying to do their best to make everything work. Because of my family's painful experiences, I wanted to tell you our story today. We appreciate your concern and thank you for the opportunity you have provided by holding this hearing. I know that our story will help you to help others like us and especially those who have been even less fortunate.

The McMullans are the new faces of homelessness—homeless families, often decent, hardworking, previously stable families who have been victimized by economic misfortune and who are trying to piece together some semblance of family life from the resources made available to them through the social service system. In fact, as discussed in more detail later, homeless families are probably the fastest growing sector of the contemporary homeless population.

Many useful details were added to the McMullans' story in their oral testimony. Their most severe recurring problem was finding shelters that would take intact families, especially families the size of theirs. In many cities, no such shelters exist. In these cases, the husband is shunted off to a shelter for homeless men, or perhaps to a mission, the wife and small children are sent to a shelter for women and children, and the teenaged children are sent to a facility for homeless adolescents. However desperately the family might wish to remain intact, the existing social service system sometimes simply does not allow it.

Mrs. McMullan: The social worker looked at me and she says well, I think I may be able to find a place for you and the children, but what is your husband going to do? And I looked at this lady and I said, lady, we have been through everything together. We are one of the more fortunate families, that my husband has not walked out. He has stayed with the family through thick and thin. And I said, and I am not going to throw him out to a car now. I said, you're going to have to do something better.

The McMullans were more fortunate, perhaps, than most. The Salvation Army did provide a room where the entire family could stay. But, in solving the immediate problem, new problems arose:

Mrs. McMullan: You're so stressed out, you're angry, you're frustrated, and you're walking around just a bundle of nerves. And it makes it even harder. And you've got emotionally handicapped people in there. You've got a time limit on how long you can stay. There are roaches, the kind that walk. We ran into trying to stabilize some kind of routine, which is really hard, because kids need that, they need a stable environment, they need to know who is in control of their lives.

As adults in the shelter environment, the McMullans must live by many rules not of their own making; they are, evidently, not even in control of their own lives, much less the lives of their children. Any concept of familial or parental authority is impossible to maintain in such a situation.

> *Mr. Coats* (ranking Republican on the committee): Mr. and Mrs. McMullan, I want to commend you for making a valiant effort to keep your family together, through obviously some very, very trying circumstances. You are an exception to the rule. . . . What is your current situation now?
>
> *Mrs. McMullan:* I am presently unemployed, looking for work, and my husband is collecting unemployment.
>
> *Mr. McMullan:* I haven't got it yet. I was just laid off, due to weather and materials cutbacks, material that wasn't on hand. And I just talked to my supervisor yesterday and he said 2 or 3 weeks.
>
> *Mr. Coats:* Are you presently receiving other benefits? AFDC?
>
> *Mr. McMullan:* WIC.
>
> *Mr. Coats:* WIC? How about food stamps? School lunch subsidies?
>
> [*No response.*]
>
> *Mr. Coats:* Are you in the process of applying for these other benefits? Am I missing something?
>
> [*Pause*]
>
> *Mrs. McMullan:* One of the things is that we are trying not to get caught up in the welfare system, because it seems like from what we've heard, once you get in, it's hard to get out. We want to be on our own . . . We don't want it to be made cushiony so that we lose that eagerness to get out there and make it on our own.
>
> *Mr. McMullan:* You become institutionalized. . . . You're giving up something when you start getting into the welfare system.

Homeless families, like the McMullans, comprise perhaps a quarter or more of today's homeless problem. Although they are as homeless as Radar, their needs and their prospects are obviously very different. Radar wants a drink, Guy and Lisa McMullan want a chance. For them, the American dream has become something of a nightmare, although the McMullans dream still. Here is their voice one final time:

> *Mrs. McMullan:* I don't think the government owes me a home. "Here, you are to give me a home, you are to feed my family, you are to do all this." But we're at the point where we need help—a helping hand, that's all. Because once you [become] homeless, people look at you like you don't even register as a human being any longer.

If you're on welfare you're at least on the bottom of the scale. You tell people that you're living in a *shelter,* and they do not hire you. They do not hire people who are living in the shelter. For whatever reason—bu it's like you no longer exist as a human being.

And it's not fair to us or our children. Because I've got two kids who are extremely ambitious. And they are still holding a straight B average in school, even though they've transferred schools three times [this year]. Everybody wants something better for their kids. . . . We're not any different.

A WOMAN'S FACE

As we see in a later chapter, more than one homeless adult in four is a woman, and among homeless adult women, one fourth have dependent children in their care. One such is Sheila, mother of four children; the oldest is Robert, age 12.[3] Sheila and her family are living in a shelter for homeless women and children in the Boston area. They have been homeless for a year and a half. The immediate cause of their homelessness was eviction from a previous apartment; Sheila's boyfriend had threatened some of the neighbors, who in turn complained to the landlord, with the result that a woman and four small children were dumped onto the streets.

Prior to coming to Boston, Sheila, the children, and the children's father had lived in a trailer in the Midwest. The father was alcoholic and physically abused the entire family, so Sheila packed up the children and left. Like Mrs. McMullan, she had also lost a fifth child. As a result of the loss of a child, the brutal home situation, and the recent dissolution of the family unit and move East, Sheila suffers chronic depression and is unable to work. While housed in the apartment, she and the children were largely dependent on the boyfriend's income.

Since eviction, the family has not lived any longer than 3 months in any one place. All of the children, Robert particularly, show obvious signs of distress as a result of their uncertain and disordered living conditions. Upon being interviewed, Robert admitted that he hates school and is bored there. He also worries that his classmates will discover his dark, shameful secret—that he has no real home like normal children have. He hates the shelter with equal intensity and, despite the obvious problems, recalls fondly the trailer in the Midwest.

Robert describes himself as "ugly" (he is somewhat overweight) and admits that he often thinks about killing himself. "Robert further stated that he has no friends, has already repeated a grade and is now failing again in school. He is constantly teased by peers and criticized by adults. Finally, since coming to the shelter, he has difficulty sleeping because of unfamiliar sounds and violent nightmares" (p. 40).

The care of dependent children in a shelter or street environment is only the most obvious of the many unique problems that homeless women such as Sheila or Mrs. McMullan face. Unlike Mrs. McMullan, most homeless women do not enjoy the support of an adult partner; they are on the streets alone or with their children. Being women, they are constantly vulnerable to sexual assault; according to one study, the rate of sexual assault on homeless women is twenty times the rate among women in the general population.[4] As we will discuss later, mental illness is about twice as common among homeless women as among homeless men, further increasing their vulnerability and adding still more to the difficulties of their existence.

Aileen Ross has written a sad, moving book about the lives of homeless women, *The Lost and the Lonely.*[5] The Table of Contents alone says volumes:

One of the lost and lonely is Lily, age 30, single, a high school dropout, child of an alcoholic father, and a drug addict herself. "Lily had a good job until she broke her leg skiing four years ago. The intense pain made her take to drugs and she has been an addict ever since. The result is much confusion and deep depression. She has made several suicide attempts. She lies constantly, steals, and shoplifts. At times she is dangerously violent. She tried to choke her mother, stabbed her boyfriend, attacked one of the shelter staff viciously, and is violent when apprehended by the police" (p. 109).

In the course of a single year, Lily was found to have been in the hospital eighteen separate times, usually in the aftermath of a suicide attempt or a drug overdose, once after swallowing 30 Valiums and 30 Seconals simultaneously. Several of her nights in the hospital were spent on respirators after having the drugs pumped from her stomach. Twice she became comatose but recovered both times. The last suicide attempt of the year followed a vicious beating by a man with a piece of wood. In the same year, incidentally, she was found to have been in jail or before the court seven times, usually on theft or shoʃ lifting charges.

Lily is routinely banned from various shelters around the city. Tʃ next to last entry on her reads as follows: "Evicted from her apar ment. Had trouble with her neighbors and beat up a man."

A DEAD FACE

Bill was a white male born in 1930 who, like Radar, suffered from severe alcohol dependency. He was disheveled and unkempt, a client in one of the local projects of the national "Health Care for the Homeless" program, a demonstration program funded in 1984 by the Robert Wood Johnson Foundation and the Pew Memorial Trust to establish "health care for the homeless" clinics in 19 large American cities.[6]

Bill was seen in the HCH clinic for the first time on July 9, 1985. As was usual, he was very intoxicated and came to the clinic complaining about his knee. He said that he drank "whatever I can get my hands on." He had no address since he lived down by the river. He was much too drunk to talk to or examine, and so was asked to come back the following day.

The next day, Bill was still drunk, evidently malnourished, unsteady on his feet; his speech was slurred. He was referred to a local shelter for homeless men but refused with some agitation, stating that he hated the shelter and "would rather die on the street." His condition and attitude the following day were no different.

A month later, on August 8, Bill was found out on the streets with an infected lip wound and broken dentures. Subsequent questioning revealed that he had been mugged and beaten up by three men who stole two sacks of empty aluminum cans that Bill was taking to the recycling center. The cans, apparently, were his sole source of income.

Staff members at the HCH clinic treated the lip wound and suggested that Bill enter an alcohol treatment program. On August 12, an appointment was made to get his dentures replaced. During this visit, he expressed the fear that "I won't live another night."

Later that evening, Bill was rushed to the emergency room, where doctors found that his ribs had also been fractured in the mugging, puncturing his lungs. Because his lungs were filling with fluid, Bill was catheterized and intubated; he had trouble breathing and was very belligerent and incoherent. During the night, he died.

The hospital discharge notes list "cardiac arrest secondary to alcoholism" as the cause of Bill's death, but the medical examiner chose to treat it as a homicide instead. Bill, it appears, may well have been beaten to death for twenty pounds of empty aluminum cans, worth maybe a couple of dollars.

A CHILD'S FACE

Another witness at the House Select Committee hearings on homelessness was Yvette Diaz, a lovely 12-year-old Hispanic girl living with her mother and three siblings at one of the large welfare hotels in midtown Manhattan. Yvette is a charming young lady with an engaging smile and coal-black shoulder-length hair, dressed this day in a freshly ironed smock. She is soft-spoken, evidently somewhat intimidated by her surroundings, but firm and very sweet. Her prepared statement is as follows:

> My name is Yvette Diaz. I am 12 years old. I live at the Martinique Hotel, at 49 West 32nd St. I live in rooms 1107–1108. There are two rooms. I live here with my mother, two sisters, 9 and 7, and my 3-year-old brother. We have lived in the Martinique Hotel for almost 2 years now. I am living at the Martinique Hotel because my aunt's house burned down and we didn't have any place to live.

> We were living in my aunt's house in Brooklyn because my father was discharged from the United States Air Force in the state of Washington and the family came back to New York where we originally came from. We couldn't find an apartment right away so we stayed with my aunt. The house burned down and we went to the Martinique Hotel.

> Since we are in New York at the Martinique Hotel, I have been going to P.S. 64 which is on East 6th Street in Manhattan. When I first started school here, I was absent a lot because the bus that took us to school in the morning was late a lot of the time, and other times I did not get up on time. We did not have an alarm clock. Finally, my mother saved up to buy one. This school year I have not been absent many times because the bus is on time, and we have an alarm clock.

> I don't like the hotel because there is always a lot of trouble there. Many things happen that make me afraid. I don't go down into the street to play because there is no place to play on the streets. The streets are dangerous because there are all kinds of people who are on drugs or crazy. My mother is afraid to let me go downstairs.

> Only this Saturday my friend, the security guard at the hotel, Mr. Santiago, was killed on my floor. He was shot by another man and killed. Anyway, people are afraid to open the door to even look out. There are a lot of people on drugs in the hotel. I once found needles and other things that drugs come in, in the hallway.

Our apartment was broken into when we were out. They stole our radio and alarm clock. We have a TV but they didn't get that because we hid it in the closet under other things every time we leave the rooms.

We can't cook in the apartment. My mother sneaked in a hot plate b cause we don't have enough money to eat out every night. They, tl hotel management, warned us that if we are caught cooking in tl rooms we might be thrown out.

I play in the hallway with friends from other rooms on my floor. Sometimes even that isn't safe. A boy, about 15 or 16, came over to me and wanted to take me up to the 16th floor. I got frightened and ran into my room and told my mother. She went to the police and she was told this same boy was showing his "private parts" to girls before, and that it was reported to them. If he bothered me again I was to tell the police.

The five of us live in two rooms at this hotel. There is only one bathroom. We don't have mice or rats like some of the other people who live in the hotel because we have a cat.

I go to the extended school program at my school, P.S. 64. We go from 3–6 P.M. every weekday except Friday. I get help with homework for 45 minutes every day and then we have computer, arts and crafts, dancing, gym and game room. I like it and we also get a hot dinner every night before we go home on the bus. I finish all my homework here as the teacher helps me and it is quiet so I can really understand what I am doing.

If I could have anything that I could want I wish that we could have our own apartment in a nice clean building and a place that I could go outside to play in that is safe. I want that most of all for me and my family.

IMAGINE

Normal middle-class people, such as those expected to be reading this book, have a great deal of difficulty fathoming the peculiarities and degradations of a homeless existence. I hope that the preceding case histories impart a better, if not more sympathetic, understanding. Many of us regard the act of scavenging in trash cans for something to eat as bizarre, to say the very least; we know not what it means to be that hungry. Likewise, urinating in public strikes most people as bizarre and offensive, but in a nation that does not routinely provide public restroom facilities, what is the alternative? We see filthy, lice-infested, disheveled people on the streets and turn our heads. But with no home and therefore no shower or bathtub, what is a homeless person to do?

Imagine that you have just awakened, that you have yet to open your eyes. You have no idea where you are, except that it is definitely not where you were yesterday morning. Are you inside or outside? In a bed or on the floor? What time is it? What day is it?

Your eyes open. You are in a bed in a large shelter. Which shelter is it? What rules are you expected to live by this morning? Is this a shelter that serves breakfast, or will you stand in line for an hour at the soup kitchen before you eat? Will you be able to shower? How about the guy in the bunk next to you? Will he rob you before you get out of bed? Will he infect you with some exotic disease?

You're up, showered, fed, and on the streets. Now what? Shall you look for a job? Panhandle some strangers? Go sit in the park? How about another trip to the welfare office, to see how your application is proceeding? Or perhaps a trip to the health clinic to have your leg ulcer soaked? Or a trip to the plasma center to see if you can sell a pint of your blood? Whichever you choose, plan on doing a lot of walking, and once you get there, plan to stand in line.

It is time for lunch. Will you spend the last 3 dollars in your pocket for a hamburger and a cup of coffee? Or go back to the soup kitchen and stand in line again? Three bucks, after all, is a bottle of cheap wine or a six-pack of beer. Will you get drunk again today, or stay sober and save the money for tomorrow? But what's the point in staying sober? Tomorrow will take care of itself, and in any case, by tomorrow you, like Bill, could be dead.

The day latens. Where will you sleep tonight? What's the weather going to be—warm and pleasant, or cold and rainy? How will you even find out? Is a weather report worth the price of a newspaper? Shall you try another shelter or sleep in the park? The shelters are warm and dry, but they are also crowded and dangerous, and if you have gotten drunk, they may not even let you in. Perhaps your buddy will let you crash with him for the night. Do you have change in your pocket for the phone call?

You decide to forget about the shelter and its rules and regulations; the park bench will do just fine. But this is no good: you are rousted by the police and told to move on. In moving on, you are accosted by a small band of thugs and relieved of your remaining change. You find a deserted alley—no one around, nothing suspicious. Some old newspaper laid out behind a dumpster is your bed for the night.

You wake up. You have no idea where you are, except to know that it is not where you were yesterday morning. Are you inside or outside? In a bed or on the floor? And thus begins the next day of your life.

Or imagine that you are a poor young woman with two children who has just left your husband because of persistent physical abuse

of both you and your children. You have never been homeless before, but without your husband's income you can't possibly keep
your apartment. You go to a battered women's program for advice
and are told to apply for AFDC.

Sure, it's welfare, but with two small kids, what else are you going
to do? At the AFDC office you are assured that you are eligible and
that help is on its way, but that it will be 2 months before the paperwork clears and a check is available.

Now what? You can't stay where you are, and until the AFDC
checks start coming, you can't rent a new place either. So you go to
a shelter for homeless women with children. It is a "transitional shelter." You are welcome to stay there, but only for 21 days. Okay, 3
weeks is better than nothing.

Suddenly, there is a range of new and difficult issues to face. Do
you enroll your school-age child in the local school, knowing that
she will have to be transferred to yet another school in 3 weeks? Or
do you try to keep her in her old school, clear on the other side of
town? How will you get her there and back? You want to look for a
job, but the shelter rules strictly forbid mothers leaving the shelter
without their children. Can you go on job interviews with the 4-year-
old in tow?

It is 3 P.M. Both children are hungry and cranky. Lunch is served
from noon to 1 P.M., dinner from 6 to 7 P.M. No foodstuffs are allowed
in the rooms (it attracts cockroaches). The children remain hungry
and cranky until 6 P.M.

The 3 weeks is up; your social worker has found a room for you in
a welfare hotel, where you can stay until you find an apartment.
Once the AFDC paperwork clears, you will also receive food stamps
and a Section 8 housing certificate that will help enormously with the
rent. But can you stick it out another month? The hotel is in a run-
down, seedy, and dangerous part of town—no place for children, to
be sure, but what is the option? So you go and stick it out. At last,
AFDC comes through. You are still poor, still a "welfare mother," still
uncertain about what your future might hold. But at least you are not
homeless.

Or imagine that you are a young man just released from prison.
Your dues are paid: you hope to put the past behind you and get on
with your life. While in prison, your parents have split up; Dad is
nowhere to be found, and Mom has no room in the tenement. You
have a little gate money; you get a room for the night. Tomorrow,
you will look for a job.

You quickly learn that applications for jobs at the minimum wage rarely ask about your prison record; applications for jobs beyond the minimum wage invariably do. At the minimum wage, you will barely clear $100 a week; the cheapest apartment you have so far seen advertised is $450 a month. The gate money is running out, so you head for a shelter for homeless men. Now you are both an ex-con and a homeless person.

Being young and in reasonable health, with no recent employment record, you learn from the case worker in the shelter that you are probably not eligible for any welfare programs. Food stamps are about all that can be obtained. But with no place to live and therefore no place to cook, what good are they? You, of course, quickly learn that they can be traded for cash at a discounted rate, and so you apply anyway.

The weeks pass. An assortment of odd jobs, temporary work, and a little panhandling keeps some spare cash in your pocket, but a steady job and a decent, affordable apartment have yet to be found. All your old friends are either in jail themselves, dead, or have left town. Your family, however willing, has no resources with which to help. Your situation becomes progressively more desperate. And then comes the revelation: Prison was better than this.

Or imagine that you are mentally ill, perhaps schizophrenic, but no obvious danger to yourself or others. You have spent your life in and out of psychiatric treatment centers, halfway houses, and the like, and now you are living on your own, on the street. Being mentally ill, your grasp of reality is uncertain anyway; the world at large is a strange and frightening place. To survive, you must depend on shelters and food lines, but if your behavior is too "inappropriate," the shelters and soup kitchens will not let you in. You sleep where you can, eat what you can, do whatever you can to pass the hours. The days and weeks blur into a continuous collage of disconnected experiences and forgotten conversations. How old are you? What is your social security number? Where were you born? Where do you live?

My point in this chapter has been that there are many kinds of homeless people. Here you will find an alcoholic skid row bum, there, a muttering schizophrenic. Elsewhere, however, you will find a disabled 33-year-old Vietnam veteran suffering from posttraumatic stress disorder, or perhaps a pregnant 15-year-old runaway whose father has raped her and beaten her once too often, or a febrile infant in the arms of her homeless mother. Look further and you will see an entire family that has been "turned out" because the factory where the father worked was shut down, and beside them an arthritic old gentleman who lost his room in the welfare hotel because he was beaten savagely and relieved of his social security check. These are the contemporary homeless—young and old, male and female, deserving and corrupt.

Many of us find it impossible to imagine being so down on our luck or out of resources, both economic and otherwise, that we would be reduced to an existence of the sort described in this chapter. But is it really so inconceivable? How much stands between any of us and a homeless existence? How far wrong would things have to go?

Look one last time, over there, under the dirt and grime and lice, beneath the tattered clothes, behind the three day stubble. Are you absolutely certain that is not someone you know?

NOTES

1. Radar's story was first recounted in J. Wright and J. Knight, *Alcohol Abuse in the National "Health Care for the Homeless" Client Population* (Washington, DC: National Institute of Alcohol Abuse and Alcoholism, 1987). The version appearing here was published in J. Wright and E. Weber, *Homelessness and Health* (Washington, DC: McGraw Hill, 1987), pp. 65–67, and is used with permission of the publisher.

2. The following material is taken from *The Crisis in Homelessness: Effects on Children and Families*. Hearings before the Select Committee on Children, Youth and Families, U.S. House of Representatives, 24 February 1987 (Washington, DC: U.S. Government Printing Office).

3. The material on Sheila and her family is from the Massachusetts Committee for Children and Youth, *No Place Like Home: A Report on the Tragedy of Homeless Children and Their Families in Massachusetts* (Boston: MCCY, 1986), pp. 39–40.

4. J. Kelly, "Trauma: With the Example of San Francisco's Shelter Programs." Ch. 5 (pp. 77–92) in Brickner *et al.*, *Health Care of Homeless People* (New York, Springer, 1985).

5. *The Lost and the Lonely: Homeless Women in Montreal*. Published by McGill University Printing Service, 1982 (mimeo'd).

6. The National Health Care for the Homeless Program is described in detail in J. Wright and E. Weber, *Homelessness and Health* (Washington, DC: McGraw Hill, 1987), from which Bill's case is taken. Material used by permission of McGraw Hill.

CHAPTER TWO

Homeless in America: The New American Nightmare

During the past decade a disturbing and largely unexpected new problem has arisen in American cities—the "new homeless." Homeless derelicts like Radar and Bill would be found in most times and places; indeed, a rich ethnographic literature focusing on skid row was produced in the 1950's and 1960's. But the seemingly sudden appearance of homeless women, children, and whole families on the streets and in the shelters was, in retrospect, a clear signal that something had gone very seriously awry.

The sudden intensity and increased visibility of the homelessness problem took most observers by surprise. Ten or fifteen years ago, a walk along the twenty-odd blocks from Madison Square Garden to Greenwich Village would have been largely uneventful, a pleasant outing in an interesting part of New York City. Along the same route today one would encounter an assortment of derelict and indigent people—old women rummaging in the trash for bottles and cans, kids swilling cheap wine from paper bags, seedy men ranting meaninglessly at all who venture near. Who are these people? Where did they come from? What, if anything, can or should be done to help them?

The popular mind brims with stereotypes about the homeless population: "They're all crazy people who have been let loose from mental hospitals;" "they're all broken down old drunks;" "they're lazy, shiftless bums who could do better for themselves if they really wanted to;" "they're welfare leeches, living off my taxes." The fact is that while all of these stereotypes are true of some homeless people, none of them is true of all homeless people. As is true of any large group in the American population, the homeless are a diverse lot; no single catchphrase or easy myth can possibly describe them all.

Most homeless people in America today are men, but a sizable fraction are women and a smaller but still significant fraction are the children of homeless adults. All told, the women and children total somewhere between one third and two fifths of the homeless population. Indifference to the plight of homeless adult men comes easily in an illiberal era, but indifference to the plight of homeless women and children, groups society has traditionally obligated itself to protect, comes easily only to the cold of heart.

Alcohol abuse and homelessness are tightly linked in the popular stereotype, but the best available studies confirm that less that 40% of the total homeless population abuses alcohol to excess. The majority do not. Focusing just on the adult men, the studies show that alcohol abuse runs only to about 50%: just about half the men, that is, are chronic alcoholics, the other half are not.

In like fashion, mental illness is certainly a significant problem within the homeless population, but severe chronic psychiatric disorder characterizes only about one third of the homeless group; the remaining two thirds are *not* mentally ill according to any meaningful clinical standard.[1]

Being among the poorest of the poor, it is also true that many homeless people receive government assistance in the form of general relief, food stamps, disability pensions, and the like. And yet, nationwide, studies show that only about half the homeless receive any form of social welfare assistance; the remaining half survive on their own devices.

In sum, some of the homeless *are* broken down alcoholics, but most of them are not. Some *are* mentally impaired, but most of them are not. Some *are* living off the benefit programs made available through the social welfare system, but most of them are not. Clearly, none of the popular mythologies provides an adequate portrait of the homeless in America today.

Figuring out what to do about homelessness requires, first and foremost, a detailed understanding of the problem. We can scarcely solve problems that we do not comprehend, least of all when the existing rudiments of our understanding amount, at best, to simplistic categorizations that divert our attention from more fundamental causes.

My purpose in this book is straightforward. Concurrent with the recent rise of homelessness in American cities has been an impressive outpouring of studies and research. These studies, like the homeless themselves, are varied. Some have been conducted by advocacy organizations, others by academic researchers. Some are casual and haphazard; others represent state-of-the-art research. But all contribute some share to a better understanding of the problem at hand.

The research of the past decade has not answered all the important questions, but it has settled a number of them. Certainly the prospects for a more complete understanding of who the homeless are, how they became homeless, and what we can do to help them are much brighter today than they were a decade ago. My aim is thus to review the important studies that have been done, and to render their findings into a relatively complete but strictly nontechnical portrait accessible to anyone who is interested in this problem.

DEFINITIONS AND NUMBERS OF HOMELESS

While it is apparent that we need to define a phenomenon before we can study or understand it, defining homelessness has proved to be a sticky business. It is easy to agree on the extremes of a definition: an old man who sleeps under a bridge down by the river and has nowhere else to go would obviously be considered homeless. But there are also many ambiguous cases: What of persons who live in rooming houses or boardinghouses or flophouse hotels? Even if they have lived in the same room for years, we might still want to consider them homeless in at least some senses of the term. What of persons who live in abandoned buildings, in tents or shacks made from scrap materials, or in cars and vans? What of a woman in the throes of divorce, with children, who can no longer afford rent on an apartment and who has an offer from her family "to live with us for as long as you need?" What of people who would otherwise be homeless except that they have temporarily secured shelter in the homes of their families or friends? Or those who would otherwise be homeless except that they are temporarily "housed" in jails, prisons, hospitals, or other institutions? What of a person living on a fixed income who rents a cheap hotel room three weeks a month and lives on the streets or in the shelters for the fourth week, the pension being adequate to cover only three quarters of the monthly room rent?

Clearly, to be homeless is to lack regular and customary access to a conventional dwelling unit. The ambiguities arise in trying to define "regular and customary access" and "conventional dwelling unit."

The examples given above demonstrate that *homelessness is not and cannot be a precisely defined condition.* A family who sleeps in its pickup truck and has nowhere else to go would be considered homeless by almost everyone. A long-distance trucker who sleeps regularly—perhaps 3 or 4 nights a week—in the cab of his $100,000 rig, who earns $30,000 or $40,000 a year, and who has a nice home where he sleeps when he is not on the road would not be considered homeless by anyone. The trucker has options; the homeless family living in its pickup does not.

Thus, choice is implied in any definition of homelessness, although clearly not in the manner suggested by Ronald Reagan's words a quoted in the Preface. In general, people who choose to live the wa' they do are not to be considered homeless, however inadequate thei housing may appear to be. Likewise, those who live in objectivel\ inadequate housing—in makeshift quarters or cheap flophouses o in the shelters and missions—because they do not have the resources to do otherwise *would* be considered homeless in most definitions, certainly in mine.

"The resources to do otherwise" implies yet another aspect of my definition of homelessness: true homelessness results from extreme poverty. One hears from time to time of street people who are found to have a locker in the bus station stuffed with cash, or of vagabonds who, in a former life, traded stock on Wall Street but cashed in for the unfettered romance of life on the road. In some sense these people are homeless, but they are homeless by choice. They comprise no important part of the homeless problem in this nation and I shall say nothing further about them.

Poor people living in objectively inadequate housing because they lack the means to do otherwise number in the tens of millions. Indeed, if we adopt a sufficiently inclusive definition of "objectively inadequate housing," virtually the entire population of the country living in poverty would be encompassed within the homeless category, a population numbering some 35 million people.[2] And yet, being homeless means more than just being poor, although, surely, being poor has a lot to do with it.

It is therefore useful to distinguish between the *literally homeless* and the *marginally housed,* a distinction first drawn by Peter Rossi in his study of the homeless of Chicago.[3] By literally homeless, I mean those people who, on a given night, have nowhere to go—no rented room, no friend's apartment, no flophouse—people who sleep out on the streets or who would sleep out on the streets except that they avail themselves of beds in shelters, missions, and other facilities set up to provide space for otherwise homeless people. By the marginally housed, I mean people who have a more or less reasonable claim to a more or less stable housing situation of more or less minimal adequacy, being closer to the "less" than the "more" on one or all criteria.

This distinction certainly does not solve the definitional problem, but it does specify more clearly the subgroups of interest. In epidemiological terms, we can say that the literal homeless are those who are at any one time actually afflicted with the disease of homelessness, whereas the marginally housed represent the population at high risk of the disorder. Following the analogy, we can also assert that both groups are relevant to the public policy discussion of the issue.

Thus it can be confirmed that there is no one, best, correct, easily agreed upon definition of homelessness, and no single correct answer to the question, "How many homeless people are there?" There is, rather, a continuum of housing adequacy or housing stability, with actual cases to be found everywhere along the continuum (that is, it is a continuum with no natural break points). Just where in the continuum one draws the line, defining those above as adequately if marginally housed and those below as homeless, is of necessity a somewhat arbitrary and therefore disputable decision.

Nonetheless, despite the unavoidable arbitrariness, the discussion calls attention to three groups who are pertinent to the themes of this book: in decreasing order of size they are (1) the poverty population as a whole, (2) the subset of the poverty population that is marginally housed, and (3) the subset of the poverty population that is literally homeless. It is useful to get some feel for the relative sizes of these three groups.

We focus on Chicago, Illinois, only because appropriate data for that city are at hand. According to United States government statistics and definitions, the poverty population of Chicago amounts to about 600,000 persons. Of these, approximately 100,000 are poor enough to qualify for general assistance (welfare) under the strict Illinois guidelines. A recent study of general assistance recipients there found that fully half resided with relatives and friends—that is, they were not literally homeless mainly because of the largess of their social networks, but were at high risk of literal homelessness in the face of the merest misfortune.[4] Certainly it would be appropriate to let this group, some 50,000 persons, represent the marginally housed. Finally, the most recent, systematic, and sophisticated attempt to census the literal homeless population of Chicago reports about 3000 genuinely homeless persons on any given night.[5] Taking these numbers at face value, the ratio of poor persons to marginally housed persons to literally homeless persons, at least in one large American city, is on the order of 600 to 50 to 3.

A number of useful points follow. First, it is transparent that homelessness is only a small part of the larger poverty problem in the nation. Most poor people, even most of the very poor, manage to avoid literal homelessness and secure for themselves some sort of reasonably stable housing situation. Just how they do this given recent trends in the housing economy is an important mystery that we shall try to clear up later in the book.

At the same time, as we also see later, the literally homeless ar the poorest of the poor, many of them surviving on less than on quarter of the poverty level income. Thus, while not the most numer ous subgroup of the poverty population, they tend to be the mos indigent and certainly the most visible. My focus in this book on the homeless, however, should not be misconstrued as ignorance of or indifference to the much larger problem of poverty as it is being confronted in America today.

A second point is that the number of literal homeless at any one time is much smaller than the number of potentially homeless (or marginally housed) people. The evidence from Chicago suggests a pool of 50,000 persons who might easily become homeless on any given day; actually, the true pool of risk is doubtlessly larger.[6] Even with a literal homeless count of 3000, the city of Chicago is hard-pressed to come up with sufficient shelter space. (Not to mention sufficient subsidized low-income housing; in many cities, such as Atlanta and Boston, the waiting list for subsidized public housing is as long as 7 or 8 *years*.) The point is that however bad the homelessness problem has become, it could easily be worse by one or two orders of magnitude. In short, the *potential* homelessness problem in contemporary America is many times worse than the *actual* problem being confronted today.

There is, of course, a sense in which this could be said of any social problem—AIDS, overpopulation, crime, and so on. Things, after all, are never quite as bad as one can imagine them being. However, if the housing and poverty trends described in the next chapter continue for another decade, and there is every reason to think that they will, then the large-scale spread of homelessness into what I am calling the population at risk is inevitable. What now appears as only a worrisome potential will inexorably become reality a decade hence.

Similarly, the number literally homeless *on any given night* is not a true indication of the magnitude of the overall problem, that number, by definition, being smaller than the number homeless *in any given month* or over the span of *any given year*. To illustrate, in the Chicago census of the literally homeless, 31% were found to have been homeless less than 2 months, whereas 25% had been homeless for more than 2 years. Homelessness is a heterogeneous mixture of transitory short-term and chronic long-term housing problems. Some people become homeless only to reclaim a stable housing arrangement in a matter of days, weeks, or months; some become homeless and remain homeless for the rest of their lives. In the research literature, the distinction is between "chronic" and "situational" homelessness.

The transitory or situational component adds further ambiguity to the numbers question. To illustrate, it is estimated that in Chicago the number ever homeless in the span of a year exceeds the number homeless on any given night by an approximate factor of three. A recent study by the RAND Corporation in California gives similar results. Three separate counties were included in that study; the estimated ratios of annual to nighttime homeless in the three counties were about 2:1, 3:1, and 4:1, respectively.[7]

It is easy to see how the "turnover" rate clouds the numbers issue. Imagine a shelter operator with a 200-bed facility, with every bed full every night. If the population served by this shelter is perfectly stable, such that the same 200 people sleep in the shelter every night, then the operator's annual count is the same as the nightly count: 200 homeless people served. If, on the other hand, the population served by the shelter is completely unstable, such that every client sleeps there for one and only one night, then the yearly count is 365 times the nightly count, or some *73,000* homeless people served.

To repeat, empirically, the homeless population is neither perfectly stable nor perfectly unstable; it is a mixture of short- and long-term homeless people. But adequate understanding of the larger problem requires that we know more about the precise nature of the "mix," most of all because we can assume that the needs of short-term homeless people are very different from the needs of those whose homelessness has become a permanent feature of their existence. The relative proportions of chronically versus situationally homeless is thus a topic to be taken up again later. As it happens, the majority of the homeless are *not* chronically homeless, and this fact has very important implications for social policy.[8]

THE BOTTOM LINE

All the preceding notwithstanding, it is still important to have some sense of the approximate dimensions of the homeless problem in America today. As Alfred North Whitehead observed in *The Aims of Education* (Macmillan, 1957), "It is no use saying the nation is large—how large? It is no use saying radium is scarce—how scarce?" And it is likewise no use saying that homelessness has become a big problem in this country if we cannot say anything about just how big a problem it is.

Unfortunately, there is no national study that provides even an approximate answer to this question. Some efforts to systematically enumerate the homeless were tried in a few cities in conjunction with the 1980 census, but the effort was in vain; the problems in a national enumeration of the homeless were found to be nearly insur mountable. Without exception the available information concerning the number of homeless is restricted to studies done in single cities. Moreover, many of the single city "studies" are so casual and haphazard that they do not yield reliable results; many of them have been conducted by advocacy organizations whose agenda is to persuade citizens and leaders of the urgency of the situation, rather than to inform them about the precise dimensions of the problem.

Setting aside the seriously deficient and the obviously polemical, I have located six city-specific studies that represent reasonably thorough and systematic efforts to census the one-night, literally homeless population.[9] No two of these studies employ the exact same definition of homelessness; they also differ in method, approach, and completeness of coverage. But as these kinds of studies go, the six employed here are the best of the lot. The cities, the homeless counts, and the 1980 U.S. census estimates of the number of people living in poverty in each city are as follows:[10]

	Homeless count	Persons in poverty	Ratio
Chicago	2700	601,400	.0045
Baltimore	1160	176,500	.0066
Boston	2863	106,800	.0268
Nashville	836	55,000	.0152
Phoenix	1813	86,700	.0209
Washington D.C.	2562	113,400	.0226

The rightmost column simply divides the homeless count in each city into the city's poverty population; it expresses the size of the homeless population as a proportion of those in poverty. As can be seen, the experience of these six cities suggests that the homeless comprise between ½ and 2½% of the poverty population. The 1980 census tallied a total of 35,000,000 persons in poverty in the United States. Using the above results, the total national homeless population on any given night can be estimated at somewhere between (.005 × 35,000,000) 175,000 and (.025 × 35,000,000) 875,000. If we take an average across the six studies as our best guess, the figure (.0161 × 35,000,000) is 563,500 homeless people.

I conclude that the total homeless population of the nation on any given night numbers in the hundreds of thousands, although probably not in the millions. As a rule of thumb, we will probably not be too far off if we speak of half a million homeless people in America at any one time. And if the ratio of one night to annual homelessness estimated for the city of Chicago (on the order of 3 to 1) can be generalized, then the *annual* homeless population of the nation is on the order of one and a half million. In any case, this is the most reasonable guess we can muster.

"Reasoned guesses" by advocacy groups invariably posit much larger numbers than these. None of the studies on which my estimates are based could be considered definitive, so it is certainly possible that the true numbers are much larger than the ones cited here. Most of the researchers whose results I have summarized, however, began their studies expecting to find many more homeless people than they actually did, and almost all of them would have been more satisfied with their results had they done so. In any case, there is no compelling *evidence* of which I am aware that implies numbers of homeless substantially larger than those I have cited. Until such evidence appears, the estimate of half a million homeless on any given night can be considered a reasonable compromise.

With what might these figures be compared? How do the victims of homelessness stack up in numerical terms against the victims of other misfortunes? Just where on the agenda of political priorities should the problem of homelessness be located? How big a number is half or one-and-a-half million?[11] Consider the following:

In 1983, there were approximately 7.5 million persons between the ages of 18 and 24 enrolled in institutions of higher education in this country. For every five college students, there is one American destined to be homeless at least once in the course of a year.

In all of 1982 a total of 224,000 persons spent at least some time in jail, and another 385,000 were incarcerated in state and federal prisons. Thus, the number of homeless on a given night rivals the total correctional population in a given year.

There are more homeless people than there are social workers (407,000 in 1983) or computer scientists (276,000); in fact, there are just about as many homeless people in America on any given day as there are doctors (519,000) or insurance salesmen (551,000).

In 1983 (our baseline year), the total population of the country was about 234 million people; 1.5 million homeless in the stretch of a year thus equals $1.5/234 = .0064$, or something less than 1% of the total national population. In 1984, 6.6% of a sample of adults said that someone had broken into their home in the previous year.[12] Thus, the annual odds of being burglarized are about ten times, but *only* ten times, greater than the odds of being homeless.

By the above calculation, the odds of being homeless in a given year are about six per thousand. In 1980, the odds of American households suffering a damaging home fire were about four per thousand; the odds of suffering a serious flood, about three per thousand; and the odds of experiencing an earthquake, less than two per thousand.[13]

This last set of comparisons is particularly interesting because the principal federal agency charged with relief and rehabilitation in the aftermath of natural disaster is the Federal Emergency Management Agency (FEMA). It so happens that, until recently, FEMA was also charged with dispensing funds under the emergency food and shelter program to aid the homeless, which was the single largest federal initiative on behalf of the homeless population until about 2 years ago. In recent years FEMA's annual expenditures for natural disaster relief and rehabilitation have averaged about one billion dollars annually. In calendar years 1983 and 1984 *combined,* the total expenditure under the emergency food and shelter program for the homeless was about 90 million dollars, or about a tenth of the annual disaster relief expenditure.[14]

So, just how big *is* the homeless problem? In sheer numerical terms, it is not as big a problem as poverty is; to repeat, the homeless problem is encapsulated within the poverty problem. Likewise, homelessness is a lesser problem than crime, but a larger problem than victimization by floods or earthquakes. There are many more homeless people than there are persons with AIDS; there are more homeless people each year, by far, than there are suicide or homicide victims; the number homeless on any given night exceeds the number of persons killed in automobile accidents in a year by a factor of ten.[15] Thus, while the problem of homelessness is clearly dwarfed by *some* of the other problems that confront the nation, it in turn exceeds other problems that have long been accepted as urgent national priorities.

Until recently, little federal attention was given to the homelessness problem, despite its apparent and growing severity. As late as 1985, the General Accounting Office was able to describe the federal role as largely "supplemental" to various state, local and private efforts. This is now changing. In all, 32 separate bills were introduced in the 100th congress dealing in one way or another with homelessness: some focused on housing and housing subsidies, some on emergency housing and shelter, some on homeless youth or homeless children, some specifically on homeless families, some on expanding existing social welfare programs to provide more complete coverage among the homeless, still others on nutrition, or health care, or homeless veterans, or homeless women. None of these bills could be said to represent a coordinated national policy with respect to the problems of the homeless; if enacted, this package of legislation would distribute federal authority over the issue to literally dozens of different agencies, bureaus, and programs. To be sure, a fragmented, chaotic, piecemeal policy is far better than no policy at all, which has been the federal posture for most of the Reagan era. But as we come to know more and more about the larger problem of homelessness, the rationale for ad hoc solutions dims.

IS HOMELESSNESS A NEW PROBLEM?

I began this chapter by referring to the growth of "a disturbing and largely unexpected new problem," namely, the problem of homelessness. But is this a new problem? And is it a growing one?

Strictly speaking, homelessness is definitely *not* a new problem, in that homeless people have always existed in American society (and, for that matter, in most other societies as well). In the recent past, the homeless were seen to consist mainly of hoboes (transient men who "rode the rails" and whose life-style was frequently romanticized in the pulp novels of an earlier era) and skid row bums (older, usually white men whose capacity for independent existence had been compromised by the ravages of chronic alcoholism). Scholarly interest in skid row spawned a large amount of academic literature on the topic, but the homeless received no sustained policy attention; they and their problems were largely invisible to social policy makers and to the American public at large.

Surprisingly, even during the war on poverty waged in the middle 1960's, little or nothing was written about the *homeless* poor. The most influential book ever written about poverty is probably Michael Harrington's *The Other America*, published initially in 1962. Despite several readings of that fine, sensitive volume, I am unable to find a single word about the homeless poor. Many of the processes discussed in the next chapter, particularly the displacement of the poor to make way for urban renewal and downtown revitalizations are taken up in considerable detail, but the apparent implication that some of the displaced would become *permanently* displaced, and therefore *homeless*, goes unstated.

Harrington brushes lightly against this "apparent implication" in a single haunting passage. This occurs in the midst of a discussion of displacement and why many of the displaced did not relocate in the public housing projects. He writes, "Still another group . . . simply do not know about the opportunity. Long-time citizens of the other America, they assume that there is no real hope, that no one is going to help them, and they vanish. That is one reason why over half of the people displaced by [development] projects in the United States are listed on the records as—address unknown" (pp. 145–146).

Recent historical research on homelessness confirms that the problem dates back at least to the Colonial era, when there were sufficient numbers of "wandering poor" at least to raise popular alarms and inspire legal measures to deal with them.

In Massachusetts, the chosen mechanism was the process of "warning out." Names of transients, along with information on their former residences, were presented to the Colonial courts. Upon judicial review, the person or family could then be warned out (that is, told to leave town). Some of the more populous towns actually hired persons to go door-to-door seeking out strangers. These methods were designed to control the size of relief rolls; up until 1739, a person was eligible for poor relief in Massachusetts if he or she had not been warned out within the first 3 months of residency. The modern-day equivalent has come to be known as Greyhound therapy, whereby transients and derelicts are given a bus ticket that will take them and their problems elsewhere.

A corollary process was that of "binding out," whereby transients could be, in essence, indentured to families needing laborers or servants, a Colonial-era version, perhaps, of what we now call workfare. These methods were used to control homelessness in Massachusetts until they were ended by legislation in 1794.[16]

As in the present day, the wandering poor of Colonial times were largely single men and women, although two-parent families were surprisingly common (comprising between 28 and 68% of those warned out across the towns and years covered in Jones' study). They, too, were drawn from the bottom of the social hierarchy; the men were artisans, mariners, or laborers; the women were mostly domestic servants. Except for the overseas immigrants (mostly Irish), they came from towns within a 10-mile radius. Interestingly, there were as many women as men among those warned out. Similar findings appear in several historical studies of indigent and homeless populations throughout the nineteenth and early twentieth centuries.[17]

The Great Depression marked the last great wave of homelessness in this country. Peter Rossi has pointed out that in 1933, the Federal Emergency Relief Administration housed something like 125,000 people in its transient camps around the country. Another survey of the time, also cited by Rossi, estimated that the homeless population of 765 select cities and towns was on the order of 200,000, with estimates for the entire nation ranging upward to perhaps one-and-a-half million (much as the estimates of today). Most of the homeless of the Depression were younger men and women moving from place to place in search of jobs.[18]

The outbreak of World War II in essence ended the Depression and created immense employment opportunities for men and women alike, an economic boom that continued well into the middle of the 1960's. This boom caused, at least in one account, the virtual extinction of homelessness.[19] While residual pockets of homelessness remained in the skid row areas, the residents of skid row were less and less the economically down and out and more and more debilitated alcoholic males. Based on the urban renewal efforts of the 1960's and the obvious aging of the residual skid row population, the impending demise of skid row was widely and confidently predicted.

The postwar real growth in personal income ended in 1966, as the Vietnam war heated up. Between the war-related inflation and decay of living standards, the 1973 Arab oil embargo, and other related developments in the world economy, the country entered an economic slump that was to last until 1980. During this period, double-digit inflation *and* double-digit unemployment were not uncommon, and the national poverty rate, which had been steadily declining, began, just as steadily, to climb back up. By 1983, the poverty level was the highest recorded in any year since 1966. (More on this in the following chapter.) And thus, by the late 1970's and certainly by the early 1980's, the problem of homelessness—the most extreme manifestation of poverty—reappeared on the national scene.

Some indication of the sudden upwelling of concern about the problem is provided by the listings under "homelessness" in *The Reader's Guide to Periodical Literature*. In 1975, there were no listings, and in 1980, also none. In 1981, however, there were three listings; in 1982, fifteen; in 1983, twenty-one; and in 1984, thirty-two. The early 1980's witnessed an outpouring of concern over homelessness that had not been seen since the Great Depression and that has not abated.

Homelessness, in short, is not a new problem in the larger historical sweep of things, but the current rash of homelessness certainly
exceeds anything witnessed in this country in the last half-centur
More, perhaps, to the point, the last major outbreak occurred as
consequence of the worst economic crisis in American history; th
current situation exists in the midst of national prosperity literally ur
paralleled in the history of the world.

Not only did homelessness make a comeback in the early 1980's,
but the character of homelessness also changed; this is another
sense in which today's problem could be described as new. In 1985,
my colleagues and I had occasion to review medical records of men
seen in a health clinic at the New York City Men's Shelter, in the very
heart of the Bowery, for the period 1969 through 1984. Among the
men seen in the early years of this period (1969–1972), almost half
(49%) were white and 49% were documented alcohol or drug abusers; the average age was 44 years. Among men seen at the end of the
period (1981–1984), only 15% were white and only 28% were documented alcohol or drug abusers; the average age was 36 years. Thus,
during the 1970's and early 1980's, the homeless population changed
from a largely white, older, alcohol-abusive one into a population
dominated by younger, nonsubstance-abusive, nonwhite men. Between the Great Depression and the 1980's, the road to homelessness
was paved with alcohol abuse; today, many alternative routes have
been opened.[20]

In *Homelessness in America*, P. H. Rossi presents a detailed comparison of results from studies of the homeless done in the 1950's
and early 1960's with those undertaken in the 1980's, thus contrasting
the "old" homeless and the "new." The first point of contrast is that
homeless of today suffer a more severe form of housing deprivation
than did the homeless of twenty or thirty years past. Bogue's 1958
study in Chicago found only about 100 homeless men sleeping, literally, out on the streets, out of a total homeless population estimated
at 12,000. Rossi's 1986 survey found nearly 1400 homeless persons
sleeping out of doors in a total population estimated at about 3000.
Thus, nearly all of the old homeless somehow found nightly shelter
indoors (usually in flops and cubicle hotels, most of which have disappeared), unlike the new homeless, sizable fractions of whom sleep
in the streets.

A second major difference is the presence of a significant number
of women among today's homeless. In 1958 Bogue estimated that no
more than 3% of the city's skid row population were women; in the
middle 1980's, one homeless person in four is a woman. A third im-

portant point of contrast concerns the age distribution, the elderly having disappeared almost entirely from the ranks of the new homeless (a point discussed in Chapter 4). Studies of the 1950's and 1960's routinely reported the average age of homeless persons to be somewhere in the middle fifties. Today, it is the middle thirties.

Rossi points out two further differences: first, the substantially more straitened economic circumstances of the new homeless; second, the changing racial and ethnic composition. In 1958, Bogue estimated the average annual income of Chicago's homeless to be $1,058; Rossi's estimate for 1986 is $1,198. Converted to constant dollars, the average income of today's homeless is barely one third of the income of the homeless in 1958. "Thus, the new homeless suffer a much more profound degree of economic destitution, often surviving on 40% or less of a poverty-level income" (Rossi, p. 27).

Finally, the old homeless were mostly white—70% in Bahr and Caplow's well-known study of the Bowery, 82% in Bogue's study of Chicago. "Among the new homeless," Rossi points out, "racial and ethnic minorities are heavily over-represented" (p. 28).

We speak, then, of the "new face of homelessness" and of the "new homeless" to signify the dramatic transformation of the nature of the homeless population that has occurred in the past decade. Today's homeless, to return to an earlier theme, are *not* just old, broken-down alcoholic skid row men, although this remains an important subgroup. Today's homeless are surprisingly young, in their early to middle thirties on the average, relatively well educated, and heavily dominated by racial and ethnic minorities. Distressingly large numbers of them are homeless women, homeless children, and homeless family groups. And while alcohol abuse remains a leading problem and an important contributory factor, it is nowhere near as important a root cause of homelessness as it has been over the past 50 years.

Is Homelessness a Growing Problem?

Granted that the character of homelessness has changed, what evidence is there that the magnitude of the problem has in fact been increasing? Certainly the amount of attention being devoted to the topic has grown, but what of the problem itself?

Since, as has been stated, we do not know precisely how many homeless people there are in America today, it is difficult to say whether that number is higher, lower, or the same as the number of

homeless 5 or 10 or 20 years ago. The case that homelessness is a
growing problem is therefore largely inferential. The pertinent evidence has been reviewed in some detail by the U. S. General Ac
counting Office.[21] The GAO's conclusions are:

> In summary, no one knows how many homeless people there are ii
> America because of the many difficulties [in] locating and countin;
> them. As a result, there is considerable disagreement over the size of the
> homeless population. However, there is agreement in the studies we re-
> viewed and among shelter providers, researchers, and agency officials
> we interviewed that the homeless population is growing. Current esti-
> mates of annual increases in the growth of homelessness vary between
> 10 and 38 percent (pp. 12–13).

The most recent evidence on the upward trend in homelessness in
the 1980's has been reviewed by Freeman and Hall.[22] Between 1983
and 1985, they report, the shelter population of New York City increased by 28%, and that of Boston by 20%. Early in 1986, the U.S.
Conference of Mayors released a study of 25 major American cities,
concluding that in 22 of the 25, homelessness had indeed increased.
There has also been a parallel increase in the numbers seeking food
from soup kitchens, food banks, and the like. Thus, while all indica-
tors are indirect and inferential, none suggest that the size of the
homeless population is stable or declining. "Even more strikingly, the
number of homeless families seems to have increased especially rapidly since 1983" (Freeman and Hall, p. 8).

How Did It Come To Be?

To ask how homelessness came to be is to ask about its causes,
and while this is an easy and appropriate question to ask, it is a frus-
tratingly complicated one to answer. The snag, as N. Smith has aptly
put it, is that homelessness is "not one problem but many."[23] In
point of fact, "the" problem of homelessness is a complex array of
many different problems: it is, simultaneously, a housing problem,
an employment problem, a demographic problem, a problem of social disaffiliation, a mental health problem, a substance abuse prob-
lem, a criminal justice problem, a family violence problem, a
problem created by cutbacks in social welfare spending, a problem
resulting from the decay of the traditional nuclear family, and a problem intimately connected to the recent increase in the number of
persons living below the poverty level. No one of these can be sin-
gled out as "the" cause of homelessness; probably none of them

could even be fairly cited as the single most important factor. They interact in complex ways to produce the homeless problem we confront today.

We can at least begin to grasp the complexity, however, by stating an obvious point: homeless people are people without housing, and thus, the *ultimate* cause of the problem is an insufficient supply of housing suitable to the needs of homeless people (a point taken up in detail in the next chapter). This means, principally, an inadequate supply of low-income housing suitable to single individuals, but, as we shall see, the housing problem cuts even more deeply.

Saying that the homeless lack housing is like saying that the poor lack money: the point is correct, even valuable, but it is by no means the whole story. There is both a supply and a demand component to be taken into account: as we will see, the supply of low-income housing in the central cities has been decimated in the past decade, but this would not cause problems if the low-income population had itself declined at a proportionate rate. However, as the supply of low-income housing has declined, the actual size of the poverty population of the cities has *increased*. A second set of factors to take into account are those suggested by the recent increase in the American poverty rate. They include the continuing erosion of demand for low-skilled labor, the migration of American capital toward the South and outside the country, the reduction in eligibility and benefit levels for many of our social welfare programs, chronically high unemployment among central city nonwhite youth, the so-called "feminization of poverty," and a host of related developments.

In Chapter 2, I argue that these large-scale housing and economic trends have conspired to create a housing "game" that increasing numbers are destined to lose. Specifically who will lose is a separate question, and on this point, attention turns to various personal characteristics of the homeless population that cause them to compete poorly in this game. Their extreme poverty, social disaffiliation, and high levels of disability are the principal problems, issues to be raised in some detail in Chapter 4.

Whatever the root cause or causes, becoming homeless is a process that requires explication. All poor people, after all, compete for the same supply of low-income housing; most, despite their poverty, are relatively successful at it. In order to better understand why some poor people become homeless, it is important to understand why more of them do not. This will be explored in Chapter 5.

Among the various disabilities that homeless people suffer, alcohol abuse has traditionally figured prominently, and continues to do so. Today, the abuse of other recreational drugs is also important. Still a third disability, prominent in discussions of the homeless since the advent of "deinstitutionalization," is chronic mental illness; chronic *physical* illness has received much less attention but turns out to be surprisingly important. These concerns are addressed in Chapter 6.

Many people, logically enough, turn to the existing social welfare system—the system of AFDC, food stamps, welfare, housing subsidies, disability pensions, and so on—for a solution to the problem of homelessness, or at least for some amelioration of the conditions of a homeless existence. As is well known, however, there are many holes in the social welfare "safety net." In some sense, the homeless are those who have fallen through all of them. Levels of and barriers to participation in the various social welfare programs among the homeless population are matters taken up in Chapter 7.

Finally, in Chapter 8, I discuss "Who Can be Helped, and How." There is no one measure that will solve the homelessness problem, no vaccine that will inoculate the population at risk of this disease. But there are a number of things that might be done to help. Some of these are in the nature of crisis intervention, others are directed more toward long-term prevention. None of them is cheap, but the mood of the nation is ripe. The number of bills dealing with homelessness in the most recent session of Congress indicates a new willingness at the federal level to intervene with national (versus state or local) solutions. And the popular mandate to do so is clearly there. A recent survey by the Roper Organization asked a sample of the U.S. population what problems we should be spending more money on.[24] "Caring for the homeless" was the top priority item, favored by 68%. In contrast, foreign aid was mentioned by only 5%, and "military, armaments, and defense" by only 17%. It seems to me that the people have spoken. Let us hope they are being heard.

NOTES

1. Evidence on all these points is reviewed later in this book. For an overview of alcohol and mental health problems among the homeless, see J. Wright and E. Weber, *Homelessness and Health* (New York: McGraw Hill, 1987), Chs. 5 and 6.

2. This figure is derived from official U.S. government poverty statistics and definitions. Many poverty researchers feel that the official federal poverty line is set too low, and that many persons officially "above poverty" live, nonetheless, in objectively impoverished conditions. See, for example, L.

Beeghley, "Illusion and Reality in the Measurement of Poverty." *Social Problems,* 31:3 (February 1984), pp. 322–333.

3. P. Rossi, J. Wright, G. Fisher, and G. Willis, "The Urban Homeless: Estimating Composition and Size." *Science* 235: 4794 (13 March, 1987), pp. 1336–1341.

4. See M. Stagner and H. Richman, *General Assistance Families* (Chicago: National Opinion Research Center, 1985).

5. See P. Rossi, J. Wright, G. Fisher, and G. Willis, op. cit.

6. It is useful to recall that our "pool of risk" consists only of GA recipients in Chicago who are currently living with relatives or friends. Within the city's poverty population of 600,000 must be many additional persons who are in arrears on their rent, or in the midst of eviction proceedings, or living in buildings soon to be condemned or razed, or about to lose their employment and soon thereafter their housing, and so on. Thus, the true pool of risk must be wider than our estimate.

7. G. Vernez, M. Burnham, E. McGlynn, S. Trude, and B. Mittman, *Review of California's Program for the Homeless Mentally Disabled.* Santa Monica, CA: The Rand Corporation, 1988, Ch. 3.

8. That the majority of the homeless are not chronically homeless follows logically from a finding that we have just reviewed, that the number homeless in a year exceeds the number homeless on any given day by an approximate factor of three. If all homeless people were chronically homeless, then the implication is that the size of the homeless population would roughly *triple* each year. There is, to be sure, solid evidence that the homeless population *is* growing, but not at anything near such a rate. Direct empirical evidence on the point, reviewed in a later chapter, is that only about one third of the homeless are chronically homeless.

9. Since this was first written, a seventh study has appeared that would satisfy my criteria: the Vernez *et al.* (op. cit.) study of three counties in California done by the RAND Corporation. Since the results of that study are altogether in line with those reported in succeeding pages, I have not incorporated them into the following analysis.

10. My sources for the following tabulation are as follows: P. Rossi, G. Fisher, and G. Willis, *The Condition of the Homeless in Chicago* (Amherst, MA: Social and Demographic Research Institute, 1986); Health and Welfare Council of Central Maryland, *Where Do You Go from Nowhere? Homelessness in Maryland* (Baltimore, MD: Department of Human Resources, August 1986); the *Boston Globe,* 12 October 1986; Nashville Coalition for the Homeless *Newsletter* (1986); C. Brown, S. McFarlane *et al., The Homeless in Phoenix: Who Are They and What Should Be Done?* (Phoenix: Report prepared for the Consortium for the Homeless by the Phoenix South Community Mental Health Center, 1983); and F. G. Robinson, *Homeless People in the Nation's Capitol* (Washington, D.C.: University of The District of Columbia, Center for Applied Research and Urban Policy, 1985).

11. Unless another source is specifically referenced, all figures given in the following discussion are taken from the U.S. Bureau of the Census, *Sta-*

tistical Abstract of the United States (Washington, DC: U.S. Government Printing Office, 1985), various pages and tables.

12. National Opinion Research Center, *1984 General Social Survey* (Storrs CT: Roper Public Opinion Research Center).

13. P. Rossi, J. Wright, E. Weber, and J. Pereira, *Victims of the Environment: Loss From Natural Hazards in the United States* (New York: Plenum Press, 1983), p. 60.

14. See U. S. General Accounting Office, *Homelessness: A Complex Problem and the Federal Response* (Washington, General Accounting Office, 1985), pp. 32–34 for evidence on FEMA expenditures on the homelessness program. FEMA disaster relief expenditures are extrapolated from data reported in Rossi *et al., Victims of the Environment,* op. cit., p. 12.

15. As of late 1986, there were about 37,000 persons diagnosed with AIDS, although there are probably several million who have been exposed to the AIDS virus. In the U.S. death by homicide averages about 20,000 murders per year; death by suicide, about 27,000 a year; and death by automobile accident, about 50,000 a year. Indeed, deaths from all causes in the United States number about 2 million a year, so there are nearly as many homeless people as there are people destined to die in the same year. (All figures are taken from *The Statistical Abstract,* except the AIDS figure, which is from C. Norman, "Sex and needles, not insects and pigs, spread AIDS in Florida town." *Science* 234 (24 October 1986), pp. 415–417.

16. See D. L. Jones, "The Strolling Poor: Transiency in Eighteenth Century Massachusetts." *Journal of Social History,* 8: 28–54.

17. See, for example, the many interesting papers collected in E. H. Monkkonen, *Walking to Work: Tramps in America, 1790–1935* (Lincoln, NE: University of Nebraska Press, 1984), especially P. F. Clement, "The Transformation of the Wandering Poor in Nineteenth Century Philadelphia."

18. P. H. Rossi, *Homelessness in America: Social Research and Public Policy* (New York: The Twentieth Century Fund, 1988).

19. K. Hopper and J. Hamburg, *The Making of America's Homeless: From Skid Row to New Poor, 1945–1984.* Report prepared for the Institute of Social Welfare Research (New York City: Community Service Society, 1984).

20. See J. D. Wright, P. H. Rossi, J. W. Knight, E. Weber-Burdin, R. C. Tessler, C. E. Stewart, M. Geronimo, and J. Lam, *Health and Homelessness: An Analysis of the Health Status of a Sample of Homeless People Receiving Care through the Department of Community Medicine, St. Vincent's Hospital and Medical Center of New York City: 1969–1984* (Amherst, MA: Social and Demographic Research Institute, 1985), Tables Two and Fourteen.

21. *Homelessness: A Complex Problem and the Federal Response,* pp. 10–12.

22. "Permanent Homelessness in America." Washington, DC: National Bureau of Economic Research, August 1986.

23. N. Smith, "Homelessness: Not One Problem But Many." *The Journal of the Institute for Socioeconomic Studies,* 10:3 (1985), pp. 53–67.

24. .The poll results are reported in *Newsweek* Magazine for 21 September 1987, p. 7.

CHAPTER
THREE

The Root Causes: Housing and Poverty

FOR SALE: Four bedrooms, three baths on 1 acre in pleasant suburban community only two hours from midtown Manhattan. Low crime. Asking $1,400,000.

That housing in the United States has become generally more expensive in recent decades will come as no real surprise to anyone. The average price of single-family dwellings sold in 1970 was $23,000; in 1980 the figure was $62,200; and in 1983, $70,300.[1] More to the point of this chapter, the median gross monthly rent for renter-occupied units has shown an equivalent upward trend: in 1970, the median monthly rent was $108; in 1980, $243; and in 1983, $315. As is true of most other commodities, it is a fact that the price of housing, whether purchased or rented, has sharply increased over the past 10 years. The advertisement above describes the *average* home for sale in Greenwich, Connecticut, in 1988.

Poor people, of course, generally do not seek housing in Greenwich or in other affluent and equally expensive suburbs, but the rampant inflation in the housing market, top to bottom, has created a severe housing "squeeze" for the low-income population. And the new homeless population is, at least at one level of analysis, a direct consequence of this housing squeeze.

My argument can be quickly summarized: The past 10 years have witnessed a virtual decimation of the low-income housing supply in most large American cities. During the same period, the poverty population of the cities has increased. Less low-income housing for more low-income people predestines an increase in the numbers without housing. The coming of the new homeless, in short, has been "in the cards" for years and will continue unabated as long as low-income housing continues to disappear from the urban scene.

In the first line of analysis, homelessness is a housing problem. This perhaps seems too obvious to mention, except that much that has been written about homelessness makes reference to the housing problem only in passing, the greater emphasis being on problems of unemployment, or on deinstitutionalization and attendant issues of mental health, or on alcohol and other substance abuse, or on the cutbacks in social welfare spending by the Reagan administration. All

37

of these, to be sure, are important factors; viewed structurally, however, the trends discussed in this chapter concerning the poverty housing supply and the poverty population conspire to create a housing "game" that increasing numbers are destined to lose. Much of the literature is focused on who the "losers" are; my interest here is in the nature of the game itself.

It would, of course, be wrong to say that homelessness is *just* a housing problem, and likewise, wrong to think that all the problems of homelessness would be solved if we simply built more low-income housing. Like every other social problem, this one is caused or exacerbated by a large number of factors. At the same time, the low-income housing situation forms the background against which these other factors unfold. An inadequate low-income housing supply is probably not the proximate cause of homelessness in most cases, but it is the ultimate cause of homelessness in all cases.

The general effect of inflation on the supply of low-income rental housing is illustrated by the trend in the total number of units nationwide renting for $80 or less per month. In 1970 these units numbered some 5.5 million; in 1980 there were 1.1 million; and in 1983 some 650,000. A family who could afford to spend no more than $80 per month on rent would therefore have seen its supply of potential housing cut nearly in half in the brief span of 3 years, and cut by nearly 90% over the longer term.[2]

A second large-scale trend pertinent to our argument, one not nearly so well known as the trend in housing prices, is the recent increase in the percentage of United States citizens living at or below the poverty level.[3] This percentage exceeded 20% up through the early 1960's, but had fallen to 14.7 by 1966 and to 12.6% by 1970. The rate hovered between 12.6% and 11.1% throughout the 1970's, with no obvious trend in either direction. Beginning in 1980, the poverty percentage started to escalate. The 1980 figure, 13.0%, was the highest recorded since 1969, and the rate continued to climb thereafter, to 14.0% in 1981, 15.0% in 1982, and 15.2% in 1983, higher even than the 1966 figure.[4] In the most recent years for which data are available, 1984 and 1985, the rate has fallen a bit (to 14.4 and 14.0%, respectively), but remains at a much higher level than at any time since the early 1960's. These rates translate into 30 to 35 million citizens living in poverty in the United States today.

It is thus a reasonable inference, based on the evidence so far reviewed, that *never before in postwar American history have so many poor people competed for so few affordable dwelling units*. In itself, this is not news; much has been written in the past two decades about the low-income housing crisis, especially in the big cities.

What has not yet been discussed in adequate detail is the apparent connection between this housing crisis and the rise of the homelessness problem. The "new homeless," I suggest, are best seen as the losers in this increasingly unfavorable housing competition.

THE SITUATION IN THE LARGE CITIES

Homelessness is by no means exclusively an urban phenomenon, but most of the research that has been done focuses on the urban component of the problem.[5] Aggregate national data such as those so far discussed illustrate the broad outlines of the low-income housing "squeeze" but lack concrete detail of the sort readily available for specific cities through the Bureau of the Census' annual housing surveys. These surveys are taken periodically in all the nation's large cities, at roughly 5-year intervals. I have focused here only on the 20 largest American cities, and within that group, only on the 12 cities that were surveyed at least once in the 1980–1983 period.

The annual housing surveys provide a wealth of detail on a city's housing stock, both rental and owner-occupied units. My attention is exclusively on the rental stock, and even more particularly, on the number of rental units available at various levels of gross monthly rent. All rental units, including publicly subsidized units, are included in my counts.[6]

In order to work with concrete dollar values, I began with the official federal poverty levels for a family of three persons in each of the years covered in this analysis, using the three-person poverty line simply because the average American household consists of about three people. All cities covered here were surveyed at least once between 1977 and 1979, so the 1978 poverty level ($5784 for a family of three) was used as a baseline figure. All cities were then resurveyed in 1981, 1982, or 1983; the official poverty lines for each of these 3 years were used.

In order to obtain a maximum affordable gross monthly rent, and therefore an estimate of the low-income housing supply, based on the poverty figures some estimate of the maximum percentage of income a family can "afford" to spend on rent is needed, and this is a tricky (and rather contentious) question. Mortgage lenders and the U.S. Department of Housing and Urban Development routinely recommend that a household spend no more than 25% of its income on housing. It has been pointed out[7] that this would vary by income level: households with large incomes can afford to spend more than 25% on housing, since plenty of cash would still remain for other expenditures; likewise, families with extremely small incomes might not be able to afford as much as 25% on housing if the remaining 75% were not adequate to cover other necessities. (Indeed, at a sufficiently low income, such as characterizes many homeless persons one might not be able to afford *anything* for housing, assuming othe necessities are to be paid for.) It is also true, empirically, that many poor families pay considerably more than 25% of their income on rent alone, whether they can afford to or not.[8]

For present purposes, I assume that poor households can afford to spend a maximum of 40% of their out-of-pocket cash income on housing. The calculation of the federal poverty figures is based on the assumption that a poor family will spend one third of its income on food; spending another 40% on housing would leave only about one quarter of the income to be spent on all other things—on transportation, medical care, entertainment, clothing, education, and so on. Obviously, a poor family spending a third of its income on food and two fifths on housing is living very close to the economic edge.

Given the poverty lines and the assumed housing expenditure of 40%, the calculation of a maximum affordable gross monthly rent is straightforward. In 1978 the figure was $193 per month; in 1981 the figure was $242 a month; in 1982 it was $256 a month; and in 1983 it was $265 a month. It is easy to count up the number of rental units in each city whose monthly cost is at or below the affordable maximum, and thus ascertain the amount of low-income rental stock available in these cities. I also consider various measures of the size of each city's poverty population: the number of *families* below the poverty line, the number of *individuals* below the poverty line, and, having begun with a hypothetical three-person household, the number of poverty individuals divided by three.

The results of this simple exercise are dramatic and, with only a few exceptions, similar in each of the 12 cities I examined. In almost all cases, each city registered a sharp decline in the number of low-income housing units and a sharp increase in the number of low-income people.

The general pattern is illustrated in the results for Detroit and Philadelphia, the two largest cities among the 12. In the late 1970's, the Detroit housing stock included some 183,000 rental units within the means of a family at the poverty level; in the same era, there were some 58,000 poverty-level families and some 279,000 poor people. Even using the arbitrarily defined three-person "household" as the basic housing-consumer unit, the supply of low-income housing still exceeded the low-income housing demand, by an approximate factor of two.

By the early 1980's the number of low-income housing units in Detroit had declined to 135,000—a 26% decline over the late-1970's value—while the number of poor people had increased to 522,000—an increase of some 87%. Again using the arbitrary three-person unit as the measure of housing demand, these data suggest that as of the early 1980's, there were 174,000 "consumer units" competing for 135,000 affordable rentals. The apparent glut of low-income housing in Detroit in the late 1970's had disappeared by 1981, having been replaced by what appears to be an obvious and perhaps severe shortage.

The trends in Philadelphia are similar. Between the late 1970's and the early 1980's, the number of low-income rental units declined from 211,000 to 157,000—a decline of 26%. In the same period, the number of poor people increased from 516,000 to 708,000—an increase of 37%.

Across all 12 cities there were 2,522,000 poor people at the earlier time point and about 3,425,000 at the later time point. This is a percentage increase in the poverty population in these cities of 36%. At the same time, the number of low-income rental units across all 12 cities declined from 1,607,000 units to 1,128,000 units—a decline of about 30%. Given these developments, it was inevitable that the trend lines would sooner or later cross, or in other words, that a time would come when there would be more poor people than housing for them. That time arrived in the early 1980's, and the rise of the "new homeless" appears to have been one direct consequence.

It is, of course, true that these trends do not logically *require* an increase in homelessness. An increase in the average number of poor people per unit is the obvious alternative, and there is some evidence to suggest that this has also happened.[9] There is, however, some limit to the number of bodies that can be squeezed into a single hovel, and perhaps the limit has been reached.

It is also true that the characteristics of the homeless population make them relatively less probable beneficiaries of any "doubling up" tendencies. Many, for example, are profoundly estranged from their families of origin and have few if any friends they can turn to. Many, likewise, are recently deinstitutionalized chronic mental patients, many of whom were institutionalized in the first place because their families could no longer care for them. Some are chronic alcoholics or drug users; some have extended prison records; and so on. As housing gets tighter and tighter, the elements of the poverty population just sketched will tend to be the first ones "turned out."[10]

Given the "iffiness" of the many debatable assumptions that have gone into the above analysis, the inherent complexities of the urban housing economy, and the obvious fact that low-income housing a: have defined it here is by no means exactly the same as housing th would be appropriate to homeless persons (most of whom are sing individuals, not family units), there is no easy or immediate transl tion of these findings into an assessment of the dimensions of the homelessness problem in urban America. The best that can be said is that this analysis illustrates in broad outline the general character of the low-income housing squeeze. Nonetheless, dividing the number of poor people in these 12 cities by the number of available low-income housing units yields interesting results.

At the earlier time point, the formula (2,522,000/1,670,000) results in a figure of 1.569 poor people per low-income unit. At the later time point, that figure (3,425,000/1,128,000) becomes 3.036 poor people per unit. The ratio between these numbers is nearly 2:1, which is to say that in relative terms, the "squeeze" in the early 1980's was *twice* as tight as it was in the late 1970's. And since we have taken an arbitrary unit of three people as the basic housing consumer unit, the figure for the later time point also suggests an "excess" of .036 poor people in need of housing for every three who have housing, or an excess of .012 poor persons needing housing per poverty individual. A slight restatement of this result would be that 1.2% of the poor are homeless, which in turn gives an estimate of 424,000 homeless people in the country on any given day—a number remarkably close to the "best guess" number reported earlier.

The bottom line to this discussion is that between the late 1970's and the early 1980's, the urban poverty population increased sharply while the supply of low-income housing dwindled just as sharply. At virtually the same time, the *visibility* of the homelessness problem certainly increased, as did the amount of attention being devoted to it. It is hard to imagine that this is all just sheer coincidence. We have, it appears, gotten to the point where we have more poor people than can be housed in the existing low-income housing stock; the rise of the new homeless is the result.

Where Has the Low-Income Housing Gone?

What accounts for the sudden and dramatic loss of low-income housing in the large cities? Obviously the general rate of inflation in consumer prices for all commodities is a major villain. Inflation was a chronic problem throughout the 1970's, with annual increases in the Consumer Price Index of 10% or even 14% not uncommon. As it happens, inflation in the price of rentals was *not* the major contributor to the overall rate of inflation; in fact, throughout the 1970's, rents rose less rapidly than other housing costs, less rapidly than consumer prices in general, and less rapidly than consumer incomes. But to a poor family at or near the economic margin, it matters little where the larger price increases are concentrated. If the price of food, utilities, and medical care all go up, and income remains essentially constant, there is necessarily less money left to pay the rent. That rent is not increasing quite as rapidly as the price of everything else is no consolation whatever.

Inflation, however, insidious as it has been, is not the whole story so far as the low-income housing supply is concerned. Inflation will increase the price that must be paid for a particular housing unit, but at least the unit is still *there*. Not so the units bulldozed to the ground to make way for urban renewal or for the revitalization of downtown areas. What we have witnessed in the past few years is not just an increase in the average price of rental housing, but an absolute loss of low-income units through outright destruction or through conversion to other, more profitable uses.

The approximate dimensions of the rental housing loss have been estimated by Downs.[11] Between 1974 and 1979, the net loss (units created less units withdrawn) averaged some 360,000 rental units *annually*. As Downs remarks, "nowhere near enough rental units were being constructed to replace those withdrawn from use" (p. 78). Chester Hartman, in the same vein, has noted "the decreasing supply of rental housing because of inadequate construction levels, conversion of apartments to condominiums, and abandonment of rental units. . . . " (see note 9, p. 17). Most observers would agree that this situation worsened in the early years of the 1980's, and that the lost rental units have been drawn disproportionately from the low-income housing stock, as Hartman's list of causal factors directly implies.

Though national data on the types of rental units being decimated apparently do not exist, there is some information available on one particular type of low-income unit bearing directly on our concerns: the so-called "single-room occupancy" (SRO) boardinghouses that have traditionally figured prominently as the housing of last resort for the socially and economically marginal population. The elimination of SRO housing has been called "a widespread trend across the country."[12] Indeed, according to the U.S. General Accounting Office (GAO) report on homelessness, approximately one million SRO units were lost nationwide during the 1970's, nearly one half the total supply (see note 8).

Available figures for specific cities are consistent with this depition. In San Francisco a single development project (the Yerba Buer project) wiped out more than 4000 units of SRO housing (Speci Committee on Aging, p. iv). Various urban renewal efforts in Seatt caused a net loss of low-income rentals amounting to some 16,200 units—half the downtown rental housing stock. "New York suffered a 21% loss of [SRO] rooms *in a sixteen month period* in the late 1970's. [Another source, the GAO report, states that New York City lost 32,000 SRO rooms between 1978 and 1982.] Seattle suffered a loss of 15,000 units, while in Boston, the number of rooming houses dropped from almost 1000 to 37 in the past two decades."[13] In Nashville, "between September 1984 and December 1985, all but one of the few remaining SRO's were closed or demolished."[14] Philip Kasinitz has reported comparable losses of SRO units in Phoenix, Newark, Minneapolis, and Portland.[15] Similar patterns no doubt characterize many other and perhaps most American cities.

The loss of the SRO stock is particularly disturbing since, as noted above, this has long served as the housing of last resort for the down and out—for the poor, the elderly, the disaffiliated, the chronically alcoholic, and so on. With SRO housing gone, the only alternative remaining for many will be no housing at all. Thus, the eradication of SRO housing is the most obvious of the many housing trends contributing, directly or indirectly, to the rising homelessness problem.

In like fashion, a large number of rooming or boardinghouses have also been closed, many by local authorities for code violations of one sort or another. Philip Kasinitz has remarked, "The only way for many rooming houses to come 'up to code' given legal and economic constraints was for them to cease to exist" (p. 250). This has further reduced the housing options for many of the nation's extremely poor population.

The SRO's, and low-income rental housing in general, have suffered considerably in the much-lauded effort to "revitalize the cities." A recent national study of the phenomenon shows that some 5% of all residential moves in urban areas represent forced relocation (that is, unwanted displacement).[16] According to Hartman's calculation, this represents some 2.5 million displaced persons *each year* (note 9, p. 21).

Characteristics of the residentially displaced include high housing cost burdens (rents as a fraction of income), central city residence, welfare dependency, and low levels of educational achievement.

"The analysis produced a consistent picture of lower income families being most susceptible to displacement" (Newman and Owen, p. 2).

There are many factors that have been discussed in connection with the revitalization of downtown and its impact on the low-income housing supply, of which three seem particularly important: (1) *arson*, whose effect on the low-income housing supply is only dimly appreciated; (2) *abandonment* and "disinvestment"; and (3) *gentrification*. One recent study by James Brady bears particular attention: it confirms that all three of these factors are intimately connected and have had strongly deleterious effects on the stock of low-income housing in many of the large cities.[17]

"The deadly crime of arson is spreading at an alarming rate in the United States, leaving whole city neighborhoods devastated in its wake" (Brady, p. 1). While the exact dimensions of the arson problem are obviously uncertain, it is clear that this has become a serious concern. Between 1951 and 1977, the number of arson reports to the National Fire Protection Association increased from 5600 to some 177,000; these figures, in Brady's opinion, "understate the seriousness of the situation," since many arson fires are presumably never recognized as such (p. 3).

It is equally clear that arson is not a random phenomenon. In Boston at least (and presumably elsewhere), "arson is tightly concentrated within certain poor Boston neighborhoods" (p. 3). Even within arson-prone neighborhoods there is a pattern: "Arson is more common in buildings owned by absentee landlords than in owner-occupied tenements," (p. 3) and is rare in public housing projects.

Brady also discusses the process of abandonment; as it happens, abandonment and arson are closely related. "More than half of Boston's 3000 arson fires from 1978 to 1982 occurred in abandoned buildings" (p. 9). Abandonment patterns, in turn, "follow closely the discriminatory mortgage-lending policies of banks which deny credit to certain districts of the inner city"—a process well known as redlining. Abandonment, then, becomes a process by which capital is "disinvested" in the central cities and thus freed for more profitable reinvestment elsewhere.

National statistics on the number of abandoned buildings in the major cities, or on the number of buildings lost annually through arson, apparently do not exist. As of 1982, there were some 5000 abandoned buildings in Boston alone, and Boston does not appear to be uncharacteristic. All that can be said with confidence is that these burned and abandoned buildings are directly implicated in the loss of low-income housing.

In Brady's analysis, both arson and abandonment are also directly related to the gentrification of the central cities. Crudely put, gentrification is a process by which low-income housing is converted to middle- and upper middle-class housing, often via conversion to condominiums or upscale apartment complexes, or to commercial space for businesses serving a middle- and upper middle-class clientele. Gentrification thus lies at the heart of efforts to "revitalize downtown."

Philip Brickner has provided a case study involving the Greenwich Hotel in New York City that serves as the archetype of this process.[18] This building was initially erected in 1893 to provide housing for poor, single workingmen. During the 1930's it served as housing for the aged victims of the Great Depression. By the 1960's the building had evolved into a "welfare hotel," providing cheap housing for some 1200 otherwise homeless and destitute men. In 1971, due to the negative reaction of the local community to the residents of the hotel, the building was closed and its inhabitants moved elsewhere—not infrequently, into the streets and temporary shelters. In the middle 1970's the building was purchased by a wealthy New York real-estate entrepreneur, refurbished, and reopened as an upscale condominium complex called *The Atrium*. The building now serves as elegant Greenwich Village housing for an affluent, upper middle-class professional population.

The role of arson in the process of gentrification is discussed in detail by Brady (note 17, pp. 15–18). There are, as Brady puts it, three main advantages to a developer considering conversion in having a "friendly fire" on the premises. First, a good blaze renders the building uninhabitable, which provides grounds for evicting the existing low-income clientele. (Eviction of existing tenants is frequently the major obstacle to conversion in most cities.) Second, the blaze guts the interior of the building and therefore undercuts a major cost of conversion. Finally, the insurance settlement on the fire provides ready capital with which to finance the renovation.

Brady quotes then city councilman and now mayor of Boston Ray Flynn: "I am convinced that there is a correlation between building conversion and arson. There is nothing so effective as fire for circumventing eviction procedures. Just look at the money being made by conversions. It is second only to the lottery in the amount of money you can make in one shot."

Brady, of course, is not the first to remark on the effects of urban revitalization and associated processes on the low-income housing supply. "Gentrification, condominium conversion, and abandonment exacerbate the [housing] problem by removing rental housing from the market, driving up rents in the remaining apartments, and uprooting tenants from their communities." The result is a "widening shortage of housing," particularly on the low-income side.[19] Likewise, Hartman enumerates the factors involved in the housing displacement of poor central city residents: "gentrification, undermaintenance, eviction, arson, rent increases, mortgage foreclosures . . . conversions, demolition, 'planned shrinkage,' and historical preservation" (note 9, p. 21).

Revitalization along the lines being discussed here has tended to pervert the "normal" flow of housing from the more to less affluent, a flow known in the housing literature as the "trickle down" effect. Normally, "except to the extent that subsidized housing production is made available, poor people must depend on older housing that trickles down from higher-income groups. . . . The phenomenon of gentrification . . . raised the demand for older urban housing. Rather than passing to households with lower incomes, it has become common for housing to filter up to higher-income groups. The flow of older units to low-income people seems to have been short-circuited."[20]

Gentrification has itself resulted from the recent backflow of middle-class populations into the urban areas. From 1960 through about 1980, most of the large central cities progressively lost population to the surrounding suburbs, an ominous development known as white flight. Though this loss created many profound problems for the cities (not least of which being the loss of tax base), it opened up immense tracts of housing for the urban poor. Beginning in some cities as early as 1975, and in almost all major cities by 1980, however, the middle class began to return. Indeed, all but one of the ten largest American cities actually gained population between 1980 and 1984 (Detroit is the only exception), a stunning reversal of a two-decade trend (Carliner, p. 123).

During the 1960's and even well into the 1970's, families displaced by revitalization processes would often be relocated, for better or worse, in publicly subsidized low-income housing projects. In the late 1970's and especially in the 1980's, however, the federal government drastically reduced its subsidies for the construction of low-income housing.[21] Today, there is virtually no low-income housing being built anywhere; indeed, Hartman has noted that the current "budget authority for [the Department of Housing and Urban Development's] low-income housing programs is about 2% of what it was when President Reagan took office" (note 9, p. 1). In 1970 there were 127,000 subsidized housing units under construction; in 1980 there were 21,000; and in 1985 barely 6000.[22] Reagan's policies have "virtually ended all programs that directly add, through construction and substantial rehabilitation, to the stock of housing available to lower income households."

And yet the demand (i.e., the need) for low-income housing is, if anything, increasing. What, then, becomes of the displaced now that public housing is no longer a viable alternative? If the analysis re- ported here is even approximately correct, then some of displaced— no doubt the most vulnerable among them—remain more or less permanently displaced, and these, we suggest, have come to be known as the new homeless.

Does the federal government not continue to subsidize the hous- ing costs of the poor? Yes, it does, increasingly through the housing voucher program known as Section 8. But there are many problems with the Section 8 housing subsidy program.[23]

First, Section 8 certificates are given out strictly on an "as avail- able" basis; unlike many poverty programs, Section 8 certificates are *not* entitlements given to any household that qualifies. Thus, there are interminably long waiting lists. According to Carliner, as of 1985 only 22.5% of the eligible low-income renter households were actu- ally receiving Section 8 housing assistance, about one in five. In most states, Section 8 certificates are given preferentially to AFDC recipi- ents—that is, to poor mothers with children, which in turn reduces their availablity to others, particulary single males (the largest demo- graphic subgroup within the homeless population).

Perhaps the most serious problem with the Section 8 program is that subsidized households are required to find (within 2 months) apartments that meet certain strict quality standards and that are available for no more than a specific "fair market rent." Apartments good enough to meet the quality standard and cheap enough to meet the fair market rent standard turn out to be in singularly short supply. As a result "despite the large subsidy available under the pro- gram, the *majority* of households selected [to receive a Section 8 cer- tificate] are unable to find housing that qualifies . . . and must forego benefits" (Carliner, p. 121). Thus, if all who received a certificate were actually able to use it, the rate of subsidy among those eligible would fall to about one in ten.

As I have already indicated, only about one poverty household in four receives any federal housing subsidy; the number of poor peo- ple exceeds the number of subsidized units by a factor of ten (see note 6).

The essential problem with our current low-income housing policy is sadly obvious. Subsidies or not, there are simply not enough units to go around. There is an evident need for the construction of new low-income housing on a massive scale to address not only the problem of homelessness, but the much larger problem of adequately housing the nation's poverty population.

None of this should have come as any surprise. It was possible to write as early as 1972 that "the United States is in the midst of a severe housing crisis."[24] Indeed, numerous books with titles such as *Housing Crisis USA* by Joseph Fried (published in 1971 by Praeger) or *Crisis in Urban Housing* by Grant MacClelland (published in 1973 by H. W. Wilson) appeared early in the decade. In the ensuing years the urban housing situation has changed from critical to catastrophic. The above mentioned increase in the urban poverty population, coupled with a sharp reduction in the amount of low-income housing, have conspired to create a new class of urban homeless. Arising in tandem with the emergence of this class is a new tier of social service agencies, advocates, social workers, and others to minister to the human suffering that has resulted.

"What to do about homelessness?" is a question that now commands considerable attention among researchers, advocates, and social policy makers. Most of the answers that have so far been provided are ameliorative in character: the homeless need more and better shelters, food, community mental health services, alcohol education and counseling, medical care, job counseling and placement—and on through the list of basic human needs. All of these, to be sure, are genuine needs, and the effort to respond to them is compassionate and laudable. But first and foremost, the homeless need a place to live, and nothing short of providing more low-income housing will solve the homelessness problem.

This, of course, is not a simple problem. As we will see in later chapters, various groups within the homeless population have unique and highly specialized housing needs. The needs of chronically mentally ill persons will clearly not be met by building a new public housing project; alcoholics need more than additional flophouses or SRO's. That many of the homeless suffer one or another disability (physical, mental, economic, or social) and therefore have specialized needs does not, however, undercut the major point, that the principal need is for housing.

The point, it appears, is not lost on the homeless themselves. Ball and Havassy have recently reported results from a needs assessment survey based on interviews with 112 homeless people in the San Francisco area.[25] In one question, respondents were asked to identify "the most important issues you face or problems you have trying to make it in San Francisco or generally in life." "No place to live indoors" was the most common response, mentioned by 94%; "no money" was second, mentioned by 88%. These were the only re sponses mentioned by at least half the sample.

In a later section of the survey, a subset of 57 respondents knowι to have had contact with the mental health system was asked, "Wha kinds of resources or services they needed 'to get by in the commu nity and keep from having to go or be taken to psychiatric emergency centers or hospitals' " (p. 919). Contrary to expectation, the most frequent answer was not community mental health services, nor alcohol rehabilitation programs, nor crisis intervention centers, nor supportive counseling. The primary expressed need among these 57 homeless (and to varying degrees, emotionally disturbed) persons was affordable housing, mentioned spontaneously by 86%.

Every study yet done of the homeless has reported a range of social and personal pathologies. Depending upon sample, definitions, and the professional interests of the investigators, somewhere between 29 and 55% of the homeless are reported to have a serious drinking problem, somewhere between 10 and 30% are reported to have a problem with other substance dependencies, and somewhere between 20 and 84% are reported to be emotionally disturbed or mentally ill.[26] (In a later chapter I will narrow these ranges considerably.) Other common problems include prior criminal records, a history of psychiatric hospitalization, physical or sexual abuse as children, profound estrangement from family and friends, and so on.

In some sense, of course, these factors are appropriately cited as the "cause" of a person's homelessness, just as consistent bad luck can be cited as the "cause" of losing at cards. Given a game that some are destined to lose, in other words, it is appropriate to do research on who the losers turn out to be. But do not mistake an analysis of the losers for an analysis of the game itself. The material covered in this chapter suggests that in a hypothetical world where there were no alcoholics, no drug addicts, no mentally ill, no deinstitutionalization movement, no personal or social pathologies at all, there would *still* be a formidable homelessness problem, simply because there is not enough low-income housing to accommodate the poverty population.

One of the many tragedies in all this is that downtown revitalization is a desperately needed and much-lauded effort to arrest the process of urban decay that had become virtually epidemic in many of the large cities, especially in the North and East. A key element in the salvage effort, obviously, is to lure middle-class taxpayers away from the suburbs and back to the urban core, and to this end, rotting urban slums are being razed and replaced by elegant apartments, historical restorations, trendy shops, and classy restaurants—developments that many city residents look upon with understandable favor. "You can sense it downtown. Instead of 'white flight,' middle-class individuals and families are migrating back to city neighborhoods that, only a generation before, their parents had abandoned for a slice of suburbia."[27] Or, as Kasinitz has put it, "At first ignored by governmental bureaucracies and shunned by wary financial institutions, downtown revival has today become the stock in trade of a network of private corporations, state agencies, and local development corporations, encouraged by banks and insurance companies who had until recently written off the inner city."[28]

There is, however, no such thing as a free lunch, and downtown revitalization, commendable though it has been, has also created a serious crisis in the supply of low-income housing and the rise of a more or less permanently displaced class of homeless and marginally housed persons. The so-called "celebration of diversity" that is said to lie behind the backflow of the affluent into downtown clearly "does not extend to people who, for whatever reasons, make middle-class people feel uncomfortable" (Kasinitz, p. 243). Throughout the nation, the cities are being reclaimed by the middle class; homelessness among the poverty class has been the inadvertent and largely unanticipated result.

In short, what we witness in the rise of the new homeless is a form of class conflict—a conflict over housing in the urban areas between the class of persons and households whose incomes are adequate to cover the costs of their housing and those whose incomes are not. In the recent past, this conflict was held in check by the aversion of the middle class to downtown urban living and by the federally subsidized construction of low-income housing projects. As the cities are made more attractive, and as the federal commitment to subsidized housing fades, the intensity of this conflict necessarily grows, and with it the roster of casualties—the homeless.

NOTES

1. My source for all housing costs discussed here is the *Statistical Abstract of the United States*, 1985, various tables.

2. See Ellen Bassuk, "The Homeless Problem." *Scientific American*, 251:1 (1984), pp. 40–45. I focus throughout this chapter on rental housing because low-income housing consists almost entirely of rental units.

3. Throughout this discussion, I use the "official" federal poverty definitions and statistics; there is much dispute among scholars on the subject of
poverty over the adequacy of this material. Some feel that the official poverty
lines are hopelessly mean-spirited, and that objective impoverishment is tc
be found even among those whose incomes are, say, 150% of the official poverty level. It is true, on the other hand, that the poverty calculation is based
on personal income only and does not make allowance for "income in
kind;" that is, benefits received by the poor through government social welfare programs. How to adjust the poverty data to take these benefits into
account (known collectively as Supplemental Income Programs, or SIP's) is a
matter of much controversy. Some analysts have argued that the SIP's have
effectively eliminated poverty in a meaningful sense.

The total annual expenditure on social welfare programs for those of limited
income is, to be sure, a staggering sum; in 1983, it amounted to $127 billion.
Divided among 35 million poor people, this amounts to more than $3000 for
every poor man, woman, and child in the country. On the other hand, many
of the programs included in this calculation are not targeted exclusively or
even primarily at the poor. For example, various veterans' programs, guaran-
teed student loans, rural housing loans, community health centers, and so
on.

It is also somewhat misleading to consider many SIP benefits as "income in
kind" in any realistic sense. By far the single largest SIP program is Medicaid,
the 1983 expenditure for which was $35 billion (more than a quarter of the
total SIP expenditure). None of these billions went into the pockets of the
poor as spendable cash; all of them went to doctors, hospitals, and other
health care institutions in exchange for the provision of services. It is true
that in the absence of Medicaid, a serious illness could easily wipe out a
poor family's finances (if, indeed, they could afford any medical attention at
all). That Medicaid pays the health bill, however, does not mean that the
family is suddenly somehow "better off" in terms of its spendable cash income. As Leonard Beeghley has correctly and wryly observed, absent Medicaid, the poor would be poor *and* sick, rather than just poor.

Several of these points are taken up again in Chapter 7.

4. *Statistical Abstract*, 1985, p. 454.

5. One leading exception is D. Roth and G. J. Bean, "New Perspectives on
Homelessness: Findings From a Statewide Epidemiological Study." *Hospital
and Community Psychiatry*, 37:7 (1986), pp. 712–719, which does discuss
urban-rural differences.

6. In the annual housing surveys, "gross monthly rent" equals the contract rent *plus* the estimated montly costs of utilities in units where utilities
are not included in the contract rent. In publicly subsidized units, the
amount of the subsidy is deducted from the gross monthly rent. The estimated gross monthly rents used here therefore approximate the actual out-
of-pocket housing costs to the tenant, regardless of whether utilities are or
are not included in the rent and regardless of whether the unit is or is not
subsidized.

It is a common misconception that most poor people receive at least some housing subsidy. In fact, the proportion of poor households living in subsidized units is only about 25–30%. See A. Downs, *Rental Housing in the 1980's* (Washington, DC: The Brookings Institution, 1983), pp. 19–20. In 1983, there were 2.2 million subsidized units in public housing projects, and an additional 1.2 million privately owned units subsidized through the Section 8 housing program. The total stock of subsidized housing therefore amounts to 3.4 million units altogether, compared to 35 million persons living below poverty.

7. In M. Stone, "The Politics of Housing: Mortgage Bankers." *Society*, 9:9 (July-August, 1972), pp. 31–37.

8. In fact, one commonly cited indicator of the housing squeeze for poor people is the proportion of low-income families paying 70% *or more* of their income for housing. In 1975, 21% of the poor spent over 70% of their income on rent; in 1981, 25%; and in 1983, 30%. See the U.S. General Accounting Office, *Homelessness: A Complex Problem and the Federal Response*, p. 25.

9. See C. Hartman, *America's Housing Crisis* (Boston: Routledge and Kegan Paul, 1983), p. 24.

10. The points just made suggest in turn that the housing needs of the homeless, or many of them, would be best served by single-person housing units; indeed, as will be emphasized in the following chapter, the largest subgroup within the homeless population is comprised of single, disaffiliated males. Attention thus turns to rooming and boardinghouses and single-room occupancy (SRO) hotels (perhaps with resident social services) as the type of housing needed most. As we see later, this is precisely the type of housing that appears to have been most severely affected by the housing trends of the early 1980's.

11. Downs, op.cit., pp. 77–78.

12. Special Committee on Aging, *Single Room Occupancy: A Need for National Concern*. An information paper prepared for the U.S. Senate Special Committee on Aging. Washington, DC: U.S. Government Printing Office, 1978, p. 24.

13. T. Fodor, "Toward Housing the Homeless: the Single Room Occupancy Alternative." Unpublished paper.

14. Nashville Coalition for the Homeless. *Newsletter*, March, 1986, p. 3.

15. P. Kasinitz, "Gentrification and Homelessness: The SRO Occupant and the Inner City Revival." *Urban and Social Change Review*, 17 (Winter, 1984), pp. 9–14. References in the text are to the reprinted version appearing as pp. 241–252 in J. Erikson and C. Wilheim (eds.), *Housing the Homeless* (Rutgers University: Center for Urban Policy research, 1986).

16. S. Newman and M. Owen, *Residential Displacement in the U.S.: 1970–1977* (Ann Arbor, MI: Institute for Social Research, 1982).

17. J. Brady, "Arson, Urban Economy, and Organized Crime: the Case of Boston." *Social Problems*, 31:1 (October, 1983), pp. 1–27.

18. "Health Issues in the Care of the Homeless." Ch. 1 (pp. 3–18) in P. W. Brickner *et al.* (eds.), *Health Care of Homeless People* (New York: Springer, 1985). The story of the Greenwich Hotel is found on pp. 10–13.

19. J. Atlas and P. Dreier, "The Housing Crisis and the Tenant's Revolt." *Social Policy,* 10:4 (1980), p. 14.

20. M. Carliner, "Homelessness: A Housing Problem?" In R. Bingham, F Green, and S. White (eds.), *The Homeless in Contemporary Society* (Beverl Hills: Sage Publications, 1987), pp. 119–128. The material quoted in the text i on pp. 121–122.

21. "Since 1980, the federal government has been shifting its low-incom housing aid away from subsidies for constructing and operating public housing in favor of providing vouchers for persons to find existing rental housing on the private market" (GAO homelessness report, p. 25). The reference here, of course, is to the so-called "Section 8" housing voucher program discussed later in the test.

22. *Statistical Abstract,* 1987, p. 717.

23. This discussion borrows heavily from Carliner, op. cit., pp. 125–127.

24. M. Stone, op. cit., p. 31.

25. Ball and Havassy, "A survey of the problems and needs of homeless consumers of acute psychiatric services." *Hospital and Community Psychiatry,* 35:9 (September, 1984), pp. 917–921.

26. These numbers are taken from Alcohol, Drug Abuse, and Mental Health Administration, *Alcohol, Drug Abuse, and Mental Health Problems of the Homeless: Proceedings of a Roundtable.* U. S. Department of Health and Human Services, Public Health Service, Rockville, MD (31 March and 1 April, 1983).

27. W. Von Eckhardt, "New Mood Downtown." *Society,* 16:6 (September-October, 1979), pp. 4–7.

28. Kasinitz, op. cit., p. 243.

CHAPTER FOUR

Who Are the Homeless?[1]

There are, as I have stressed, many different kinds of homeless people: men, women, and children; young, middle-aged, and old; white, black, and Hispanic; short-, medium-, and long-term homeless. But what are the relative proportions? How many are women, how many are elderly, how many are long-term?

Corresponding with the rise of public concern about the homeless has been an upsurge of research interest; a large number of recent studies, which are very uneven in coverage and quality, has resulted. Much of the work has been applied research on easy-to-reach populations (mainly shelter users), and with relatively few exceptions, serious attention to technical matters such as sampling, measurement, or generalizability has been missing. I will *not* attempt to cover the many methodological issues involved or engage in any systematic study-by-study critique, but I do slant my discussion heavily toward those studies that set the highest research standards. In the relatively few cases where the reported results of the various studies are "all over the map," I rely on the *average* result across studies as the most reliable guide.

One of the largest and most geographically dispersed samples of homeless people available is that contained in our study of clients seen in the National Health Care for the Homeless Program (referred to briefly in Chapter 1).[2] Data for the first year of the HCH program describe nearly 30,000 people seen in health clinics in sixteen large cities all over the country. Because of its size, geographical dispersion, and my familiarity with the results, I use the findings from this study extensively in the following discussion.

A second study upon which I draw heavily is the Rossi *et al.* survey of the homeless in Chicago (some results from which were presented in Chapter 2).[3] One problem in many studies of the homeless is that they are based exclusively on shelter users; it has long been recognized that the shelter users are only one of two important components of the literally homeless population, the other being "street homeless" who, for whatever reason, rarely or never make use of the shelter system. Among the many virtues of the Rossi *et al.* survey is its thorough and systematic sampling of the street homeless. This, coupled with the breadth of topics covered and the general degree of sophistication in the conduct of the research, makes the Chicago survey especially useful.

Because neither of the above two sources provides answers to all the important questions, in many cases I have relied on the rich and increasingly large body of published results from other research efforts. The studies that I employ vary widely in definitions, scope of coverage, and methodological sophistication, and as a result the findings are not always strictly comparable, or, for that matter, completely reliable. In all cases, I have sacrificed technical niceties for completeness of understanding, knowing full well that new and better research will no doubt change the picture at least in small details.

ONE THOUSAND HOMELESS PEOPLE

As a presentational convenience, it is useful to begin by imagining a sample of a thousand homeless people, drawn at random from the half million or so homeless people to be found in America on any given evening. Based on the research sketched above, we can then begin to dissect this sample in various ways, so as to portray as graphically as possible the mosaic of homelessness in this country.

The social portraiture of homelessness that follows is intended to serve several purposes. First is to answer the simple descriptive question posed in the title of this chapter, Who are the homeless? Various subgroups of them, as we will see, have sharply different social origins, background characteristics, and needs. Thus, the portrait points to groups within the larger homeless population who become homeless in different ways; more importantly, it also shows the sometimes unique needs that each group faces. A second purpose is thus a more refined targeting of services and assistance.

A third purpose is to respond to Stuart Bykofsky's implicit challenge as it was reviewed in the Preface, that is, to make some empirically defensible statement about the relative proportions of "deserving" and "undeserving" homeless people. How many of the homeless are just down on their luck, victimized by large-scale forces that they do not control, and thus deserving of generosity and compassion? And likewise, how many are, in Bykofsky's words, "just plain shiftless," people who could do better for themselves if they wanted to but are simply unwilling to make the effort, and therefore deserving of his, and our, contempt?

I admit that deserving and undeserving are relative judgments in the extreme and can only be based on certain human values that not everyone shares. I also admit that my basic instinct is to give everyone the benefit of the doubt, and in this Bykofsky and I clearly differ. In my scheme, a homeless person is deemed deserving if I can find one good reason to be sympathetic to his or her condition. Readers will decide for themselves whether they share my sympathies and adjust the result accordingly.

HOMELESS FAMILIES

Among the sad histories reviewed in Chapter 1, that of the McMullans' is to my mind the saddest—an intact family unit consisting of a wife, her husband, and their four dependent children, victims of unemployment and economic misfortune struggling in the face of long odds to maintain themselves as a unit and get back on their feet again. How many McMullans can we expect to find among our sample of a thousand homeless people?

Although the rapidly rising number of homeless families has become a matter of considerable policy concern, evidence of their proportion in the larger homeless population is hard to come by. Most of the pertinent research has been done in homeless family shelters (or in facilities for homeless women and children), and while this material is useful for descriptive purposes, it does not tell us anything about relative proportions.

Some useful information appears in the HCH study. Across the 16 cities covered, 16% of all clients seen were described as members of homeless family groups. In six of the sixteen cities, however, family status was not systematically reported; among the 18,842 clients seen in the remaining ten cities, 28% were members of homeless family groups. Thus, somewhere between 160 and 280 of our thousand homeless people will be members of homeless families—whether male or female, adult or child. Let us take the midpoint of the range, 220 members of homeless families, as our best and final estimate. The remainder, of course, are lone individuals.[4]

The HCH study further suggests that among the 220 members of homeless families, 99 will be children (under age 16) and 121 will be adult; among the adults will be 83 adult women and 38 adult men. Our first important conclusion, then, is that a tenth of the homeless on the streets of American cities today are homeless children in the care of their adult parent or parents. (Later I will add children on the streets by themselves to this figure.)

A second important conclusion follows from the relative preponderance of women to men among the adult family members: most homeless families consist of single mothers with their children rather than intact nuclear families. (There are also a few single fathers with children, but their numbers are miniscule in all studies.) If each of the 38 adult men is coupled with one of the 83 adult women, the talley becomes 38 male-female pairs and 45 single females among the total of 121 adult family members. Thus, somewhat more than half of the homeless families are in fact single-parent (typically, single mother) units; somewhat less than half are intact nuclear families.

Most of the intact nuclear families, as it turns out, have dependent children, but only about half of them actually have their children with them. The most common arrangement among the remainder is that the children are living with other relatives; in some cases the children are in foster care. Thus, only 17 or 18 or the intact male-female pairs would also include children as part of the family unit; the 99 children are therefore distributed among, say, 18 mother-father pairs and 45 single parents (mostly mothers). It follows that most homeless children live in broken families, one among the many distinctive problems homeless children face.

Studies of the effects of homelessness on children paint a bleak picture. According to Ellen Bassuk, developmental delays of varying severity are observed in more than half.[5] My own research has confirmed that homeless children suffer various physical disorders at rates two to ten times those seen among children in general.[6] Some of the problems encountered by homeless children are portrayed in the case studies reviewed in Chapter 1: depression, anger, anxiety, low self-esteem, and uncertainty about life are common problems at the psychological level; inadequate nutrition, dangerous living conditions, violence and abuse, lack of parental authority, lack of a quiet place to do homework, and so on are the problems encountered at a more concrete, palpable level. Young Yvette's dream is for a clean apartment and a safe place to play out of doors. This does not seem too much to ask.

Bassuk once remarked in a conference presentation, "Nobody in their right mind would think that homelessness was actually *good* for children. What surprises me is just how bad it is." The large numbers of homeless children being seen in the shelters and soup kitchens means that the homeless of the twenty-first century are already being created.

As for the adult members of homeless family units, the picture is somewhat brighter; among both the men and the women, rates of alcohol and drug abuse, and mental illness, are lower than they are among lone homeless individuals. The adult family members also suffer fewer chronic physical disorders, are more likely to be short-term (or situationally) homeless, and are rated as having better housing and employment prospects than the lone homeless are. In general, their prospects for the future are much brighter.[7] Many of these families, like the McMullans, need little more than a helping hand to get them through a rough stretch; many of the single mothers with dependent children need little more than an expedited AFDC process. While helping hands and more efficient AFDC processing would not solve all the problems these families face, they would help considerably.

In sum, members of homeless families constitute a significantly large fraction of the homeless population, comprising approximately one-quarter of the total, nearly half of whom are homeless children. While most people, I think, would look on homeless families as most deserving of help, there is reason to believe that they need the least help (in that they appear to have the fewest disabling problems and tend generally to be the most intact), and that even relatively modest assistance would make a substantial difference in their life chances and circumstances. If the available resources are such as to require triage, then homeless families should be the top priority.

THE LONE HOMELESS: WOMEN AND CHILDREN

By the above calculations, there remain in our hypothetical sample of one thousand some 780 lone homeless persons—single individuals on the streets by themselves. Based on the HCH study, some 6% of these are children or adolescents age 19 or younger (which amounts to 47 additional children in the sample of a thousand), 20% are adult women (156 additional women), and 74% are adult men (which leaves, from the original sample, only 580 adult males not members of homeless family groups).[8] Adding these to the earlier results, we derive two significant conclusions.

First, among the sample of homeless persons, 146 will be children aged 19 or younger—approximately one in every seven. Second, among the remaining 854 adults, 229 will be women, which amounts to 27% of all adults. Combining all figures, homeless children and homeless adult women themselves comprise 375 of the original thousand—three of every eight. Thus, while adult men comprise the majority of the homeless, a sizable minority—nearly 40%—are women and children.

Most of the lone children found in the above calculations are teenagers, which is to say that nearly all homeless preteen children are still living with one or both of their parents. However, children as young as 12 or 13 will be found in sizable numbers in these data. Although men predominate among homeless adults, boys and girls are found in equal numbers among homeless children and teen-agers; in the HCH data that form the basis for the above calculations, 51% of the lone homeless aged 19 or younger are boys and 49% are girls; among all children (under age 16) in these data (whether lone individuals or members of homeless family groups), the split is the same. The heavy preponderance of males to females is observed only among the adults.

Although precise numbers are hard to come by, there is little doubt that many of these homeless teenagers are runaway or throw-away children fleeing abusive or otherwise unacceptable family situations. Among the girls the rate of pregnancy is high: 9% of the girls aged 13–15, and 24% of the girls aged 16–19, were pregnant at or since their first contact with the HCH clinic system; the rate for 16- to 19-year-olds is the highest observed in any age group.[9] There is impressionistic evidence (but no hard evidence) to suggest that many of these young girls (and, not incidentally, many of the young boys) are reduced to prostitution in order to survive; many will thus come to possess lengthy jail records. Drug and alcohol abuse are also common problems. The rate of known drug abuse among the 16- to 19-year-old boys—some 16%—is the highest rate recorded for any age group in the HCH data.[10]

The teenage years, to be sure, are not easy for anyone; it is a time of uncertainty and transition in the best of cases. But it is the rare adolescent who, in addition to the normal concerns of the teenage years, must also worry about where to sleep at night, or where the next meal is coming from, or who is going to assault them next. What hope for the future can be nourished under such conditions? Many of these adolescents—tough kids on mean streets, but just kids nonetheless—face an unending downward spiral of booze, drugs, crime, and troubles with the law. They too must surely be counted among the deserving homeless; anything that can be done to break the spiral and set them on a path to an independent and productive adult existence should be done.

To reiterate, among the 854 adults remaining in our initial sample of one thousand homeless will be 229 adult women, or 27% of all adults. I stressed earlier that this is not a new phenomenon; studies by D. L. Jones in Massachusetts and by P. F. Clements in Philadelphia confirm sizable fractions of women among the homeless at least since Colonial times.[11] Compared to homeless adult men, homeless women are younger by an average of about 2 years; 42% of the adult HCH women, but only 30% of the adult men, are under 30. Compared to the men, the women are much more likely to have psychiatric impairments, but much less likely to abuse alcohol and drugs. (Data on this point are presented in a later chapter.)

There are, of course, many different kinds of homeless women, and it is therefore a mistake to think that all homeless women face the same problems. One large and important subgroup is comprised of lone mentally impaired women from whom the "bag lady" stereotype has been derived. This is the subset of homeless women that in some sense has been created by deinstitutionalization and related changes in our mental-health treatment system. A reasonable guess is that they constitute about one third of all homeless women. They are relatively older (median age of the group = 40) and predominantly white (58%). Their principal need, of course, is for vastly improved mental-health services, including aftercare housing as a top priority.

A second important subgroup, accounting (as we have seen) for more than one quarter of the total, are mothers with dependent children in their care. These women tend to be young (median age = 27), and their rates of mental disorder and substance abuse are relatively low. Only about half receive AFDC; many would presumably be employable if day care were available.

Yet a third group are homeless teenage girls, some of whose problems have already been discussed. The remainder of the women fall into a residual "other" category; the distinctive feature of this group is that alcohol (and drug) abuse is much more widespread than among the other women, rivaling the rates generally found among homeless men.[12]

Most people would probably feel comfortable counting the adult women among the deserving homeless. Just as women and children are the first to be evacuated from a sinking ship, so too should women and children be the first to be rescued from the degradations of street life or a shelter existence. If we add to the group of deserving homeless the relatively small number of adult men in homeless family groups, then our initial cut leaves but 580 persons from the original thousand to account for.

LONE ADULT MEN: THE ELDERLY

What is to be said about those who remain, the 580 lone adult males who are not members of homeless families? A small percentage of them, much smaller than most people would anticipate, are elderly men over age 65; in the HCH data, they comprise about 3% of the group in question, or 17 elderly men. In fact, among all HCH adults, just about 3% are over age 65; the lone adult men are no exceptional in this respect.

Since about 12% of the national population as a whole are over 65 our 3% figure means that there are many fewer elderly homeless that. would otherwise be expected—a "shortage" or "deficit" of elderly homeless that has been remarked in several studies.[13]

What explains this apparent shortage? First, a number of entitle- ments become available to people once they turn 65, chief among them being medicare and social security. It is possible that these benefits are adequate to get most older homeless persons off the streets or out of shelters and into some sort of reasonably stable housing situation. A second possibility is premature mortality; home- less persons may only rarely survive to age 65 in the first place.[14]

Though little research has been done on mortality among the homeless, the few studies that are available suggest that the mortality hypothesis is not to be taken lightly. Alstrom and his colleagues fol- lowed 6032 homeless Swedish men for a 3-year period. Observed mortality during the study period ($N = 327$ deaths) exceeded the age-adjusted expected mortality ($N = 87$ expected deaths) by approx- imately a factor of four. The average age of death among the 327 men was about 53 years.[15] My own study of the topic has produced a sim- ilar result; among 88 deaths occurring among clients seen in the HCH program, the average age of death was 51.[16] Based on these findings, we can conclude that homeless men die some 20 or so years earlier than they should given normal life expectancies. Thus, premature death must certainly account for at least some portion of the elderly deficit.

The shortage of over-65's is not the only striking aspect of the age distribution of the homeless; the fact is, homeless people are gener- ally very *young*. The median age of all HCH adult clients is 34 years, very close to the average figure (35 years) reported in a number of recent studies.[17] Indeed, virtually all recent demographic studies of homeless populations have remarked the low average age, perhaps because the stereotypical expectation is that the homeless tend to be old. As noted earlier, our study of trends in the age of homeless men seen in the New York City Men's Shelter shows that the average age has apparently been declining by about 6 months per year over the past decade. Today, the average homeless adult male is somewhere in his early to middle thirties.

The low average age of the homeless sustains an important and often overlooked conclusion; namely, that the rise of the new homeless is in some sense a result of the so-called baby boom, the immensely large generation born in the United States between 1947 and 1964. As a cohort, the average age of this group is now the early thirties, almost identical to the average age of homeless people.

The baby boom has posed numerous problems for virtually every institution it has touched in the course of its life span, beginning with the crisis in elementary education that commenced in the early 1950's, continuing to a serious national housing shortage today, and ending ultimately with what will be a shortage of burial space around the year 2020 and thereafter. The more affluent members of the baby boom generation have come to be known as "yuppies" (young urban professionals), whose housing preferences and purchasing power are in many respects responsible for the current housing crisis. What is often overlooked in discussions of the yuppies is that they sit at the upper end of an income distribution, the other end of which reaches down into the poverty population. In the lowest levels of this income distribution one finds the new homeless, whose numbers have clearly begun to strain the capacity of the existing social welfare system. (I have more to say about the young men later in this and subsequent chapters.)

As to the elderly, surely they are to be included within the deserving group. As it happens, only about half of them receive social security.[18] Many of those find that no housing can be purchased or rented within their means. Well over half have chronic physical health problems that further contribute to their hardships. Certainly they are among those homeless deserving our sympathies.

LONE ADULT MEN: THE VETERANS

We are now left with, let us say, 563 nonelderly lone adult men, at least a third of whom (188) are veterans of the United States Armed Forces. Indeed, over a number of recent studies, the percentage of veterans among the men varies from a low of 32% to a high of 47%.[19] The one-third figure is clearly conservative; the true figure might be as high as one half. As a point of comparison, 41% of all American adult men are also veterans; in this respect, the homeless are not much different.

The studies reviewed by Robertson (see note 19) show that the homeless veterans are slightly older and have higher proportions of whites than homeless nonveteran men; compared to the national veteran population, Vietnam-era veterans are somewhat overrepresented among the homeless. About one in five have service-relatec disabilities sufficiently serious to prevent them from working Service-related psychiatric difficulties, while not always disabling, ar(also widespread: among the Vietnam-era veterans, posttraumati(stress disorder is perhaps the most common of these problems. Mos_ of the veterans, especially the younger ones, report chronic unemployment problems as well. No more than about a third receive any form of assistance from the Veteran's Administration.

Most homeless veterans are drawn from the lower socioeconomic strata, having enlisted to obtain, as Robertson has put it, "long term economic advantages through job training as well as postmilitary college benefits and preferential treatment in civil service employment" (p. 64), only to find that their economic and employment opportunities remain quite limited after they have mustered out. The lure of military service proves to have been a false promise for many of these men. "Despite recruitment campaigns that promote military service as an opportunity for maturation and occupational mobility, veterans continue to struggle with postmilitary unemployment and mental and physical disability without adequate assistance from the federal government" (p. 79). One of the Vietnam veterans in Robertson's study sums up as follows: "If they expect the youth of America to fight another war, they have to take care of the vets" (p. 79).

Many homeless veterans would fall easily into Stuart Bykofsky's group of "the drunk and the addicted," if not among the "just plain shiftless." Alcohol and drug abuse are common among homeless veterans, many of whom have deteriorated steadily since their service days and have ended up on the streets. Some were dishonorably discharged in the first place (and are therefore not eligible for any veteran's benefits). Still, despite their many current problems and disabilities, these men were there when the nation needed them. I do not think it is overly generous or sentimental to say that they at least deserve a return of the favor.

LONE ADULT MEN: THE DISABLED

Based on the admittedly conservative estimate that one-third of the nonelderly lone adult men are veterans, then 375 nonelderly nonveteran adult men are all that remain of the initial one thousand. Sorting out this subgroup in the HCH data, I find that one third are assessed by their care providers as having moderate to severe psychiatric impairments—*not* including alcohol or drug abuse. (I deal at length with the homeless mentally ill in a later chapter.) Many of them have "fallen through the cracks" of the community mental health system.

In the vast majority of cases, the homeless mentally ill pose no immediate danger to themselves or to others (and thus are generally immune to involuntary commitment for psychiatric treatment). At the same time, their ability to care for themselves, especially in a street or shelter environment, is marginal at best. Compassion dictates that they too be included among the deserving group.

Just what they deserve is hotly contested; I cannot do justice here to the many complex issues involved. Some, like Mayor Koch of New York City, think that they deserve involuntary commitment if their lives or well-being are imperiled by the material conditions of their existence; civil libertarians think they deserve the right to die on the streets if they want to.[20] Many mental health professionals, along with Bykofsky, seem to feel that reopening the large state mental institutions is the only viable solution; others think that fulfilling the promise of community based mental health care—the explicit promise upon which deinstitutionalization was justified—is the only morally defensible approach. But all agree that for many of the mentally ill homeless, the "least restrictive treatment" doctrine has meant a life of scavenging food from street sources and sleeping in alleys and gutters. And this no one intended.

Subtracting the 125 or so mentally disabled men from the remaining group of 375 leaves 250 of the original thousand. Among these 250 will be (according to the HCH data) 28 men who are *physically* disabled and incapable of working. They include the blind and the deaf, those confined to wheelchairs, the paraplegic, those with amputated limbs, and those with disabling chronic physical illnesses such as heart disease, AIDS, obstructive pulmonary disease, and others.

Men with work histories who are disabled and incapable of working are theoretically eligible for SSDI (disability insurance) benefits; among the physically disabled homeless in the HCH study, only about 18% actually received such benefits. Other physically disabled persons, those without sufficient work histories to qualify for SSDI, are presumably eligible for less generous Supplemental Security Income (SSI) payments, but fewer than half of the disabled homeless receive even SSI. Of the physically disabled HCH homeless, 40% receive neither SSI nor SSDI benefits. Like the mentally disabled, the physically disabled must be counted among the deserving. Subtracting them leaves a mere 222 persons from the original thousand—nonelderly, nonveteran, adult males with no mental or physical disability.

LONE ADULT MEN: EMPLOYMENT STATUS

Of these 222 men, approximately half—112 to be precise—will in fact be found to have some sort of job: the HCH data suggest that 7 will have full-time jobs, 27 will have part-time jobs, and 78 will be employed on a sporadic basis (seasonal work, day labor, odd jobs, and the like). The remaining 110 men are unemployed, and among these, some 61 will be looking for work (according to their health care providers). All told, then, among the 222 men there will be 173 who are at least making an effort; they are looking for work, but so far unsuccessfully, or have a job but do not earn enough to allow them to afford stable housing.

This leaves 49 people from the initial one thousand who are not members of homeless families, not women, not children, not elderly, not veterans, not mentally or physically disabled, not currently working, and not looking for work. Call these the "undeserving homeless," or, if you will, the "just plain shiftless." They account for about 5% of the total—a mere one in every twenty.

There are, to be sure, many undesirables among the various groups within the homeless that I have deemed deserving. Overall, perhaps 40% of the homeless (50% of homeless men) abuse alcohol; one tenth abuse other drugs; one third are mentally ill; many have lengthy prison records; most have chronic unemployment problems; most are estranged from their families and disaffiliated from the larger society. Still, all but a residual fraction merit our compassion on one or more counts.

RACIAL AND ETHNIC COMPOSITION

Several dozen studies have reported information on the racial and ethnic makeup of the homeless population. While the findings from these studies are extremely variable, it is clear that the racial and ethnic composition of a city's homeless population usually reflects that of the city's larger poverty population. The closest we have to a genuine national sample is the sixteen-city HCH study, wherein the racial composition is 45% white, 40% black, 11% Hispanic, 2% American

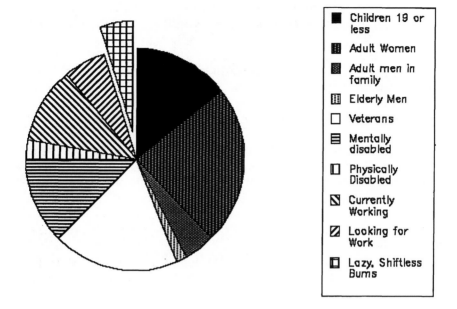

Legend:

- ■ Children 19 or less
- ▦ Adult Women
- ▓ Adult men in family
- ▥ Elderly Men
- □ Veterans
- ▤ Mentally disabled
- ◫ Physically Disabled
- ◩ Currently Working
- ▨ Looking for Work
- ◘ Lazy, Shiftless Bums

FIGURE 4.1   The worthy and unworthy homeless.

Indian, and 1% Asian, with the remainder in a catchall "other" category. Since in the national population as a whole blacks comprise 11.7%, Hispanics 6.4%, and American Indians 0.6%, racial and ethnic minorities are heavily overrepresented among the homeless, as they are in the poverty population at large.[21]

The preponderance of ethnic minorities among the homeless is itself a relatively new phenomenon; most studies done before the middle 1970's reported the homeless to be largely white.[22] The current overrepresentation of minority groups, both among the homeless and the larger poverty population, calls attention to persisting discrimination against minorities in the employment and housing markets as yet another factor that contributes to the homelessness problem.

EDUCATION

The common view of the homeless is that they are a largely uneducated group; in fact, however, every recent study of the homeless has reported higher-than-expected levels of educational attainment. In the HCH data, for example, just over half (53%) of the adults have a high school diploma or better; nearly one in five has attended 1 or more years of college as well. At the same time, nearly half, 47% have something less than a high school education. (Among all adult in the United States age 25 and older, 66.5% have a high school di ploma or better and 31.9% have attended 1 or more years of college among adults older than 25 below the poverty line, the comparabl figures are 42.4 and 17.5%.) As in the general population, levels or education are higher among the younger homeless and drop off in the older age groups.

The general demographic patterns that I have been discussing sustain several important conclusions. First, the stereotype of home-lessness tends to be one of an older, predominantly white, over-whelmingly male, uneducated and alcoholic population, or, in the more conventional parlance, the skid row bum. Whatever the histor-ical merits of this stereotype, it is clearly inadequate as a portrait of today's homeless, who are unexpectedly young, well-educated, and dominated by racial and ethnic minorities; a sizable fraction of the homeless are women and children. The same point has been made by many others.[23]

Second, the obvious heterogeneity of the homeless with regard to age, race, gender, and other social characteristics correctly implies that it is misleading to speak of "the" homeless as though they were a single, unitary group. The homeless are comprised of many differ-ent subgroups, each with its own characteristic circumstances and problems.

FAMILY BACKGROUND AND AFFILIATIONS

That homeless people are generally disaffiliated from family ties is widely reported in most research studies. About half the homeless prove never to have married; of those who have married, most are separated, widowed or divorced. In my own study of these topics, only 11% of the women and 6% of the men were currently married and living with spouses; if unmarried partners are added, the figures are 18 and 9%. Most homeless people, in short, exist without the financial or emotional support of an adult partner. Most are also ap-parently without extended kin networks; more than half have mini-mal or nonexistent levels of contact with their families (making contact with the family rarely or never); less than one quarter main-tain regular contact.

Similar findings appear in the Chicago survey. Few of the Chicago homeless had ever formed their own households through marriage, and most who had were no longer married. A mere 9% were currently members of household units, and this small group was made up almost exclusively of homeless women and their children.

Contact with families and relatives again tended to be minimal. Although almost nine out of ten (88%) had parental family members and relatives who were living, only three out of five (60%) maintained minimal contact with any of them—visiting, writing, talking with or telephoning at least once every 2 or 3 months. Similarly low levels of contact were registered with spouses, ex-spouses or children: 55% had such persons, but only one in three maintained minimal contact. The end result is a pattern of isolation: one in three had no contact with *any* relatives and almost one in four (24%) had no contacts with either relatives *or* friends.

The implication is that the homeless do not have access to the buffering effects of extended kin or friendship networks, rendering them especially vulnerable to the ups and downs of fortune occasioned by changes in employment and changes in physical or mental health.

GEOGRAPHY

The geographic origins of the homeless are relevant because it is not uncommon in public policy discussions to hear the claim that the homeless are a geographically mobile group. State or city leaders often express the sentiment that "the homeless are somebody else's problem." The general idea is that the homeless population of a particular city or state originated elsewhere and migrated in; therefore, responsibility for the problem must also reside elsewhere. A variant on the hypothesis is that many people of marginal skills have been drawn to the Sunbelt cities by the spectacular economic growth there over the past decade and by the consequent promise of unlimited opportunities for work, only to find that their opportunities remain severely restricted, with another episode of homelessness the ultimate result. A third variant is that homeless people are attracted to states (or cities) with the most generous welfare benefits or with the most fully developed social services for the homeless; this concern tends to be voiced whenever a city or state is thinking of expanding the range of services and benefits offered to homeless people.[24]

Despite the frequency with which these hypotheses have been voiced, there is relatively little available data on the geographic ori gins of homeless people. In the Chicago survey, most respondent were long-term residents of Illinois and of Chicago, with more thai 70% either born in the state or residents of the city for more than 1(years. Among HCH clients whose geographic origins are known more than a third (35%) were born in their current city of residence, with another 15% born elsewhere in the same state. Thus, almost half the homeless, at least in the HCH study, are indigenous to their current state of residence. Another 42% were born elsewhere in the United States; the remaining 8% were born overseas.

The U.S. census publishes similar data for the population as a whole and for specific cities. The percentage of a given city's population that was born in the current state of residence averages about 60% across the cities included in the above calculation. In other words, roughly four in ten of the current residents of the cities analyzed here were born in other states; among HCH clients in those cities, the equivalent number is five in ten. Thus, homeless people are not much more mobile than urban persons generally.

Overall migration differences between the Rust Belt and Sunbelt cities are surprisingly modest. Among Rust Belt HCH clients, 54% are indigenous to their current state, 39% were born in other states, and 7% were born overseas; among Sunbelt clients, the figures are 45, 46, and 8%, respectively. The in-migration difference between Sunbelt and Rust Belt homeless is thus on the order of 9%; even in the Sunbelt cities, nearly half the HCH clients (45%) were born in-state.

Our study also asked about length of residence "in the local area" for HCH clients born out-of-state. We found that 28% of the in-migrants had lived in the state for more than 5 years, and an additional 22% had been there for more than 1 but less than 5 years. The more recent migrants (those living in-state for less than a year) amount to approximately half the total migrants, and thus to about one quarter of the total homeless population.

Although overall migration varied little between Rust Belt and Sunbelt cities, recency of migration varied sharply, with 71% of the Sunbelt migrants living in-state for less than 1 year (as compared to 33% of the Rust Belt migrants). We therefore estimate that $.54 \times .71 = 38\%$ of the Sunbelt homeless are recent in-migrants to the Sunbelt cities; for the Rust Belt cities, the equivalent proportion is $.46 \times .33 = 15\%$. Thus, many of the Sunbelt homeless *are* recent in-migrants to the Sunbelt regions; outside the Sunbelt, the large majority of homeless tend to be indigenous to or relatively long-term residents of their current state.

CRIMINAL BACKGROUND

The homeless consist predominantly of young, nonwhite central city men, so it should be expected that many of them will have had criminal backgrounds. In the Chicago survey, 41% of the homeless respondents reported that they had served time in a city or county jail, 28% said they had been placed on probation by a court, and 16% indicated they had served a term in a state or federal prison, presumably on felony charges. The HCH data again produce similar results. About half the men and one quarter of the women have been sentenced at least once to a prison or jail term; 29% of the men and 8% of the women have at least one felony conviction.

Another question asked where the client had lived just prior to the most recent episode of homelessness. "In jail or prison" was mentioned for 7% of the men and 4% of the women. Still another sequence asked for assessments by care providers of the principal causes of the client's homelessness. "Just released from prison or jail" was noted as a contributory factor for 14% of the men and 5% of the women. These and similar data reported in other studies make it plain that some share of the homelessness problem, especially among men, results from inadequate discharge planning in the American prison system, more specifically, release without adequate provision for housing or subsequent social service follow-up.

EXTREME POVERTY

The Chicago survey contained a number of questions on income, employment status, and means of support. Median income from all sources for the month prior to the interview was just under $100; mean income for the same period was $168. The 1985 poverty line for single persons under 65 was $5250 (annual income), 2.6 times the mean income and 4.4 times the median income of Chicago's homeless. The homeless are thus among the poorest of the poor, surviving on less than 40% of a poverty-level income.

The link between literal homelessness and extreme poverty is easily demonstrated. In 1985, the average monthly rent for Chicago SRO rooms, among the cheapest accommodations available, was $195, or $27 *more* than the mean income of the sample.[25] The average homeless person could spend all available income on housing and still come up short. Consider too that fares on Chicago Transit Authorit buses and trains are $0.90; a single round-trip bus fare would there fore consume more than half the average daily income. That the Chi cago homeless manage to get by at all is attributable to the shelters soup kitchens, and charitable organizations that provide them witl requisite necessities.

All this is not to say that the Chicago homeless made no contribu-tion to their own support. Although only a small percentage (3%) held full-time jobs, almost two in five had worked for some period of time over the month preceding the survey, mostly at casual, poorly paid, part-time jobs. Work and other economic activity was, in fact, the source of 29% of all income.

Despite their extreme poverty, surprisingly few were on public as-sistance; about one in four (28%) were on AFDC or General Assis-tance (mostly the latter). These income transfer payments accounted for 30% of the total income of the literal homeless. Another 21% of their income is accounted for by pension and disability payments, re-ceived by less than one in five (18%).

The job histories of the homeless show them to have been among the extremely poor and unemployed for years. On the average, it was more than 4.5 years (55 months) since their last steady full-time job (one lasting more than 3 months), with the median being 3.3 years (40 months). However, the homeless had been unemployed much longer than they had been homeless, by an average of about 3 years. This finding suggests that many unemployed single persons are helped out by their families and friends for relatively long periods, but that the patience, forbearance, or resources of these benefactors eventually runs out, with literal homelessness the result.[26]

NATURE AND DURATION OF HOMELESSNESS

Homeless people are differentiated not only according to their background and demographic characteristics but also in terms of the nature, duration, and circumstances of their homelessness. My study asked care providers to assess the nature of HCH clients' homeless-ness as chronic (more or less continuously homeless since the first episode of homelessness), episodic (recurring episodes of homeless-ness punctuated by occasional and variable periods of a more or less stable housing situation), or recently homeless for the first time (such that no pattern has yet been established).

The popular view of homelessness would certainly include chronicity as an important part of the depiction; the image is of persons who have been "down on their luck" for years. In contrast, recent research shows these people to be a mixture of chronic long-term and transitory short-term homeless: in Chicago, 31% had been homeless less than 2 months, 25% for 2 or more years. Homelessness, therefore, is *not* a stable condition in all cases; over any reasonable time span, there is considerable movement into and out of the homeless state. A further implication is that the chronically homeless will *not* constitute the overwhelming majority of any sample of homeless populations.

Consistent with the point just made, the majority of homeless HCH clients (52%) were judged to be episodically homeless; 29% (barely more than one quarter) were judged to be chronically homeless; about one fifth (19%) were recently homeless for the first time. Men were more likely than women to be chronically homeless (33–19%); women, in contrast, were more likely to be either episodically homeless (55–51%) or recently homeless for the first time (26–16%).

Among the major ethnic groups, whites are most likely to be chronically homeless (by about ten percentage points over either blacks or Hispanics). The chronically homeless are also the oldest of the three groups (average age is 42), followed by the episodically homeless (40 years), and the recently homeless (38 years). Thus, the chronically homeless tend to be older white men; and the recently homeless, younger women.

Independent data on the duration of the client's current episode of homelessness show an equivalent picture. About one third of the men (32%) and one fifth of the women (19%) have been homeless for more than a year; in contrast, 27% of the men and 37% of the women have been homeless for a month or less. The correlates of duration are essentially identical to the correlates of chronicity as reported above: the long-term homeless are older and have a higher percentage of whites than the short-term homeless.[27]

A recent study by the Institute for Research on Poverty at the University of Wisconsin[28] has shown just how transitory the state of homelessness is. The IRP researchers initially interviewed a sample of homeless persons and then reinterviewed the sample 6 months later. "Astonishingly, although the second interviews were only 6 months after the first, three-fourths of the homeless had found places to live at least once. Furthermore, among those who did so, the majority became homeless one more time during the same period, and 55 percent of these managed to exit [from homelessness] again" (p. 23).

Thus, the most common case in these data is two episodes of homelessness and two periods of having housing all in the span of a half-year.

Another question in the HCH study asked whether the client wa currently seeking permanent housing. In some 15% of the cases th client was reported to already have permanent housing, and thus wa not homeless at the time of the study. Of those without housing, the split was nearly 50–50 between those looking and those not. Consistent with the relative recency of their homelessness, the women were more likely to be seeking permanent housing than the men.

A final question asked for an assessment of whether the client's current homelessness was likely to be short-term or long-term. Overall, the split was the same: 53% of the clients were assessed as short-term homeless; 47% as long-term. These assessments also show the expected gender difference: the women were more likely to be assessed as short-term homeless (62%) than the men (49%).

Statistical analysis of the "short- versus long-term" assessments showed interesting results. The strongest effect was for level of contact with family; those in regular or frequent contact were significantly more likely to be assessed as short-term homeless than others. The apparent implication is that maintenance of family ties is one, possibly *the*, critical variable in shortening the duration of a person's homelessness (or, as we see in the next chapter, preventing it in the first place). A second significant factor is ethnicity (as suggested above); other factors held constant, nonwhites were significantly more likely to be judged short-term homeless than whites. Having a dependent child in one's care also reduced the likelihood of a long-term prognosis. Thus women, especially women with dependent children, those who maintain regular contact with family, and nonwhites are the least likely candidates for long-term homelessness.[29]

Where did HCH clients live before they became homeless? The most common prior arrangement was either one's own place (26% of the men, 38% of the women), or with family (18% of both men and women), or with friends (15% of the men, 14% of the women). A substantial fraction of the men (14%) lived in rooming houses; no other prior housing arrangement characterized as much as a tenth of the sample for either sex.

Given the emphasis that has been placed on deinstitutionalization of the mentally ill as a cause of homelessness, it is worth noting that only 3% of the homeless men and 5% of the homeless women lived in mental institutions prior to their current homelessness. Combining all institutional living arrangements (mental institutions, prisons and jails, and the category of "other institutions"), we find that 14% of the men and 12% of the women were in institutions just prior to their current episode of homelessness.

DISABILITIES

It should be apparent that the homeless suffer numerous disabilities—physical, psychological, economic, and social—that interfere with normal functioning in a complex society. Some of these have already been noted: half, for example, have less than a high school education; many have extended jail or prison records; most are unemployed; nearly all have incomes well beneath the poverty line. Mental and physical disabilities are also widespread, as are alcohol and drug abuse. In the Chicago survey, more than one in four reported some health condition that prevented their employment. Prominent among these conditions were mental illness, cardiovascular conditions, and gastrointestinal disorders. More than one in three (37%) reported themselves as being in "fair" or "poor" health, a level of self-reported ill health more than twice that found in the general adult population (18%). More than one in four reported a hospital stay of more than 24 hours over the previous year.[30]

Much has been written on psychiatric disability among the homeless. In the Chicago data, almost one in four (23%) reported having been in a mental hospital for stays of over 48 hours, more than four times the rate in the general population. Among those who had been in mental hospitals, three out of five (58%) had been in more than once. Nearly one in five (16%) reported having attempted suicide some time in the past. Scores on two standard psychiatric epidemiology scales were also very high.

All told, more than four out of five (82%) of the Chicago homeless were estimated to have one or more of the disabilities noted above; a majority had had two or more such experiences or conditions. Although these data are obviously not precise, they suggest that the prevalence of disabling conditions among the homeless must be several magnitudes above that encountered in the general adult population or even among persons in poverty.

REASONS FOR HOMELESSNESS

As I have already emphasized, the causes of homelessness are many. At one level, homelessness is a problem rooted ultimately in the political economy of the nation; at another, it is the consequence of various personal pathologies and failings. To determine the relative significance of some of the factors that contribute to homeless ness, we gave HCH care providers "a list of factors that ar sometimes involved in a person's becoming homeless" and aske them to rate the importance of each in regard to the particular clier in question. Twenty-two possible factors were included.

The results showed the predictable mix of personal and structural causes. Alcohol and drug abuse was the single item cited most often (although the major or most important factor in only about half the cases), followed by general money problems, chronic mental illness, loss of employment and other job problems, and a general inability to find housing. Decaying interpersonal relationships also figured prominently in the results, especially the breakup of a former relationship and estrangement from one's family of origin. Eviction for nonpayment of rent completes the list of nine most frequently cited reasons.

In the various discussions of the causes of homelessness, surprisingly little attention has been given to poor physical health. In contrast, poor mental health would be included in any comprehensive listing (as, indeed, it should be, given these and many other results). It is nonetheless obvious that chronically poor health can interfere dramatically with labor force participation and therefore with the ability of a person to lead an independent and stably domiciled existence. It is therefore of great interest that chronic physical disorder finished tenth on the list, being only slightly less important than evictions for nonpayment of rent and finishing *ahead* of commonly cited factors such as loss of entitlements (eleventh) or recent deinstitutionalization from mental facilities (fifteenth). In all, poor physical health plays some role in the homelessness of about 21% of the HCH clients and is a major (or single most important) factor in the homelessness of about 13%. Thus, approximately one homeless adult in eight is homeless at least in major part as a result of chronically poor physical health.

Additional analysis of these data showed that employability provides the link between poor physical health and the condition of homelessness. Those of particularly poor health find it impossible to hold down a regular job; lacking the steady income that employment provides, one's housing is also eventually lost. In an earlier era, the linkages among ill health, employment, and homelessness would have been broken, at least for many, by Social Security Disability Insurance (SSDI) benefits. It is plausible to assume, therefore, that the

SSDI eligibility and benefit level rollbacks of March 1981, have in-creased, at least in part, the importance of poor physical health as a reason for homelessness.

Who, then, are the homeless? As this chapter should make clear, there is no one answer to this question. Aside from extreme poverty and the absence of stable housing, there is no single characteristic that all homeless people share. Some are old men, some are young women, some, indeed, are infants and children. The homeless con-tain runaway teenage girls, drug-addicted adolescents, mentally im-paired women, and physically disabled men. The group contains honorably discharged U.S. veterans as well as recently released con-victs—both heroes and villains, if you will. Some of the homeless have been homeless for decades, others for only a few weeks or months.

Amidst the obvious heterogeneity of the homeless, however, three salient and widespread conditions do stand out: first, the extreme level of poverty characteristic of the group; second, the high levels of disabilities of all sorts; and third, the excessive degree of social isolation common to most, if not all. These, at least in the opinions of many analysts, are the factors most directly implicated in the pro-cess of becoming homeless.

NOTES

1. Some of the material in this chapter originally appeared as "The Wor-thy and Unworthy Homeless." *Society,* 25:5 (July-August 1988), 64–69, and is used with permission of the publisher.

2. See J. Wright and E. Weber, *Homelessness and Health* (Washington, DC: McGraw Hill, 1987), for a complete description of the HCH program and the client data base.

3. P. Rossi, G. Fisher, and G. Willis, *The Condition of the Homeless in Chicago* (Amherst, MA: Social and Demographic Research Institute, 1986).

4. This result is consistent with most other studies of the topic; the rule of thumb employed by most researchers is that 20–25% of the homeless are members of homeless family groups.

5. E. Bassuk, L. Rubin, and A. Lauriat, "Characteristics of Sheltered Home-less Families." *American Journal of Public Health,* 76 (September, 1986): pp. 1097–1101.

6. J. Wright, "Homelessness is Not Healthy for Children and Other Living Things." *Journal of Child and Youth Services* (forthcoming, Spring, 1988).

7. See J. Lam and J. Wright, "The Homeless Family: A Contradiction in Terms." Unpublished paper. Amherst, MA: Social and Demographic Re-search Institute, 1987.

8. To arrive at these results, I simply dropped all HCH clients from the data base who were known to be members of homeless family groups and then calculated the age and sex distributions for those that remained. The sample size for the calculations is 17,633. (Also omitted are all clients whose date of birth is unknown.)

9. J. Wright, *Selected Topics in the Health Status of America's Homeless* Special Report to the Institute of Medicine, National Academy of Science May, 1987, Table Six.

10. Ibid., Table Two.

11. D. L. Jones, "The Strolling poor: Transiency in Eighteenth Century Massachusetts." *Journal of Social History,* 8 (1974), pp. 28–54; P. F. Clements, "The Transformation of the Wandering Poor in Nineteenth Century Philadelphia." In E. H. Monkkonen (ed.), *Walking to Work: Tramps in America* (Lincoln, NE: University of Nebraska Press, 1984).

12. All figures on homeless women are derived from J. Lam, *Homeless Women in America: Their Social and Health Characteristics.* Unpublished Ph.D. dissertation, Department of Sociology, University of Massachusetts, Amherst, 1987.

13. See P. Rossi *et al.,* op cit., pp. 61–62.

14. The "entitlements" explanation is pursued in greater detail in P. Rossi and J. Wright, "The Determinants of Homelessness." *Health Affairs,* 6:1 (Spring, 1987), pp. 19–32.

15. C. H. Alstrom, R. Lindelius, and I. Salum, "Mortality Among Homeless Men." *British Journal of Addictions,* 70 (1975), pp. 245–252.

16. J. Wright and D. Weber, op. cit., Ch. 8.

17. J. Knight and J. A. Lam, "Homelessness and Health: A Review of the Literature." Unpublished manuscript, Amherst, MA: Social and Demographic Research Institute, 1986.

18. Why only half? Many of the elderly homeless have insufficient work histories to qualify for social security; a lifetime of unsteady and temporary work without FICA deductions means that they are nonentities so far as social security is concerned. Some who are technically eligible move around so frequently that there is no place to send their checks (lack of a mailing address is a recurring problem for homeless people of all ages); others are so disoriented, debilitated, or otherwise destroyed that they have never successfully negotiated the social security paperwork.

19. M. Robertson, "Homeless Veterans: An Emerging Problem?" Ch. 4 (pp. 64–81 in R. Bingham, R. Green and S. White (eds.), *The Homeless in Contemporary Society* (Beverly Hills, CA: Sage Publications, 1987).

20. The arguments on both sides of this issue are, to my mind, almost equally compelling, which is why this is a complex, difficult issue. The case in favor of Mayor Koch's position has been argued most persuasively by Charles Krauthammer in *Time* Magazine (2 December 1985):

"Liberty counts for much, but not enough to turn away from those who are hopelessly overwhelmed by the demands of modern life. To permit those who flounder even in the slowest lane to fend for themselves on very mean streets is an act not of social liberality but of neglect bordering on cruelty. In the name of a liberty that illness does not allow them to enjoy, we have condemned the homeless mentally ill to die with their rights on."

The opposing case, just as forceful, is made by Henry Mitchell in the Washington *Post* (3 January 1986):

"The freedom not to be carted off by the cops without a specific warrant, or in the presence of a crime, is an important freedom. It should not be fiddled with simply because in some rare case it might be a good thing."

(This material appears in F. S. Redburn and T. F. Buss, *Responding to America's Homeless: Public Policy Alternatives* (New York: Praeger, 1986), pp. 136–137.

21. The racial composition of the national poverty population in 1983 was roughly 68% white, 28% black, and 4% "other." Among the poor, 12% are of Hispanic origin (which, by U.S. census definition, may be of any race.) Thus, racial and ethnic minorities are clearly overrepresented among the homeless even in comparison to the racial and ethnic composition of the American poverty population. See U.S. Bureau of the Census, *Statistical Abstract of the United States*. Washington, DC: U.S. Government Printing Office, 1985: p. 456 (for the racial composition of the poverty population) and p. 17 (for the racial composition of the national population).

22. See, e.g., D. J. Bogue, *Skid Row in American Cities* (Chicago: Community and Family Study Center, University of Chicago, 1963); H. Bahr and T. Caplow, *Old Men Drunk and Sober* (New York: NYU Press, 1974).

23. See, for example, M. Hope and J. Young, *The Faces of Homelessness* (Lexington, MA: Heath and Company, 1986); J. Erikson and C. Wilhelm (eds.), *Housing the Homeless* (Rutgers University: Center for Urban Policy research, 1986); C. T. Mowbray, "Homelessness in America: Myths and Realities." *American Journal of Orthopsychiatry*, 55:1 (1985), pp. 4–8.

24. In public discussions of the Health Care for the Homeless program, the question is regularly asked whether I have seen evidence of a sizable influx of homeless people migrating to the HCH cities in order to avail themselves of free health services. (The answer, incidentally, is NO.)

It is worth a mention, if only in passing, that the Sunbelt states, particularly the southern and southwestern states, have relatively more stringent eligibility criteria for most benefit programs and generally lower benefit levels; in contrast, the states in the Northeast have relatively less stringent eligibility rules and higher benefit levels. The lure of more and better jobs in the Sunbelt may therefore be offset by the distinctively less generous package of social welfare benefits available there.

25. Community Emergency Shelter Organization and Jewish Council on Urban Affairs. *SROs: An Endangered Species*. Chicago, 1985.

26. Similar findings are reported in the M. Stagner and H. Richman study of welfare recipients in Chicago. See *General Assistance Families* (Chicago: National Opinion Research Center, 1985).

27. Perhaps needless to say, nature and duration of homelessness are strongly correlated, so the similarity in results is not surprising. More than

four out of five of those judged chronically homeless have been homeless for more than one year; 88% of those judged recently homeless have been homeless several months or less.

28. "Tracking the Homeless" (no author stated). *Focus*, 10:4 (Winter, 1987-1988), pp. 20–24.

29. The effect of having a dependent child in one's care is of particular interest. In the Chicago survey, it became apparent that many homeless women were in fact homeless primarily because they were waiting for the AFDC paperwork to clear and that once the AFDC benefits were available, their literal homelessness would cease. Virtually any homeless woman with a dependent child will be *eligible* for AFDC, regardless of the strictness of regulations in the specific state; and yet, only about half the HCH women with dependent children are in fact currently *receiving* AFDC (J. Lam, *Homeless Women in America*, unpublished Ph.D. dissertation, University of Massachusetts, Amherst, 1987). In many states, the process of getting enrolled in AFDC is a lengthy one, with delays between application and receipt of benefits of more than a month not uncommon.

30. The self-reported health status of the adult population in the U.S. for 1982 is reported in R. W. Johnson Foundation *Special Report*, 1, 1983. Additional data on the health status of the homeless are reported in P. W. Brickner, L. K. Scharer, B. Conanon, A. Elvy, and M. Savarese (eds.), *Health Care of Homeless People* (New York: Springer Publishing, 1985); J. Wright *et al.*, "Homelessness and Health: Effects of Life Style on Physical Well Being Among Homeless People in New York City," in M. Lewis and J. Miller (eds.), *Research in Social Problems and Public Policy*, Vol. 4 (Greenwich, CT: JAI Press, 1987).

CHAPTER FIVE

How People Become Homeless

The many different kinds of homeless people become homeless in many different ways. It is, however, wrong to suggest there are no common threads on this tapestry. People become homeless for specific reasons, and the task is to figure out what those reasons are.

It is obvious that people become literally homeless because they are extremely poor and cannot successfully compete for a dwindling supply of low-income housing. When the cheapest housing available is priced at 70 or 80% or even more of one's income, there will often be no alternative to homelessness. It can be seen immediately, however, that this is not the whole story, as there are many extremely poor persons competing for the same inadequate low-income housing supply who are not literally homeless. Consider the following:

The annual income cutoff for General Assistance (welfare) eligibility in the city of Chicago in 1985 was $1848 for a single person (this amounts, incidentally, to about $35 a week); the General Assistance rolls for the city numbered some 100,000 recipients, most of them single males. The GA income cutoff is approximately equal to the mean annual income of homeless people in the city as measured in Rossi's survey of the Chicago homeless, so it can be fairly said that those 100,000 GA recipients are equally poor. And yet, the best estimate from the Chicago study is that there are not more than about 3000 persons literally homeless in Chicago on any given night. Thus, the immense majority of the extremely poor manage to secure housing despite their extreme poverty and the tightness of the low-income housing market; nationwide, as discussed in Chapter 2, the literally homeless probably do not comprise more than 1 or 2% of the larger poverty population.

Properly to understand why some of the extremely poor are literally homeless, then, we need to know why more of them are not. *The puzzle is not that there are so many homeless people, but that there are so few.*

One important clue to this mystery is contained in Chapter 3; in note 8 to that chapter, I pointed out that in 1983, some 30% of the nation's poverty population spent *70% or more* of its income on housing costs alone. The rule of thumb in the real estate business is that households should spend no more than one quarter of their incomes on housing. This, indeed, is the standard that banks use to calculate the size mortgage a family can afford. If the nation's poverty population were to adopt such a standard, it is obvious that literal homelessness would increase by many magnitudes very quickly

Even using a 40% criterion, the number of "affordable" units has dropped sharply in comparison to the number of poor families; if we used a 25% criterion, the disparity would obviously be many times worse. In the first line of analysis, then, many poor families avoid literal homelessness by spending a lot more on their housing than, in principal, they can actually afford. My colleague Peter Rossi and I have referred to this phenomenon as "overspending" on housing.[1]

THE POVERTY LINE

It is useful at this point to look at how the federal poverty lines are determined, so as to indicate something of what it would mean to a poor family to spend, say, 70% of its income on housing. As already noted, there is much dispute among researchers and government officials about how poverty should be defined, a definitional issue that is complicated by the many transfer payments and income-in-kind provisions of federal, state, and local social welfare programs. In fact, the official federal poverty lines are set in the following manner:

First, the U.S. Department of Agriculture publishes something called the "emergency temporary low-budget diet." This is *not* the same as the so-called "minimum daily adult requirements" diet. The latter is the minimum nutrient intake needed to assure proper bodily functioning over the long term. The former, the "emergency temporary low-budget diet," is the minimum nutrient intake necessary to sustain human life over short periods. The diet comprises so many grams of protein and carbohydrates, so much fat, so many milligrams of various vitamins and minerals, etc.

Once the nutrient components of this emergency diet have been determined, USDA shoppers go to a selection of supermarkets and other food outlets in several of the major cities, attempting to determine the cheapest possible way to purchase those dietary components. How little is it possible to spend, that is, to obtain foodstuffs containing so many grams of protein and carbohydrates, so much fat, so many milligrams of various vitamins and minerals, and so on? Comparing results across cities, shoppers, and supermarkets, analysts then derive a dollar figure: the minimum amount a family can spend to purchase an "emergency temporary low-budget diet."

Once the emergency dietary dollar figure has been set, the calculation of the poverty line is straightforward: the line is set at three times the dietary cost. Why? Because studies in the 1960's showed that the average poverty family spends about one third of its income on food. The poverty line is further adjusted according to family size, region of the country, and urban-rural residence (because the price of food and most other commodities varies by region and city size).

In 1983, the above procedures led to a poverty line of $7938 in annual income for a three-person household in an average urban area. One third of that is $2646, which is what the government figures it would take to purchase the emergency low-budget diet. Feeding three people for each of 365 days of the year therefore yields a food budget of about $2.42 per person per day, or $16.94 per week (or, if you assume three meals a day, 81 cents a meal). The daily per-person food budget for a poverty family is less than what a middle-class person would expect to pay for a single cocktail at a reasonably nice restaurant.

Studies by the federal government, incidentally, show that this is in fact just about what poverty families actually spend on food—$16.90 per household member per week according to one study.[2] The same study also found that only about 42% of the nation's low-income households participated in the food stamp program. One final result of note: "Less than 40 percent of the low-income households met the RDA [Recommended Dietary Allowances] for all 11 nutrients [studied]" (p. 2).

Let us again consider a family at the poverty line that is spending 70% of its income on housing, leaving 30% to be spent on all other things. If that family shops as aggressively and as conscientiously as the USDA shoppers shop, seeking always to maximize nutritional content for minimum cost, and, moreover, if that family also spends all of its remaining income (30%) on food alone, the food budget would *not* quite allow the family to purchase an "emergency temporary low-budget diet" (since, by the logic detailed above, a family at the poverty line would need at least 33% of its income to purchase such a diet).

Remember also that we are dealing with a family right *at* the poverty line; most poverty families (by definition) must be somewhere *below* the poverty line, some of them quite far below it. In fact, the *median* income for poverty households is just about 50% of the official poverty line. At this level, a family spending 70% of its income on shelter would be spending (70% × 50%) =35% of the poverty line figure on this item, which by the same logic would leave 15% of the poverty line figure for food. Such a family would only be able to buy about half the nutrients of the "emergency temporary diet" even if it spent all of its nonhousing dollars on nourishment.

Based on the above logic, if a family at the poverty line purchased the minimal diet, two thirds of its income would be left to purchase all other things. Thus, if housing consumes 67% or more of the income, and the family is to continue purchasing the minimal diet, then housing and food alone will consume the entire income.

Or let us assume, as in Chapter 3, that a poverty family spends 40% of its income on housing and also purchases the minimal diet. For a three-person household, that would mean (.40 × 7938)/12 = $265 per month for housing and, as above, $2.42 per person per day for food. In this case, food and housing alone consume 73% of the income, or, for a family right at the poverty line (.73 × 7938) = $5821, leaving ($7938 − 5821) = $2117 *for everything else.* Divided among three people and 365 days, this comes to $1.93 per person per day for everything other than food and housing. One round-trip on public transportation would consume most or all of that amount in most cities.

To summarize, any poverty family spending 40% of its income on housing and eating a minimal emergency diet will be left with very little income to use on anything else, be it transportation, medical care, child care, clothing, allowances for the children, entertainment, insurance, automobile payments, savings, purchases of household and consumer goods, and so on. Any poverty family spending 67% or more of its income on housing (and eating the minimal diet) will be left with *no* income to use on anything else. This situation appears to characterize about one third of the nation's poor families.

It is therefore easy to see that most of the routine monthly expenditures of a middle-class family represent luxuries to a poverty family in the best of circumstances and hopelessly unattainable items to a poverty family in average circumstances. Once housing and a minimally adequate diet have been purchased, what remains to a poverty family is somewhere between very little and nothing at all.

As I have already stated, a three-person household right at the poverty line in an average American city has an annual household income of $7938. If that family, like one third of poverty families, is spending 70% of its income on housing, then the annual housing expenditure is (.70 × 7938) $5557, or $463 per month. Even allowing such a high percentage of income for shelter, in other words, leaves a per-month housing budget that is, at best, barely adequate; in most cities there would be at least some apartments renting at or below that figure, but not many. Assuming our hypothetical family found one, the housing costs alone would leave only $2381 to divide among three persons to cover all other living expenses, or $2.17 per person per day.

I can now state an obvious but essential conclusion: *Any poverty family (or, for that matter, poverty individual) spending anywhere close to 70% of its income on housing alone cannot possibly survive on the income that remains.* Poor people can avoid literal homelessness by overspending on their housing *only because* they can often rely on social services, their network of family and friends, private charities, and the like to provide essentials that their incomes cannot. Absent this range of supplementary resources, homelessness, or starvation, or both, would be unavoidable. To repeat, poor people who have access to such resources will be able to avoid literal homelessness by overspending on housing; poor people without access to such resources obviously will not.

RESOURCES OF THE HOMELESS

What, then, of "access to resources" among the literally homeless? How does this differ from access to resources among the poor in general?

Setting aside for the moment participation in social service and welfare programs that are considered at length in Chapter 7, it is useful to review once again Stagner and Richman's study of Chicago General Assistance (GA) recipients, because it gives some additional and very important clues to this question.[3] That study showed GA recipients to be similar to the literal homeless of Chicago in demographic composition. Most of them, like most of the homeless, are male (68%), black (71%), and unmarried (91%). One difference is that the GA recipients are somewhat younger (average age was 34) than the homeless (average age of about 40). Still, both the literal homeless and the GA recipient populations of Chicago consist overwhelmingly of relatively young, nonwhite single males.

GA recipients contrasted strongly with the literal homeless, however, in three important respects:

1. GA recipients appeared to be considerably more integrated socially, half of them living with relatives and friends and an additional 30% receiving financial assistance from such sources. By definition, of course, none of the homeless were living with

family or friends and virtually none of them reported cash assistance from family or friends as a means of their support.

2. Disability levels among GA clients were much lower; far fewer, for example, had physical health conditions that prevented their employment (9 versus more than 25% of the homeless); far fewer had been in mental hospitals (1 versus 23% of the homeless). Compared to Chicago's literal homeless, in short, the GA recipients were much less impaired.

3. Median time unemployed was much lower among GA clients (19 months) than among the literal homeless (40 months); the period of dependency, that is, was longer for the homeless by a factor of about two.

Given the price of housing in Chicago and the average incomes of GA recipients, many of them are clearly at high risk of becoming literally homeless; at minimum, as suggested in Chapter 2, their numbers provide a reasonable guess about the size of the precariously housed population in that city. The key finding from the Stagner and Richman study is that *half of the GA recipients in the city are presently housed mainly through the generosity of relatives and friends; an additional one third receive economic assistance—private subsidies, in a word—from the same sources.*

These data make it apparent that kin and friendship networks provide the most important line of defense against literal homelessness for the extremely poor; the homeless are those among the extremely poor for whom this defense has failed. The apparent reason there are not more homeless, in short, is that most of those who might otherwise be homeless avoid that fate through the generosity of their family members and social networks.

THE DYNAMICS OF HOMELESSNESS

The Stagner-Richman and Rossi studies of Chicago indicate little of the dynamics, the actual processes, involved in all this, but it is obvious that having family or friends who will provide shelter whatever your income is a powerful safeguard against literal homelessness. We can imagine that many of the GA recipients living with family and friends make occasional contributions of some kind to the household that supports them; in such cases their de facto housing costs may be only a small percentage of their incomes; their housing costs are in essence subsidized by a familial and social network.

This is, no doubt, a precarious arrangement in many cases, depending for its continuation on the goodwill or economic health of the subsidizing household. Precarious or not, however, it appears to be the short-term safeguard that keeps perhaps 50,000 poor people in Chicago off the streets. To refer to it as precarious is also to imply that these arrangements collapse periodically, with an ensuing incident of literal homelessness the consequence. For the episodically homeless, who comprise more than half the total, it is an arrangement that is destined to collapse again and again.

In light of the above discussion, the "broken circle" of kith and kin networks characteristic of most homeless people, as discussed in the previous chapter, assumes added significance. The picture is not at all bright. First, many homeless people do not have any family. A reasonable guess is that maybe a tenth of the homeless were orphans at birth or were orphaned sometime early in childhood, which is to say that they have been homeless in some sense from the day they were born.

Many who do have family are so profoundly estranged from them that they in effect have no family at all. Few of the homeless have ever married; most who have are now either separated, widowed, or divorced. Many of the homeless who have had children do not even know for sure where their children are, having had no contact with them in years. Most of the friends of homeless people are other homeless people with no resources to spare.

In a very deep sense, to be homeless *is* to be without family or friends that can be relied upon in times of crisis or need. Robert Frost once wrote, "Home is the place where, when you have to go there, they have to take you in."[4] It is not a bad definition; to be homeless, by the same logic, is to be without such a place. Most of us probably know at least *someone* that we could turn to in the face of disaster; the homeless are those for whom this cannot be said.

There is much concern expressed these days about the breakdown of the American family, and at least since 1965, when the so-called Moynihan report was published, there has been a particular concern with the social disorganization characteristic of the poverty family. Even today, two decades later, high divorce rates among poverty families, the rapid increase of single-parent families among the poor, the increasing rates of out-of-wedlock teenage pregnancies, and other related developments are still routinely cited by conservative analysts as evidence that the poverty family has become, in some sense, a pathological institution.

There is little doubt that the above analysis is pertinent *in a few cases,* since the destruction of social networks, chief among them family networks, is clearly a key element in the process of becoming homeless. At the same time, however, it is the apparent *strength* of the poverty family (indeed, American families in general) that literally keeps hundreds of thousands, or even millions, of the poor off the streets, that keeps the homeless population from being orders of magnitude larger than it already is. The homeless constitute that small fraction of the total poverty population whose ties to family and friends have been destroyed.

This point deserves an even more forceful statement. If we deem each literally homeless person in Chicago, of which there are about 3000 on any given night and some three times that number in the span of a year, to represent a failure on the part of some poor family to sustain its dependent adult members, then by rights we must judge each marginal and dependent person who is *not* literally homeless as a success on the part of some other family. The Stagner and Richman study shows that there are some 80,000 successes—extremely poor adult welfare recipients in Chicago who are *not* literally homeless at least in major part because they are subsidized by their social networks, either through direct provision of housing (in 50,000 cases) or through cash assistance (30,000 cases).

Even if we consider the estimated *annual* homeless population of Chicago, the failures only add up to about 10,000: the successes, in short, outnumber the failures by at least eight to one. This is a much better success rate than any federal poverty program has ever been able to attain and is all the more remarkable when one takes into account the obviously meager resources at the disposal of the subsidizing families. There are, let us remember, 600,000 people in Chicago who live below the poverty line. All things considered, that only about 10,000 of them are ever without housing in the course of a year has to be considered a stunning achievement on the part of the city's low-income families.

There is little doubt that the destruction of social support networks characteristic of most homeless people is in its turn strongly related to their high levels of personal disability. Roughly two fifths (as discussed in the following chapter) are chronic alcoholics; about one third are mentally ill; some 10% are drug abusers; almost all are chronically unemployed. In comparing the GA results and the homeless results, we get some sense of the process of network destruction. The average homeless person has been unemployed two or three times as long as the average GA recipient; the average homeless person is three or four times as likely to have a physical disability that prevents employment. Based on the criterion of hospitalization for mental problems, the average homeless person is perhaps twenty times as likely as the average GA recipient to have a psychiatric disability that either precludes or at least complicates labor force participation.

Most middle-class families, of course, could absorb many years of dependency among their adult children if they were inclined to do so; it is mostly a question of patience, not of resources. It must therefore be stressed that the friends and kin of the very poor are likely to be poor themselves and would normally have very limited resources to share with others. The proportional burden of taking on the support of an additional adult, that is, would be relatively high, and the line of defense against literal homelessness correspondingly thin.

If the person in question also presents behavioral difficulties (for example, mental illness, episodes of drunkenness, trouble with the police) and the prospect of being dependent more or less indefinitely (for example, as the period of unemployment lengthens or as chronic physical disabilities set in), the line would become thinner still. At some point, all lines of defense snap—all resources *and* patience are exhausted—and another case of homelessness then appears on the streets.

We can thus begin to piece together a theory of homelessness that synthesizes structural and personal elements. Structurally, as seen in Chapter 3, society has created a housing "game" that increasing numbers are destined to lose, partly through the economics of housing, partly through the economics and sociology of labor, and partly through the unwillingness of government to redress these structural problems. Attention then turns to the factors that determine who the losers will be. In the present case, the critical factor appears to be the presence or absence of support networks to draw on in times of economic, psychiatric, or personal crisis. The losers in the contemporary housing game are those whose supportive networks have been destroyed or exhausted.

Literal homelessness is thus a function of extreme poverty in a housing market that has an inadequate supply of very low-cost housing to offer, especially to single individuals. Low incomes and high housing costs create a population at risk for homelessness, principally among those who are unaffiliated with households and other social networks and among those who have been extremely poor for long periods of time. The homeless are the long-term very poor who have been unable to maintain supportive connections with (or have been rejected by) their parental families and friends and who have not been able for a variety of reasons to establish their own households.

Long-term abject poverty, rejection by family and friends, and difficulties in establishing and maintaining normal social networks are in turn related to disability levels. Persons with serious disabilities such as those characteristic of the homeless will obviously experience difficulties obtaining stable employment and functioning in the reciprocal manner characteristic of a social network.

It is therefore misleading to say that a person is homeless because he or she is extremely poor; it is economic poverty *coupled with* inadequate social resources that lies at the heart of the problem. Likewise, a person is not homeless simply because he or she is an alcoholic or mentally ill, but because these disabilities exhaust the patience or resources otherwise available in one's social network. Unemployment per se does not create homelessness; the problem is the inability of many poor families to maintain their members through long periods of unemployment. And thus we see that homelessness is not primarily an economic problem, not primarily a housing problem, and not primarily a psychiatric problem. It is, fundamentally, a *social* problem in the richest sense of this much-abused term. In painting the picture of homelessness in America today, poverty, inadequate housing, personal disabilities and the like are the pigments, but the destruction of social networks is the brush.

This is not to say that all homeless people become estranged from social networks in the same way. Rossi and his colleagues draw a useful distinction between "family leavers" and "family rejects," the latter being those who are in some sense expelled from the network, the former those who leave of their own accord. One interesting question asked in the Chicago survey was whether respondents would like to go back and live with their families of origin, and if they did, whether they thought they would be welcome. Most of the *men* said they would like to return but doubted that they would be taken in; most of the *women*, in contrast, did not want to go back in the first place, having fled from a domestic situation so profoundly brutalizing that life on the streets became the preferred alternative. One may thus either lose or reject the resources otherwise available in the social network; either path to homelessness is open.[5]

Lacking access to the resources of a viable social network, a poor person is faced with trying to find housing that can be afforded within his or her income and supplementing that income to the extent possible with various social services, programs, and benefits. Almost anyone below the poverty line is eligible at least for food stamps; sustenance can be purchased at a subsidized rate, thus freeing some portion of the income for housing. Occasional (or regular) meals at soup kitchens or breadlines would conserve even more income. Various amenities and superfluities such as an automobile, entertainment, insurance, savings, and the like can also be foregone. Used clothes, even free clothes, are obtainable.

But what if, in the face of every conceivable economy, the monthly income is *still* not enough to purchase even the cheapest available housing? And what if, in addition, the resources of a person's social network are exhausted or unavailable? And what if, in addition to all that, one is a relatively young, single male who is therefore not eligible for much in the way of social services other than, say, food stamps? Is there any alternative to homelessness under these conditions?

These "what ifs" may seem too restrictive, but in fact they are not. Let us imagine a young, single male working steadily at the minimum wage, which is now $3.35 per hour. For a 40-hour week the gross pay is $134; in a 50-week working year the annual gross income is $6700—somewhat above the poverty line for a single person, but not by much. Subtract 15% in federal and state incomes taxes, and about $114 per week remains.

We calculated earlier that it takes at least $2.42 a day to feed oneself even a minimally acceptable emergency diet; over a 7-day week, that totals at least $17. Supposing an occasional meal each week whose nutritional content falls short of the emergency level, let us say that after food and taxes, $100 per week remains at the absolute outside. Month to month, *half* of that would have to be spent for the average SRO hotel room in the city of Chicago. (As I remarked in an earlier chapter, the average monthly cost of an SRO room in Chicago is $195, and that is the cheapest housing available.) If one were to live in a halfway decent apartment, the cost would be at least twice what it costs to live in a flophouse, and the rent would therefore consume everything that taxes and food did not.

All that, keep in mind, is for a *single* person working 40 hours a week and 50 weeks a year at the minimum wage. If the person in question were also supporting a wife and one child, then 40 hours a week and 50 weeks a year of work at the minimum wage yields an income about $1000 *below* the official federal poverty line for a family of three in an average American city. A minimum wage, indeed.

A single person working less than 40 hours a week, or less than 50 weeks a year, or at less than the minimum wage, would obviously be in more straitened circumstances still. The worst case is for those not working at all. In the decade of the 1970's, unemployment rates above 10% were not uncommon, and even now in the economic boom years of the 1980's, the unemployment rates usually run to 5 or 6%. Among young, nonwhite central city men, rates of 40 and even 50% are commonplace. Such a young man—with no job and no income—will be stably housed only so long as he has family or friends who will house him.

One should not make the mistake of supposing that unemployment compensation somehow makes up the difference. An article in the New York *Times* for December 12, 1987 (p. A28) reported that in the previous month, almost three quarters of the nation's unemployed workers received *no* unemployment insurance benefits, "the greatest percentage recorded in more than 30 years." Of the 6.8 million persons who were unemployed in October 1987, 5.1 million received no unemployment benefits. (Nearly one million of the total had been unemployed for more than 27 weeks, the cutoff for eligibility in many cases.)

Since the average length of unemployment in the Chicago General Assistance study was about 19 months, we might infer that the average minimum "grace period" (the acceptable period of dependency) is on the order of a year and a half. And since the average period of unemployment among the Chicago homeless was 40 months, we might infer that the average maximum grace period is seldom more than 3 or 4 years. In round numbers, we might therefore conclude that a young central city nonwhite male with no job, no unemployment benefits, and therefore no income might well remain domiciled through the generosity of family or friends for a period of one to four years, but rarely beyond that. (There would obviously be much variation around these averages: some people, that is, would be turned out the day they lost their jobs, others would remain with their families or friends indefinitely.) As the period of dependency came to exceed some critical value (defined in a broad sense by the resources, both economic and psychological, available to the host household), the odds of literal homelessness would increase.

The obvious point here is that a young male, not eligible for welfare or most other social services, who cannot find a steady job and therefore has no regular source of income, will have no alternatives to homelessness other than those offered by his social network. Such is the precariousness of a life of poverty and unemployment in this country. An entire class of individuals exists for whom homelessness is the near-inevitable consequence of the merest misfortune.

But Why Now?

The above would, of course, be true in all times and all places throughout history. What makes the present-day situation unique compared, say, to that of the 1950's or 1960's? Given that the poverty rates were even higher in the 1950's and early 1960's than they are today, why is homelessness a more visible problem now than it was then?

The answer to this question lies in part in the virtually complete disappearance of a formerly widespread urban social system known generically as skid row. Skid row areas, of course, continue to exist; indeed, it is where the homeless tend to concentrate in most cities. I am talking, however, not about the disappearance of skid row *areas*, but about the disappearance of the skid row *social system*.

Skid row has always been inhabited by unattached, unaffiliated, single men. There were many significant elements to the old skid row, but two are of particular interest: the flophouses, rooming houses, missions, and such that provided extremely cheap housing to the skid row population; and the day-labor outlets that provided casual employment.

The employment provided through the day-labor outlets was largely unskilled work; loading and unloading trucks, trains, and boats was perhaps the most common. The income to be earned through such work was also minimal. At the same time, the flops were extremely cheap, and cheap meals were widely available. Often, rooms could be rented for as little as fifty or sixty cents a night; a dime would purchase a sandwich and a cup of coffee. In those times and in this particular social system, one could pick up a dollar or two a day working at casual labor, and, more to the point, *get by* on a dollar or two a day. It was unquestionably a poverty level existence, but it allowed for a roof over one's head and a meal or two each day.

The disappearance of SRO or flophouse housing has already been discussed. The disappearance of day-labor outlets has been no less complete. Most of the work once done in this fashion has been mechanized; many hundreds of thousands of day-labor opportunities were wiped out by the invention and widespread adoption of the forklift, containerized shipping, and, of course, the unions. The unionization of the construction and stevedore industries in particular has made day labor in these sectors obsolete. The function formerly served by the day-labor outlets has been assumed by large temporary help corporations such as Manpower (in the United States) or Industrial Overload (in Canada). These are sanitized temporary help outlets located far from the skid row areas; they are no longer part of the skid row social system, at least not in most North American cities.

Thus, while the process of becoming homeless today must be much the same as it has been throughout history, the historical means to avoid literal homelessness have been largely removed from the urban social scene. The flops and the SRO's are mostly gone and nothing has replaced them. Their housing function has beer taken over by the large temporary overnight shelters that now exist ir nearly every city. Opportunities for casual day labor are also largely gone, and nothing has replaced that either. The income function o casual labor has been replaced by scavenging from trash cans and by panhandling. The organized social system of skid row, in short, has been replaced by the disorganized existence of homelessness.

In the meantime, low-income housing continues to disappear and unemployment, especially among young central city men, continues to run to 30 or 40%. The net consequence has been the creation of a more or less permanently displaced and unaffiliated urban homeless population whose poverty, dependency, and disabilities have destroyed the only lines of defense otherwise standing between them and the streets. These, truly, are the poorest of the poor—the new homeless—and they are best seen as the victims of large-scale social and historical trends assuredly not of their own making.

NOTES

1. P. Rossi and J. Wright, "The Determinants of Homelessness." *Health Affairs*, 6:1 (Spring, 1987), pp. 19–32. By use of the term "overspending," we do not mean to suggest that poor people are wasteful or unwise in their housing choices, only that the housing economy requires many poor people to spend much more for housing than they can afford to spend given the usual budgetary standards applied in such matters.

2. U.S. Department of Agriculture, Human Nutrition Information Service, *Food Consumption and Dietary Levels of Low-Income Households, November 1979–March 1980.* Nationwide Food Consumption Survey, Preliminary Report No. 10, p. 1.

3. M. Stagner and H. Richman, *General Assistance Families* (Chicago: National Opinion Research Center, 1985).

4. The line appears in Frost's poem, "The Death of the Hired Hand," which is included in almost any anthology of Frost's poetry. My gratitude to Peter Rossi for calling the source of the line to my attention.

5. Rossi et al., *The Condition of the Homeless in Chicago*, op. cit.

Drunk, Stoned, Crazy, and Sick

As noted in the previous chapter, research has identified personal disabilities as a key element in the destruction of social networks, and the destruction of social networks as a key element in the process of becoming homeless. There is no doubt that alcoholism, drug abuse, and physical and mental illness loom large among the personal disabilities in question. But just how large? How many of the homeless are alcoholics? How many are mentally ill? How many are physically sick or disabled?

As reviewed in Chapter 3, previous published estimates of the rates of the so-called ADM disorders (alcoholism, drug abuse, and mental illness) among the homeless have varied wildly: from 29 to 55% for alcohol abuse, from 10 to 30% for drug abuse, and from 20 to 84% for mental illness in one well-known review of the literature. One purpose of this chapter is to determine where in these broad ranges the true figure is likely to lie.

I have already stressed a principal conclusion of this chapter: Not all, not even most, homeless people are alcoholics or mentally ill. Some, however, are profoundly addicted to alcohol and some are equally addicted to other drugs; likewise, some are severely and chronically mentally ill. The subsets within the homeless who do suffer these impairments have highly specialized housing and social service needs, and it is therefore in our interests to be as precise as we can about how large these subsets are.

To note that there is a correlation between alcoholism and homelessness, or mental illness and homelessness, is not to say that either of these factors is a *cause* of homelessness. In some and perhaps many cases the causal order is reversed; alcoholism and mental illness, that is, can sometimes be the *consequence* of a homeless existence as well as a possible cause. Unfortunately, there is very little research that speaks directly to the causal question.

ALCOHOLISM

Alcohol abuse and homelessness are inextricably linked in the popular consciousness, the alcohol-impaired skid row bum representing perhaps the most common stereotypical image of homelessness in contemporary America. It is clear that the stereotype is not entirely without foundation, in that alcohol abuse is undeniably widespread among the homeless, afflicting somewhere between one third and one half. At the same time, this leaves one half to two thirds who are *not* alcohol impaired and whose homelessness must therefore result from other factors. In discussing alcohol abuse among the homeless, it is well to remember that we are dealing with a minority—albeit a large and significant minority—of the homeless population today.

There is little doubt that in an earlier era, the links between alcohol abuse and homelessness were more pronounced. Homelessness was often the ultimate fate of the chronic public inebriate, a condition punctuated only by occasional stints of alcohol detoxification and nights spent in jail.[1] Even in the small town in Indiana where I grew up in the 1950's, there was a homeless town drunk in our neighborhood. He lived nowhere in particular so far as any of us knew, drifted around town following his own inner logic, receiving in his infrequent hours of sobriety meals or spare change in exchange for odd jobs. The 1980's, however, have witnessed the rise of what we have called the new homeless, and alcohol (or drug) abuse is only sometimes a contributing factor in the homelessness of this group.

The point is illustrated by my earlier study showing that the rate of alcohol abuse among samples of homeless New York city men declined from 49% in the 1968–1972 period to 28% in the 1981–1984 period.[2] The appropriate conclusion is *not* that alcohol abuse has become an unimportant factor in homelessness, but that other factors have become more important, chief among them the strictly economic conditions discussed in Chapter 3.

Most prior studies of alcohol and homelessness focused on the question, What is the rate of alcohol abuse among the homeless population? Since there is no widely agreed-upon definition of alcohol abuse, the answers vary considerably.[3] The average rate of reported alcohol abuse over a number of recent (post-1983) studies of homeless samples is 38%, with a range of 21 to 67%; the average across 14 pre–1983 studies reviewed by Mulken and Spence was about 35%, with a range of 20 to 45%; studies reviewed in the report of the Alcohol, Drug Abuse, and Mental Health Roundtable give figures ranging from 29 to 55%.[4]

The studies that go into these summary estimates are, of course, based on very different populations, were undertaken by investigators from many separate disciplines, and use widely varying methods to measure alcohol abuse, however it is defined for purposes of any single study. Still, averaging over all available research studies, the proportion of the homeless with a significant alcohol problem is around 40%. Evidence from the Health Care for the Homeless client population confirms this estimate.[5]

The true rate of alcohol abuse among the population in this country as a whole is also not known to any degree of precision. About 70% use alcohol at least occasionally.[6] Most experts in the field use a "rule of thumb" figure of about 10% with a significant drinking problem.[7] Assuming this to be an indicative value (but see note 6), alcohol abuse is some four times more widespread among the homeless than among the domiciled population.

It is therefore important to stress that the difference in the rate of alcohol abuse between homeless people and people in general is a matter of degree. Alcohol abuse, that is, is found to some degree in all populations, including the homeless. It certainly is not as though all homeless people were alcoholics; in fact, the most plausible conclusion one could reach given the available research studies is that more than half—the clear majority—are not.

Several studies have added important details to the picture of the homeless alcoholic. A particularly useful contribution is that of Roth and Bean, a study restricted, unfortunately, to homeless persons in Ohio.[8] It is based on a sample of 979 homeless persons, of whom 204 (21%) had been drinking "some" or "a lot" in the month prior to the interview *and* who had sought help for their drinking problems at some time in the past. These 204 problem drinkers differed in many respects from the remainder of the sample. In terms of demographic characteristics, they were disproportionally male, white, and old. As would be expected, they had also had more troubled marital histories (more likely than the remainder to be divorced or separated), more run-ins with the law, and higher rates of psychiatric impairment. They tended also to have been homeless and to have been unemployed for longer periods than the remainder of the sample, were more transient, and were more socially isolated. Finally, by self-report, they also showed higher levels of physical ill health. These data support the image of the homeless alcohol abuser as multiply disadvantaged and as exhibiting disproportionally high rates of physical, mental, and social illness.[9]

Some findings from my study of health and homelessness in New York City are relevant here. Consistent with Roth and Bean, alcohol abuse was more common among homeless men (30%) than among homeless women (16%) and was also higher among whites than among other ethnic groups. Clinical data on the health problems of the sample showed that most physical disorders were much more prevalent among the heavy drinkers than the others.

Some additional information on these topics is provided by the HCH clinical data. One essential point that surfaced in the analysis is that the rate at which alcohol problems are diagnosed even in clinical settings varies greatly, and is a function of the number of client contacts. Indeed, the proportion of HCH clients identified as alcoholic increased from 17% among those seen just once to 37% of those seen five or more times, apparently because several contacts with a client are often necessary before a full and complete health picture emerges.

Under-diagnosis of alcoholism and similar disorders is a common problem in medicine, accounting in part for the wide range of results reported in the research literature.[10] We developed procedures to correct the data for this problem; the net consequence was an estimated 38% rate of alcohol problems among homeless HCH clients.

The same calculations were also applied separately to HCH men and women. One problem with many prior studies is that they are either based entirely on men or have too few women to give a reliable estimate. Using our correction procedures, we estimated that 47% of the adult HCH men and 16% of the adult HCH women were problem drinkers. There are a few other studies that also compare men and women, and they report approximately the same three-to-one differential. We were also able to confirm that homeless men of all ages and ethnic backgrounds are more likely (in the same proportions) to be problem drinkers than are the corresponding women.

In addition, we found (in both the HCH study and the New York City study) that the rate of problem drinking among the homeless is curvilinear with age, a pattern that pertains to both men and women. The highest rate of alcohol abuse comes in the middle years (ages 30 to 64); the rate is noticeably lower among both the young and the old. Thus, the stereotype of the *old* broken-down homeless alcoholic is not confirmed.

Differences across racial and ethnic groups are generally not as pronounced as the age differences, but are nonetheless worth noting. First, differences between blacks and whites were insubstantial for both sexes. The highest rate of alcohol abuse, by far, was found among homeless American Indians (both men and women): among homeless Indian men, the rate of alcohol abuse exceeded 60%. In contrast, the rate of problem drinking for homeless Hispanics and especially homeless Asians was below the average; these patterns held for both men and women.

Measurable numbers of alcohol problems are reported for homeless children as young as 6–10; among teenagers, about 8% of the girls and more than 10% of the boys already show signs of alcohol abuse.

It is also obvious, even in a casual inspection of the HCH data, that serious physical illnesses are much more prevalent among the known alcohol abusers than among the others. Along with their many other problems, homeless alcoholics tend to be very sick. Diseases that we found to be more common among alcoholics included nutritional deficiencies, injuries of all sorts, serious skin ailments, serious upper respiratory infections (such as pneumonia or influenza), liver disease, seizure disorders, diabetes, anemia, neurological disorders, eye disorders and diseases, cardiac disease and hypertension, chronic obstructive pulmonary disease, gastrointestinal disorders, peripheral vascular disease, arthritis, and active tuberculosis.

A college student once remarked, in the inimitable fashion of all undergraduates, "Homelessness is a pretty bombed-out existence, isn't it?" The imagery is not inapt; the biographies of the homeless are often strewn with rubble and devastation. It is obvious that homeless alcoholics are the most "bombed out" of them all: more socially disaffiliated, more profoundly disabled, more impoverished, and much sicker than their nondrinking counterparts. Compared to any other subgroup of the homeless, they are rated by their care providers as having by far the worst chances for the future, as being the least employable, and as most likely to be chronically homeless. If there is one subgroup that consistently frustrates the best efforts of their care providers to help, the homeless alcoholics are definitely it.

They also share one further condition: many people find it difficult or impossible to work up much sympathy for their plight, because at least to the casual eye, they are in some sense personally responsible for their miseries.

I do not wish to quarrel at length with this judgment. I do think it important to point out, however, that while many people become homeless because they drink heavily, others drink heavily because they have become homeless. One study of homeless alcoholics in Los Angeles has reported that about three quarters indeed had serious alcohol problems before the first episode of homelessness; that leaves one quarter whose drinking problems arose *after* the onset of a homeless existence.[11] Here, as in many other cases, one must take pains not to reason from correlation to cause in the wrong direction.

Whether alcoholism is a disease over which people have little control or a behavioral disorder potentially within the mastery of the individual continues to be hotly disputed among professionals in the field.[12] Alcoholics who are highly motivated to quit drinking are often successful, suggesting that mastery of the disorder is within the grasp of at least some people. At the same time, there is little doubt that many alcoholics need a drink as badly as a diabetic needs insulin the physical symptoms associated with withdrawal make it obvious that addiction to alcohol is at least partially organic. For present pur poses, let us simply admit that many homeless alcoholics probably could, in better circumstances, control their drinking behavior.

I submit that many normal, middle-class people who cluck their tongues at the rate of alcoholism among the homeless would, after experiencing this existence for a few weeks or months, come to look upon getting and staying drunk as a useful, convenient, and relatively cheap means of coping with the degradations they faced. The relief to be obtained from alcohol may well be temporary and is almost certainly illusory, but the short-term illusion of well-being is, with equal certainty, an improvement over the long-term reality of daily existence for many of these people.

Like many alcoholics and even "social drinkers" in the population at large, homeless people often drink to alleviate, however temporarily, the miseries of life—to cope, as Shakespeare wrote, with "the slings and arrows of outrageous fortune." The main difference between homeless alcoholics and the rest of us is perhaps only that their fortunes are more outrageous.

Drug Abuse

Drug abuse among the homeless, as among the population generally, has received considerably less attention than alcohol abuse, although all would agree that this is a serious and growing problem. Owing in large part to the expense of maintaining a drug habit, there are many fewer drug abusers among the homeless than there are alcohol abusers. The several studies reviewed in the Alcohol, Drug Abuses, and Mental Health Roundtable report suggest a rate of drug abuse among the homeless on the order of 10%.

Estimating a rate from the HCH clinical data again requires correction factors that take the under-diagnosis problem into account. Making these corrections, the estimated rate of drug abuse in the HCH sample is about 13%, close to the result obtained in independent studies. After the first year of the HCH program, we selected a sample of the clients and asked their care providers to fill out short questionnaires about them. In the sample data, 16% of the clients were judged to have a "moderate" to "disabling" drug problem, a rate similar to that suggested in the clinical results.

The survey also asked about the client's drug of choice, the drug used most frequently by each client with a drug problem. The first choice of 37% was heroine, methadone, or "crack"; 22% used cocaine, 21% used marijuana, and the remainder (20%) used a miscellany of other street drugs (amphetamines, depressants, PCP, and so on.) Thus, about 58% of the drug abusers (users of heroine, methadone, crack, and cocaine) are likely to be intravenous (IV) abusers, which amounts to 7 or 8% of the total client base.

Patterns of drug abuse contrast sharply with those of alcohol abuse. The rate of drug abuse is somewhat higher among homeless men than among homeless women, but the difference is slight, never more than a few percentage points. The strongest correlate of drug abuse among the homeless is age. As would perhaps be expected, rates are highest among the younger homeless and fall off with increasing age, especially after age 50. This too contrasts with the pattern for alcohol abuse, which is curvilinear with age. Across ethnic groups, the highest rate of drug abuse is observed among black men, followed by Hispanic men, then black women, then white men. Combining race, age, and gender, the group at highest risk for drug abuse is therefore young black men. Also of some interest is that rates of drug (and alcohol) abuse are somewhat lower among adult members of homeless families than among lone homeless individuals.

As with alcohol abuse, significant numbers of drug problems begin to be reported among children as young as 11 to 15; those in the next age category, 16 to 19, show the highest rates of drug abuse among any age group (at least among men in the HCH data). Thus, the drug problem is *most* pronounced for homeless men in their late teens and twenties.

Also following the alcohol pattern, most physical disorders are more prevalent among drug abusers than among the others, usually for both men and women and usually by a wide margin. Disorders significantly more common among drug abusers than nonabusers include serious skin ailments, some categories of trauma, liver disease, AIDS, seizure disorders and other neurological disorders, anemia, eye disorders and diseases, cardiac disease, chronic obstructive pulmonary disease, genitourinary disorders (both male and female), peripheral vascular disease, all categories of sexually transmitted disease, and the general category of infectious disorders. The similarity of this list to the one given earlier for alcoholics is not coincidental, since most of the drug abusers also abuse alcohol heavily.

There is little doubt that alcohol abuse and, to a lesser extent, drug abuse are leading problems among the homeless population. A reasonable guess is that half the men and one sixth of the women ar alcohol abusive, and that about one tenth of both groups are dru abusive. Compared to the nonabusive homeless, those who abus either alcohol or drugs are generally in the worst possible shape however this is to be measured: more disabled, less employable, more estranged, less intact, sicker, and with the poorest prospects for the future. There is also little doubt that alcohol abuse is heavily indicated in the premature mortality of many homeless people.[13]

Treatment of alcohol and drug disorders is difficult even under the best of circumstances, and homelessness is assuredly not the best of circumstances. The best alcohol rehabilitation and detoxification programs imaginable can have but limited success if, at the end of treatment, the homeless alcoholic returns to a life on the streets, which has been the typical case. Many homeless alcoholics, like Radar (see Chapter 1), will have been detoxified and "rehabilitated" dozens if not hundreds of times, needless to add at enormous expense to society.

The prevailing opinion among professionals in the field of alcoholism is that the key to successful treatment is to provide social (and physical) environments where sobriety is positively valued. This, needless to say, is generally not the environment one encounters on the streets, where drunkenness is often a way of life. Instead, even acknowledging that many people are homeless precisely because of a pattern of chronic alcohol or drug abuse, it is worth emphasizing that drunkenness provides many positive benefits for a homeless person, and that high rates of alcohol (and drug) abuse will continue to prevail among the homeless so long as this remains true.

It is, for example, self-evident that many homeless substance abusers drink heavily or take drugs to ease the miseries of their material and psychic existence. It is well-known that alcohol and many other drugs induce euphoria, and among the homeless, euphoria is in singularly short supply. In the Chicago study, as we saw in an earlier chapter, the average homeless person was found to have been unemployed for more than 4 years and homeless for nearly 2. That same person found it necessary to survive on a monthly income not more than about 40% of the official federal poverty line. What hope remains for people like this? What solace can they hope to find? Is there, in short, a better alternative than getting and staying drunk?

One might also suppose that some of the homeless drink heavily or use other drugs for the relief of chronic physical pain, alcohol being among the most potent pain relievers legally available without a prescription. Given the strongly elevated rates of chronic physical disorder among the homeless, this is not a hypothesis to be lightly entertained. And still others may drink heavily as a distancing mechanism, as a means of keeping an unfriendly world at arm's length.

The obvious point here is that chronic alcohol (and drug) use can serve a range of positive functions for a homeless individual. Many among the homeless drink heavily for good reasons, and as long as those reasons remain, so too will alcohol and drug problems. While outright sympathy for homeless alcohol and drug abusers may be more than many of us can muster, we should at least be able to understand that these problems are as often rooted in the existential conditions of homelessness as in the moral failings of a person's character.

MENTAL ILLNESS[14]

The rate of psychiatric impairment among the homeless is not known with much precision and is, in any case, a matter of considerable dispute.[15] The lowest figure I have seen reported in the literature is 15%, and the highest is approximately 90%. Some have argued that homelessness is largely or exclusively a mental health problem (even more particularly, a problem created by the deinstitutionalization of the chronically mentally ill); others have written on "the *myth* of pervasive mental illness among the homeless."[16]

As in all other cases involving the homeless, studies of the mental health topic are based on a wide range of samples and employ an equally wide range of definitions of mental illness. Since there is no universally accepted definition of what it means to be mentally ill (even the "official" definitions appearing in the Diagnostic and Statistical Manuals of the American Psychiatric Association are hotly contested among mental health professionals), the definitional issue is a critical one. It is therefore useful to begin by noting that under at least some definitions, nearly *all* homeless people could be considered mentally ill, and by other conceptualizations, almost *none* of them would be.

For example, in the state of Wisconsin a person can be involuntarily committed to in-patient psychiatric treatment only if that person is "dangerous to self or others." (Similar commitment laws exist in many states.) As defined by statute, "dangerous to self" specifically includes: "Inability to meet basic needs for food, shelter, medical care, or safety such that without prompt and adequate treatment

death, serious disability, physical injury, or serious physical disease
will imminently ensue." At one time or another, virtually by definition, nearly all homeless people will satisfy this criterion. Indeed, a
one time or another, nearly all poverty persons would satisfy som
element of this criterion.

There is little doubt that the life of the homeless is one of extrem
stress and deprivation. As reported in an earlier chapter, for example, the average monthly income of homeless people in Chicago is
considerably less than the average monthly cost of the cheapest
housing available. That the homeless manage to survive at all under
these constraints illustrates truly remarkable adaptation to conditions
of extreme deprivation. In at least some conceptualizations, the ability to adapt to misfortune, to cope with all that life throws at you, and
to survive in spite of everything would be taken as signs of mental
health—not of mental illness.

Lay people routinely mistake coping behavior among the homeless
for mental illness. Rummaging in garbage cans for something to eat
would strike most people as bizarre, to say the very least, but it is
sensible behavior if it is the only alternative to hunger. Urinating in
public is repulsive and, again, bizarre to most, but in a nation that
(unlike most civilized nations) does not routinely provide public restroom facilities, where else are the homeless to go? Lack of options
accounts for as much, or more, of the apparently crazy behavior observed among the homeless as clinical psychiatric impairment.

Another often-overlooked point is that many of the symptoms
of physiological illness are indistinguishable, at least on casual
inspection, from the symptoms of psychiatric illness. Persons with
uncontrolled diabetes, for example, will experience wild fluctuations
in their blood glucose levels which in turn will result in chaotic mood
swings that strongly resemble manic depression. Malnutrition, de-
hydration, and various vitamin deficiencies can also result in what
appears to be crazy or psychotic behavior. Thus, undiagnosed
and untreated physical disease will often cause patterns of behavior
or changes of mood that appear to a lay observer as psychiatric
impairment.

Many of the questions frequently used in standardized psychiatric
assessment protocols were developed and validated in normal
middle-class or clinical populations and could not in any realistic
sense be construed as indicating mental illness within a homeless
context. Some examples include: "Do you feel unhappy about the
way your life is going?" or "Do you feel discouraged and worried
about your future?" or "Do you feel so tired and worn out that you
cannot enjoy anything?" Nearly any *sane* homeless person would

have to answer yes to all of these—not because of mental disorders but because of the material conditions of their existence.

Many of the apparently crazy, bizarre, or abnormal behavioral patterns observed among the homeless are adaptations to the rigors and dangers of street or shelter existence and should not be interpreted as signs of psychiatric impairment. In a very deep sense, homelessness *itself* is an insane condition; that it exists at all is offensive to the standards of decency that prevail, or should prevail, in a civilized society. We should therefore take pains to avoid mistaking the conditions of homelessness itself, and adaptations to those conditions, for signs of mental disorder among the homeless population.

Lacking an agreed-upon definition of mental illness, most of all within the context of a homeless existence, there can be no definitive answer to the question, How many homeless people are mentally ill? Differing definitions and approaches to the question will produce markedly dissimilar results. The *clinical* data from the HCH study suggest a "best guess" value of approximately one third with a significant psychiatric impairment, and this is roughly at the midpoint of the range of values reported in other studies.[17]

Other data from the HCH project (the questionnaire data alluded to earlier) converge on about the same value. In one question sequence asking about reasons for homelessness, for example, "mental illness" was reported to be the "single most important" reason for homelessness for 16% of the sample, and was at least a contributory factor for as many as 40%. Combining the responses "major factor" and "single most important factor" yields a total of just 33% who were homeless principally or in major part because of their mental disorders, a percentage virtually identical to the "best guess" estimate.

Another question asked care providers whether the client had "significant mental or psychiatric impairments other than alcohol or drug problems." Again, the answer was "YES" for 33% of the cases. From the same sequence, it was also learned that 34% of the clients had been "hospitalized for mental, psychiatric, or emotional problems" at least once.

A final question asked for the care provider's overall assessment of the client's "mental and/or emotional condition." "No obvious impairment" was the assessment for 51%; "slight" impairment for 16%; "moderate" impairment for 18%; and "severe" or "disabling" impairment for 15%. Taking moderate through disabling impairments as the criterion, 33% are once more found to have significant psychiatric or emotional disorders. The conclusion based on several lines of evidence is that the rate of mental illness among the homeless is on the order of one third.

Concerning specific psychiatric diagnoses: Among those identified as mentally ill in the sample data, 36% were schizophrenic, 22% exhibited depressive disorders, 13% had personality disorders, 7% were manic depressive, 5% had chronic organic psychoses, 5% were mentally retarded, and the remainder were dispersed over a number of miscellaneous diagnoses.

As in all other cases, the rate of mental or emotional disorder among the homeless varies across different subgroups. The most dramatic correlate is gender: mental illness is about twice as common among homeless women as among homeless men. Psychiatric morbidity in the general population is also higher among women than among men.[18] Among ethnic groups, whites show the highest rate and Hispanics the lowest; differences across age groups are modest.

There are interesting interactions among these three variables in their effects on the rate of mental illness among the homeless. Mental illness is more common among young adult men, dropping off slightly in the older age categories; mental illness is relatively uncommon among young adult women, and much more widespread among women over 30. The net result is that the rate of mental illness among *young* homeless adults is about the same for both men and women, but is much higher for women than men in all subsequent age categories, the difference widening with increasing age. Further, the rate of mental illness is highest for whites of both genders, and lowest for Hispanics of both genders; the rate for white women, however, is particularly high. The most widespread mental health problems are therefore to be found among middle-aged white women, where the rate of psychiatric disorder easily exceeds 50%.

Analysis of the effects of mental illness on physical health showed the mentally ill to be physically sicker on most measures. While there may be some organic or physiological linkages between mental and physical ill health reflected in these results, the bulk of them must be ascribed to correlated behavioral aberrations, such as inadequate personal care, unwillingness or inability to seek medical attention or follow a treatment regimen, poor dietary practices, and increased vulnerability to assault and predation. As shown in the following section, there is a marked tendency for the mentally ill also to be disproportionally alcohol- and drug-abusive, and this too would be a factor in the results. Among the women, the mentally ill are generally older (than the nonmentally ill); this may be another complicating factor. Finally, some of the differences may reflect side effects of neuroleptic or psychotropic medications.

DEINSTITUTIONALIZATION

There is little doubt that many of the homeless mentally ill are the unintended victims of deinstitutionalization, the policy whereby institutionalized mental populations were to be freed from the large, degrading state mental hospitals and returned to their families and communities. Indeed, the existence of large numbers of chronically mentally ill persons among the homeless has been cited as proof positive that deinstitutionalization has failed.[19]

Whether or not it has failed for everyone, it has clearly failed for some; many of the formerly institutionalized were placed in mental hospitals in the first place because their families and communities could no longer care for them. What to do with or about the deinstitutionalized mentally ill who have *not* been successfully reintegrated with their families and communities and are instead living in shelters or in the streets is an exceedingly difficult and contentious issue. (Direct subsidies to the families in question, to defray at least part of the increased burden, is one largely untested possibility.)

Many of those who have written about this issue are clearly motivated by an urge to avoid institutionalization of the mentally ill at any cost. But "no institutions" is not the only alternative to large, impersonal, and degrading institutions. Smaller, more humane, and more effective institutions are another option which, stripped of all rhetoric, is exactly what the "community-based mental health services" that were to replace mental institutions were intended to be.

Distaste for the concept of an institution, and the associated imagery of the human warehouse, should not blind us to the evident need among many mentally ill homeless for a 24-hour-a-day total-care environment. Whether we call such places institutions or find some more acceptable euphemism, we are talking about badly needed ports in the storm of life.[20]

The crucial point is that while the state mental hospitals were often indescribably dehumanizing, the street existence to which some of the mentally ill homeless have been consigned is no less so. Abandonment is not liberation. To be homeless *and* mentally ill is to be victimized in every sense, most of all by well-meaning but ineffective social policies.

The direct effects of deinstitutionalization on the contemporary problem of homelessness have no doubt been exaggerated in many accounts. Indeed, it has become something of a truism among care providers for the homeless that the "never-institutionalized" mentally ill are now much more common than the "ever-institutionalized"

mentally ill. It is often overlooked that the first waves of deinstitutionalization of the mentally ill in this country occurred in the 1950'ᐤ
and accelerated in the 1960's. By the middle 1970's, almost everyon
destined to be deinstitutionalized already had been.

Thus, homeless mentally ill persons in their twenties or early thi
ties are unlikely to have been institutionalized in the first place, an
therefore are equally unlikely ever to have been deinstitutionalizeu.
Their lack of prior psychiatric institutionalization or treatment histories, however, speaks more to large-scale societal developments of
the past three decades than to their level of psychiatric functioning.

In illustrating the point, it is useful to recall some of the results
from the "reasons for homelessness" questions that were included in
the HCH client survey. (These results were initially discussed in
Chapter 4.) The leading response, by far, was alcohol and drug
abuse, the "single most important factor" for the homelessness of
32% and a "major" factor for another 22% (54% overall). Second was
"chronic mental illness," with corresponding figures of 16 and 18%
(or 33% overall). Yet another possible response was "recently released from a mental institution." This was judged the single most
important reason for the homelessness of a mere 2% and was a major
factor for an additional 4%. Thus, the number of people who are
homeless at least in part because of mental-health issues appears to
be much larger than the numbers homeless because they were recently deinstitutionalized.

To conclude, the common notion that recently released mental patients comprise a large fraction of today's homeless population is indeed a myth, or at least a significant overstatement. The idea that
many homeless people have psychiatric impairments of varying degrees of severity, however, is not.

ALCOHOL, DRUG ABUSE, AND MENTAL ILLNESS: THE OVERLAP

By my and many other estimates, approximately two fifths of the
homeless have significant alcohol problems, one third exhibit some
degree of psychiatric difficulty or impairment, and one tenth abuse
drugs. What is the pattern of co-occurrence among these three
disorders?

Since the rate of occurrence of all three disorders is itself disputed, the degree of overlap among them also cannot be known with
precision. Based on an overview of the studies that have been done,
it is probably safe to conclude that somewhere between one half and

two thirds of the homeless have one or more of these three problems, and that perhaps one quarter have two or more of them.
Among clients in the HCH program seen at least five times (for whom
the diagnostic data should be most complete and reliable), about two
thirds were either alcoholic, drug abusive, or mentally ill, and nearly
one quarter (23%) had two or more of these disorders, the combination of alcoholism and mental illness being the most common.[21]

In general, while alcohol problems are much more widespread
among homeless men than among homeless women, mental health
problems are much more common among women than men; rates of
drug abuse are approximately the same in both categories. The net
result is that the proportions with *any* of these three problems are
nearly equal. Among racial and ethnic groups, the highest rates of
co-occurrence are found among blacks, American Indians, and
whites, in that order, with lower rates among Hispanics and Asians.
Categorizing by age groups shows only a low rate of co-occurrence
among the elderly.

As it happens, all three of these disorders are positively related to
one another. That is, the alcoholic are more likely to be drug abusive
and mentally ill than the nonalcoholic; the mentally ill are more
likely to be alcoholic and drug abusive than the nonmentally ill; and
the drug abusive are more likely to be alcoholic and mentally ill than
the nonabusive. In all cases, these points are equally true of men and
women. The general conclusion is obvious: the presence of any one
of these three disorders increases the likelihood that the remaining
two will also be present.

This discussion isolates the subgroups within the homeless population for whom adequate treatment and assistance are routinely the
most problematic. Many mental-health facilities, for example, will
refuse treatment to alcoholics (on the reasonable grounds that they
are not equipped to handle alcohol problems as well). Likewise,
many alcohol and drug rehabilitation and detoxification facilities will
refuse treatment to those who are also mentally ill (on largely the
same grounds). In sum, perhaps 25% of the homeless show some
combination of alcohol, drug, and mental problems (that is, suffer
two or more of the three disorders). As the level of disability mounts,
housing needs and employment prospects also change dramatically.
Homeless people with co-occurring disorders are by far the most
in need of treatment and services, but they are also the most difficult
to treat.

In discussing the rationale for the HCH program, the foundation
brochure remarked that many homeless people are "perceived in

some sense to be 'undesirable' as patients" in many health-care institutions; this would be no less true of other social-service institution⁻
(welfare offices, job placement programs, and the like). Certainly, th
alcohol-impaired, the drug-abusive, and the mentally ill are mor
'undesirable' than others, and those who are both alcoholic (or drug
abusive) and mentally ill are the most undesirable of all. To be drunk
crazy, *and* homeless is about as low as one can fall.

PHYSICAL ILLNESS

The HCH research project, findings from which have been discussed throughout this and some of the previous chapters, produced
a wealth of information on the physical health status of homeless
people. It will surprise no one to learn that many homeless people
are physically quite ill; it would be more remarkable if this were not
the case. Indeed, it has been said, no doubt with much justification,
that the homeless possibly harbor the largest pool of untreated disease left anywhere in the nation today.

Exposure to the environment, inadequate nutrition, indifferent or
nonexistent medical care, uncertain sleeping arrangements, various
self-destructive personal habits, high rates of alcoholism and mental
illness—these and many other factors produce a health profile
among the homeless that is an insult to any standard of human decency. One does not need to believe in universal health care as a
basic civil right to feel some outrage that very ill people, some of
them terminally ill, are left to wander aimlessly and hopelessly over
the urban landscape.

This is not the place to recite the entire litany of diseases and disorders to which homeless people are prone.[22] The list below only
touches on the highlights that surface in research studies:

1. The rate of tuberculosis among the homeless in the United
States is at least 25 times, and possibly hundreds of times, higher
than the rate among the adult population as a whole.[23]

2. Diseases and disorders of the extremities—chronic infected
skin ulcers, cellulitis, edema, and other disorders associated with peripheral vascular insufficiency—are some 15 times more common
among the homeless than among the rest of the population.

3. The incidence of sexual assault on homeless women is about 20
times higher than among women in general.

4. Chronic lung disease is 6 times more common among the homeless than among the rest of the population.

5. Neurological disorders, especially seizure disorders, are 6 times more common.

Other diseases and disorders that have been found to be at least three times more prevalent among the homeless than among the population at large include nutritional disorders, tooth and mouth diseases, hepatic (liver) disorders, skin ailments and infestations (lice and scabies), and trauma (injuries) of all sorts.

It is true that some of the differences summarized here are due simply to demography (the demographic profile of the homeless population being substantially different from that of the national population); some of the remaining differences are clearly due to elevated incidences of alcohol and drug abuse. But most of the differences are due to homelessness itself, to the extreme poverty that is characteristic of homeless people, and to the unique risk factors to which these people are exposed. Eliminating those clients in the HCH data who do not abuse alcohol, do not abuse drugs, and are not mentally ill, we find the homeless still to be much sicker than the comparison group.

The broad dimensions of the health problems of the homeless can be seen in a few simple statistical comparisons. Among those seen in the HCH program, 40% were found to have serious and chronic physical health problems: included in this description are tuberculosis, AIDS, cancer, diabetes, hypertension, stroke, arterial disease, paraplegia, seriously impaired vision or hearing, seizures, chronic lung disease, and the like. Among urban adults in the National Ambulatory Medical Care Survey, only 25% were observed to have these disorders. Thus, homeless people suffer chronic physical diseases at a rate far in excess of "normal."

When we think about the reasons that a person might be homeless, it rarely occurs to us that some may simply be too physically ill to work and, lacking the stable income that work provides, too poor to afford stable housing. And yet, poor physical health was assessed by HCH care providers as at least a contributory factor in the homelessness of 21% of their clients, and as a major (or the single most important) factor in the homelessness of 13%—approximately one in every eight. As a matter of fact, 17% of the sampled HCH clients were assessed as physically disabled and incapable of working. In a later sequence, we asked care providers to assess the client's employability; among those judged definitely or probably not employable, physical disability was the reason in about one third of the cases.

Some people, in short, become homeless because of physical illness; many contract various physical illnesses because of their homelessness. The net result of both processes is that the homeless are physically much sicker than their counterparts in the general population. Among the many good reasons to "do something" about homelessness is that homelessness makes people ill. In the extreme, it is a fatal condition.

NOTES

1. There is a very large ethnographic literature dealing with homeless alcoholics. See, e.g., P. Archard, *Vagrancy, Alcoholism and Social Control* (London: Macmillan Press LTD, 1979); H. Bahr and T. Caplow, *Old Men Drunk and Sober* (New York: New York University Press, 1974); D. Bogue, *Skid Row in American Cities* (Chicago: Community and Family Study Center, University of Chicago, 1963).

2. J. D. Wright, P. H. Rossi, J. W. Knight, E. Weber-Burdin, R. C. Tessler, C. E. Stewart, M. Geronimo, and J. Lam, *Health and Homelessness: An Analysis of the Health Status of a Sample of Homeless People Receiving Care through the Department of Community Medicine, St. Vincent's Hospital and Medical Center of New York City: 1969–1984* (Amherst, MA: Social and Demographic Research Institute, 1985), p. 92.

3. Indeed, it has been said, with tongue only partly in cheek, that an alcoholic is anyone who drinks more than his or her doctor does.

4. See J. Knight, *Alcohol Abuse among the Homeless,* unpublished doctoral dissertation, University of Massachusetts, Amherst, 1987; V. Mulkern and R. Spence, *Alcohol Abuse/Alcoholism among Homeless Persons: A Review of the Literature* (National Institute of Alcohol Abuse and Alcoholism, Rockville, MD, November, 1984); Alcohol, Drug Abuse, and Mental Health Administration. *Alcohol, Drug Abuse, and Mental Health Problems of the Homeless: Proceedings of a Roundtable,* op. cit.

5. See J. Wright and E. Weber, *Homelessness and Health* (New York: McGraw Hill, 1987: Ch. 5).

6. The General Social Surveys undertaken by the National Opinion Research Center periodically contain the following question: "Do you ever have occasion to use any alcoholic beverages such as liquor, wine, or beer, or are you a total abstainer?" From 1972 through 1987, this question was asked of more than 10,000 adults. Summing results across all surveys, 72% say they use alcohol at least occasionally.

A followup question is occasionally included in these surveys: "Do you sometimes drink more than you think you should?" Of those who drink at all, 38% confess to sometimes drinking too much. Since 72% drink, and 38% of them sometimes drink too much, simple multiplication gives an estimated rate of "problem drinking" among the adult population of about 27%, a figure, I hasten to note, that lies well within the range of estimates of alcohol abuse among the homeless.

7. See N. Fisk, "Epidemiology of Alcohol Abuse and Alcoholism." *Alcohol Health and Research World,* 9:1 (1984), pp. 4–7.

8. D. Roth and J. Bean, "Alcohol Problems and Homelessness: Findings from the Ohio Study." Ohio Department of Mental Health, Office of Program Evaluation and Research, July, 1985.

9. The same image is supported by a great deal of other research. See in particular the Spring 1987 issue of *Alcohol Health and Research World,* devoted exclusively to alcoholism among the homeless. (*AHRW* is the quarterly research journal of the National Institute on Alcohol Abuse and Alcoholism, a division of the Public Health Service.)

10. See in particular R. Moore and F. Malitz, "Underdiagnosis of Alcoholism by Residents in an Ambulatory Medical Practice." *Journal of Medical Education,* 61 (January), 1986, pp. 46–52.

11. P. Koegel and M. Burnham, "Traditional and Nontraditional Alcoholics." *Alcohol Health and Research World,* 11:3 (Spring, 1987) pp. 28–33.

12. The case that alcoholism is *not* a disease, contrary to much conventional wisdom among alcohol treatment professionals, has been made by H. Fingarette, "Alcoholism: the Mythical Disease." *The Public Interest,* 91 (Spring, 1988), pp. 3–22.

13. See Wright and Weber, *Homelessness and Health* (op. cit.), Ch. 8, for a discussion of the point.

14. The following material is taken largely from J. Wright, "The Mentally Ill Homeless: What is Myth and What is Fact?" *Social Problems,* 35:2 (April, 1988), pp. 182–191, and is used here with permission of the publisher.

15. More has been written about the mental health of the homeless than about any other aspect of the homelessness problem. A particularly helpful review of this vast literature is L. Bachrach, "The Homeless Mentally Ill & Mental Health Services: An Analytical Review of the Literature" (op. cit.). Other pertinent studies not already cited elsewhere in this volume include: L. Bachrach, "Interpreting Research on the Homeless Mentally Ill, Some Caveats." *Hospital and Community Psychiatry,* 35:9 (1984a), pp. 914–916; L. Bachrach, "Conference Report: Research on Services for the Homeless Mentally Ill." *Hospital and Community Psychiatry,* 35:9 (1984b), pp. 910–913; F. L. Ball and B. E. Havassy, "A Survey of the Problems and Needs of Homeless Consumers of Acute Psychiatric Services." *Hospital and Community Psychiatry,* 35:9 (1984), pp. 917–921; N. Cohen, J. Putnam, and A. Sullivan, "The Mentally Ill Homeless: Isolation and Adaptation." *Hospital and Community Psychiatry,* 35:9 (1984), pp. 922–924; R. K. Farr, P. Koegel and A. Burnam, *A Study of Homelessness and Mental Illness in the Skid Row Area of Los Angeles* (Los Angeles: Los Angeles County Department of Mental Health, March, 1986); R. E. Jones, "Street People and Psychiatry: An Introduction." *Hospital and Community Psychiatry,* 34:9 (1983), pp. 807–811; H. R. Lamb, "Deinstitutionalization and the Homeless Mentally Ill." *Hospital and Community Psychiatry,* 35:9 (1984), pp. 899–907; F. R. Lipton, A. Sabatini and S. Katz, "Down

and Out in the City: The Homeless Mentally Ill." *Hospital and Community Psychiatry,* 34:9 (1983), pp. 817–821; S. P. Segal, J. Baumohl, and E. Johnson. "Falling Through the Cracks: Mental Disorders and Social Margin in a Youn؛ Vagrant Population." *Social Problems,* 24:3 (1977), pp. 387–400.

The National Institute of Mental Health has sponsored 10 recent studies o homelessness and mental health. These studies are reviewed in detail in R Tessler and D. Dennis, *A Synthesis of NIMH-Funded Research Concernin؛ Persons Who Are Homeless and Mentally Ill* (Amherst, MA: Social and Demographic Research Institute), August, 1988.

16. The paper whose title is cited in the text is by D. A. Snow *et al.* and appears in *Social Problems,* 33:5 (June, 1986, pp. 407–423).

17. The "best guess" value from the HCH data *is* corrected for the under-diagnosis problem discussed earlier. See Wright and Weber, *Homelessness and Health* (op. cit.), Ch. 6, for details.

18. The classic study is M. Shepherd *et al., Psychiatric Illness in General Practice* (London: Oxford University Press, 1966).

19. See, for example, H. R. Lamb, "Deinstitutionalizational and the Homeless Mentally Ill." *Hospital and Community Psychiatry,* 35:9 (1984), pp. 899–907.

20. It is interesting that the phrase "mental institution" originally came into widespread usage to replace the older phrase "insane asylum," because of the strongly negative imagery that had come to be associated with the latter. Today, institution is out of favor and asylum has begun to replace it (the qualifier, "insane," has of course been dropped).

21. The five-plus contacts are used as the most reliable guide for this reason: The best guess about the rate of alcohol abuse among the HCH population is 39%; among the five-plus contacts, the observed rate is 37%. Likewise, the best guess about the rate of drug abuse is 13%; among the five-plus contacts, the observed rate is 13.5%. Thus, among the various contact groups, those in the five-plus category come closest, empirically, to estimated rates. On the other hand, the rate of mental illness among the five-plus group, 43%, is noticeably higher than my best guess estimate of 33%; the focus on the five-plus group may therefore overstate somewhat the rate of mental illness, and thus, the rates of co-occurrence as well.

22. See Wright and Weber, *Homelessness and Health,* op. cit., for an extended discussion of all that follows.

23. In all the following discussion, the comparison is specifically to urban adults in the National Ambulatory Medical Care Survey. This is a survey of the problems people have when they go to the doctor; that is, it is a survey of patients seen in outpatient ambulatory care settings. The proper, although clumsy, phrasing of the results would thus be: Homeless people who for whatever reason seek care through the Health Care for the Homeless program suffer tuberculosis at a rate some 25 to hundreds of times higher than do normal people who seek care in out-patient ambulatory care settings. The essential point is that the comparison in all cases is between clinical populations.

CHAPTER SEVEN

To Promote the Social Welfare

Since the 1930's and the advent of Franklin Roosevelt's New Deal, the nation has made great strides in creating a social welfare safety net that assists much of the population when various misfortunes beset them, misfortunes such as physical disability, the income loss that typically comes from retirement, unemployment (at least for a time), and to a certain extent, poverty itself.

The elderly are eligible for numerous programs: social security pensions, some housing subsidy, and medicare. The poor are also eligible for many programs: food stamps, medicaid, Section 8 housing certificates, aid to families with dependent children (AFDC), supplemental security income (SSI), free school lunches for the children, and so on. Most veterans of the U.S. armed forces are eligible for yet another tier of social services: medical care and psychiatric attention at V.A. medical centers, veteran's disability payments, and the like. The disabled, whether they are veterans or not, can receive housing, medical and cash assistance benefits under the provisions of social security disability insurance (SSDI). In fact, the social welfare system in this country has evolved to the point where federal expenditures for social and human services now represent the single largest item in the federal budget, exceeding even the expenditure for defense.[1]

This being the case, it is fair to ask why the existing social welfare system is not coping with the needs of the homeless. Indeed, political leaders often assert that new programs are *not* needed. What *is* needed instead is a more complete participation among the homeless in the programs for which they are already eligible. If homeless people have unmet health needs, then enroll them in medicaid. If their nutrition is inadequate, provide them with food stamps. If their incomes are not sufficient to cover their housing costs, then provide them with Section 8 housing subsidy certificates. If they have no incomes at all, put them on welfare or general assistance. If they are disabled and incapable of working, enroll them in SSDI.

According to this view, the solutions to the problems of homeless people are already "in place," like ripe apples waiting to be plucked. All that is really needed is some aggressive case management, whereby the homeless are made aware of and then enrolled to receive the benefits, services, and programs available to them.

BARRIERS TO PARTICIPATION

What the preceding viewpoint fails to acknowledge are the many profound barriers to participation in existing social welfare programs faced by the homeless population. The fact is, the social welfare system in this country is a vast and bewildering congeries of federal, state, and local programs characterized by a truly baffling array of program benefits, eligibility criteria, and administrative procedures. Negotiating this system effectively, so as to assure that one received all the program benefits to which one was entitled, would be a daunting task for anyone, homeless or not.

Social caseworkers themselves are sometimes not aware of all the programs for which a client might be eligible.[2] Even when a client's eligibility seems obvious, there remains a truly formidable bureaucratic process of paperwork, case reviews, eligibility certification, and the like. Thus, even if the solution to a homeless person's problems is already contained somewhere within the social welfare safety net, finding that solution can itself often be a frustrating and perplexing task.

The National Health Care for the Homeless program, a program mentioned throughout this text, represents something of a test case for the issues at hand in this chapter. Although the focus of the program was primarily on physical health, its philosophy recognized that the physical health problems of the homeless could not be adequately dealt with in the absence of concern for the entire range of problems that such people face.

Health-care teams in the 19 HCH projects therefore consisted, minimally, of doctors, nurses, *and* social workers "or other appropriately trained persons acting as service coordinators." The responsibilities of the projects, as stated in the program brochure, specifically included "arranging access to other services and benefits, for example, job finding, food or housing services, and benefits available through public programs such as disability, worker's compensation, medicaid, or food stamps." The underlying concept, clearly, was to use health care as a "wedge" to expose and address a much broader range of social, psychological, and economic problems.

From the viewpoint of social service, the successes and failures of the national HCH program in plugging homeless clients into the social welfare system—a specific and well-defined program priority—should therefore indicate something about the extent to which existing benefit programs can be successfully exploited on behalf of the urban homeless population, and thus should also provide at least a partial answer to the question, Isn't the solution to homelessness not already in place?

SOME OBVIOUS BARRIERS

It takes no great analytic sophistication to appreciate some of the obvious barriers homeless people encounter in negotiating the social welfare system. The first line of the application form for any benefit program will ask for one's name; at the second line, however, one encounters a nontrivial problem: it asks for one's address. A homeless person, by definition, does not have an address as that term is typically understood by social welfare bureaucracies.

With no fixed or stable address, how is one to establish legal residency? If the program in question is state-supported or state-run, establishing legal residency in the state is essential, and usually requires documenting that one has lived at some specified place for some specified amount of time. Rent receipts are often used for the purpose. But how do you document that you have been living down by the river for the last year and a half? Or that you have been sleeping on a park bench? How do you prove legal residency when you really have not been living anywhere in particular?

There is a further problem: Lacking a stable residence, where might you keep your legal documents even if you had any? An "earnings determination" is part and parcel of the eligibility certification process for most or all income transfer programs. If you have had any earnings, have you bothered to keep the pay stubs? Did you even get any pay stubs? If you were paying rent, or even living night to night in a flophouse hotel, did you retain all your rent receipts? Do you, for that matter, know where your social security card is? Do you even have any legal identification that proves who you are?

Suppose further that all the above problems were somehow overcome, that you were able against long odds to prove who you were, document your legal residency, and certify that you were in fact eligible for the program benefit in question. Next problem: "Where do we send the check?" It thus happens that one of the singularly most useful things that missions, shelters, and other facilities ministering to the needs of the homeless can do on their behalf is to provide them with a legitimate mailing address. Otherwise, no address often means no check.

Or suppose further, in addition to the above problems, that you are also mentally impaired or chronically alcoholic. Will you have sufficient wits about you to negotiate the complexities of the welfare system? If you are told to go to the welfare office at the corner of Market Street and Third, will you know where that is or how to get there? Are you sufficiently intact to fill out the forms that will be required? Are you even well enough to spend two or three hours standing in line?

If you are told after the initial interview to return for a follow-up interview and a final eligibility determination, will you be able to remember the place, date, and time? We may be certain that the average homeless person will not keep an appointment calendar where the reinterview information will be recorded. Moreover, "Please come back next Thursday" has meaning only if "Thursday" has meaning. If the days and weeks are little more than a continuous and undifferentiated blur, "next Thursday" may have no meaning at all.

It is, to be sure, cheap and easy to poke fun at the existing social welfare system, but it sometimes seems as though much of the system was specifically designed to frustrate the unique needs of homeless people. The food stamp program, for example, is a coupon system run through the United States Department of Agriculture: needy families or individuals are given food coupons, whose dollar value is fixed according to income. Food stamps can then be used in lieu of cash to purchase food items through conventional retail outlets.

To prevent obvious abuses of the system, however, there are strict regulations concerning what food stamps can and cannot be used to buy. Cigarettes, for one thing, cannot be purchased with food stamps. Neither can prepared, ready-to-eat foods, the rationale being that poor families should not depend on the more expensive ready-to-eat items but should purchase basic foodstuffs instead and prepare meals themselves. But what is a homeless person with no access to a kitchen or any other food-preparation facility going to do with a bag of rice? Many of the food items that can be legally purchased with food stamps are of little use to someone without access to a kitchen.

Of course, there are some items that can be legally purchased with food stamps and eaten as is, such as a loaf of bread and a jar of peanut butter. Since you have no home and therefore no food storage capacity, however, it is best to buy in the smallest quantities possible, thereby, of course, minimizing the return on your food dollar. (Items packaged in smaller quantities always have higher unit prices than the same items packaged in larger quantities.) Also, lacking any food storage capacity, some of the food will eventually have to be thrown away, another obvious inefficiency in the use of the system. In sum, deriving full value from the food stamp program requires that one have a means to prepare food and a place to store it, which, virtually by definition, homeless people lack.

Another example of the difficulties homeless people face in negotiating the social welfare system is found in the SSDI (Social Security Disability Insurance) program. SSDI is a federally administered income transfer program, although eligibility rules vary considerably from state to state. SSDI is probably the most generous benefit program currently available to the needy, but it is restricted to those with work histories and with disabilities sufficiently serious to prevent them from working again.[3]

Work history for purposes of SSDI eligibility is determined according to the number of quarters a person has paid FICA (Social Security) taxes. However, a lifetime of part-time, temporary, or casual labor may often result in no documentable work history as far as social security is concerned, and thus in a determination that one is not eligible for SSDI, regardless of disability.

Moreover, the person's disability must be documented by a medical doctor, which in the best of cases at least adds one additional tier of complexity to the process. Where will a homeless person with no money and no health insurance go to obtain the requisite examination? A recent study of homeless persons seeking care in St. Louis reported that more than 70% had *no* regular health-care provider and that more than half had not received any medical attention in the previous year.[4]

Some sense of the limits of SSDI as applied to the homeless can be gotten from the HCH program data. At the end of the last chapter, I pointed out that some 17% of the HCH clients were judged to be physically disabled and incapable of working. Among this group, a mere 18% in fact received SSDI benefits. A much larger fraction, about 48%, were receiving SSI (supplemental security income), a less generous income transfer program for the disabled that does not depend on work history. Perhaps most troubling of all, 40% of those physically disabled and incapable of working received neither SSDI nor SSI, and fully 25% did not receive *any* form of social benefit or entitlement.

The inherent problems of SSDI were further exacerbated by the Reagan administration's March 1981 "crackdown on ineligibility." This crackdown resulted from a report prepared by the General Accounting Office suggesting that as many as 20% of the existing beneficiaries of SSDI might in fact be strictly ineligible for benefits under the law. According to Ellen Bassuk, somewhere between 150,000 and

200,000 persons "lost their benefits before the administration halted its review of the beneficiary rolls." It was alleged that many truly disabled people were in fact *too* disabled to respond to the termination notice and had thus been unfairly stricken from the rolls.[5]

Or consider AFDC (aid to families with dependent children). AFDC is a relatively generous program of cash assistance to families (typically single mothers) with dependent children in their care. In most states, a determination of AFDC eligibility also means automatic eligibility for medicaid; AFDC mothers are also usually given priorities for Section 8 housing certificates and in some states they become eligible for subsidized day care as well.

Thus, women who are eligible for AFDC typically receive a wide range of valuable benefits as a consequence of their enrolling in the program. And yet, as best as I have been able to determine, only about half the homeless women with dependent children seen in the HCH program were receiving (or were in the process of applying for) AFDC benefits.[6] A similar result appears in Rossi's Chicago survey.[7] Why such a low rate of participation in a relatively generous benefit program? This is particularly puzzling because nearly any homeless woman with dependent children would be eligible for AFDC benefits.

Although the answer to this question is uncertain, there is impressionistic evidence to suggest that many homeless women avoid the AFDC bureaucracy (and anything else that smacks of "officialdom") for fear that their children will be taken away from them and placed in foster care. This, moreover, is *not* an unrealistic fear in many cases. Human services providers are legally and morally obligated to bring cases of child neglect to the attention of Child Protective Services or other legal authorities. The sad fact of the matter is that the *condition of homelessness itself* comes dangerously close to satisfying the legal definition of neglect, however loving, concerned, and capable the parent might otherwise be.

Consider the following: In the state of Massachusetts, the technical legal definition of child neglect is "failure by a care taker either deliberately or through negligence or inability to take those actions necessary to provide a child with minimally adequate food, clothing, shelter, medical care, supervision, emotional stability and growth or other essential care." In Massachusetts, but not in all states, there is a further proviso that would protect many homeless women: "provided, however, that such inability is not due solely to inadequate economic resources." Absent the proviso, and *every* homeless mother would seem to satisfy the technical definition of neglect, by sheer virtue of being homeless.

Suppose, then, that you are a homeless woman with children, unversed in legal niceties, uncertain of your AFDC status, riddled with anxiety over the prospect of your children being taken away from you. How willing would you be to run the risk of coming to the attention of the authorities, even if the benefit program were a useful and generous one? Just how generous would the benefits have to be to offset the possible cost—the loss of your child?

Homeless mothers with dependent children are not the only group within the homeless population that has good reason to avoid the authorities. Homeless teenagers, for example, can be put under state custody in many states if they have yet to attain the age of majority. Some homeless men have outstanding arrest warrants; others are in arrears on child support payments. Some mentally ill homeless avoid the authorities for fear that they will be involuntarily committed to a psychiatric treatment facility.

Alienation from, suspicion about, and often outright hostility toward society and its institutions are common outlooks among homeless people and are significant barriers that all persons face in ministering to the needs of the homeless population. However generous or well-meaning a care provider or social service worker might be, there is still the ever-present chance that seeking or accepting assistance will expose one to strongly unwanted outcomes. The further and equally essential point is that in many cases, the alienation, suspicion, and hostility are well-founded in that person's prior experiences. As I once saw written on a bathroom wall, "Just because you're paranoid doesn't mean they are *not* out to get you!"

The well-known GAO report, *Homelessness: A Complex Problem and the Federal Response,* sums things up nicely: "Entitlement programs do not work for many homeless persons because:

- Most homeless are single people, and hence, not eligible for Aid to Families with Dependent Children (AFDC).
- Social Security Disability Insurance (SSDI) is available only to persons who have work histories.
- Supplemental Security Income (SSI) is available to mentally disabled persons, but they have difficulty applying for and managing their benefits, especially when they are on the streets.
- Medicare is only for aged or disabled persons with work histories.
- State Medicaid eligibility rules are often contingent upon eligibility for AFDC or SSI, or even stricter standards, which exclude some homeless people.
- Many homeless do not know how to gain access to programs for which they may be eligible.

"Shelter providers also report that the various benefit programs are not accessible to many of the homeless because:

- Some programs require applicants to have a fixed address to qualify.
- Homeless persons may not be aware of possible benefits available t(them, and they need assistance in fulfilling the necessary steps to qual ify" (from the GAO report, pp. 38–39).

The above litany, of course, pertains to federal or federally funded social welfare programs. With all the noted problems, it is not surprising that "state general assistance programs [welfare] are viewed as perhaps the 'last line of defense' for the homeless, since these are the *only* programs which provide cash assistance to non-disabled and non-aged single persons. State governments, however, since the early 1980's, have been reducing their general assistance programs, by either cutting benefits or tightening eligibility standards" (GAO report, p. 24). The report adds, "Further, few general assistance programs give aid to those who have no permanent address or are residing in temporary shelters."

A good sense of the inadequacy of state general assistance programs is given by the benefit levels in Illinois. In that state in 1985, the average monthly general assistance payment to a single individual was $154. In the city of Chicago in that same year, the average monthly cost of an SRO room, the cheapest housing available, was $195. The average general assistance payment, in a word, is $41 short of covering even the cheapest available housing cost, not to mention the costs of food, clothing, transportation, and the other necessities of life. Yet, if you are not disabled, not elderly, and not the parent of dependent children, then general assistance is likely to be all you can get.

Rossi (in *Homelessness in America*) has posed an interesting question: Just what would we expect a homeless person to spend $154 a month on? As we have just seen, trying to rent adequate housing with that sum is pointless. One could spend it for food, but free meals can usually be had in the shelters, soup kitchens, and breadlines. It certainly would not cover the monthly payments, maintenance, fuel, and insurance costs for a car. Clothing is a possibility, but free clothing is also readily available through clothing outlets, missions, and shelters. And so, what can be purchased with $154 a month—$5 a day—that cannot be had for free through the social service system? One obvious answer is alcohol. Is it therefore possible that the low welfare payment levels actually encourage alcohol abuse among the homeless? "Yes," says Rossi, "it is."

SOME NOT-SO-OBVIOUS BARRIERS

Although many of the social welfare programs that we have been discussing are federal programs, most are administered and some are cofinanced through the states, and as a result the eligibility criteria, benefit levels, administrative procedures, and the like vary greatly. One important consequence of this variability is that the usefulness of entitlement programs as a means of addressing the problems of the homeless is much higher in some states than in others. In a substantial number of states, many benefit programs are essentially nonexistent or inaccessible to homeless people.

The percentage of the homeless potentially enrollable in one or another entitlement program is indeterminable unless complex state-level differences are taken into account. *In general,* as we have already seen, eligibility criteria are easiest to satisfy for elderly persons, the disabled, and clients with dependent children, and are most difficult to satisfy for single, able-bodied young males. [Another pattern of some significance is that eligibility requirements tend to be less strict (and benefit levels more generous) in the northern and eastern states than in southern and southwestern states.]

There is also a formidable *demographic* barrier to social welfare program participation among the homeless, one whose dimensions were described in Chapter 4. Although it is true that a sizable fraction of the homeless are women, children, elderly, and homeless family group members, the majority of the homeless are unaffiliated, nonelderly, nondisabled men who will seldom be eligible for any sort of benefit program other than general relief (or perhaps, in some cases, veteran's benefits). The sheer demography of the homeless population, coupled with the eligibility criteria that govern program participation, pose strict limits on how far the existing social welfare system can be pressed in solving the problems of the homeless.

As indicated earlier, many state governments, along with the federal government, have been engaged in decade-long efforts to control social welfare spending. One common strategy has been to tighten eligibility restrictions, or in other words, to shrink the size of the eligible recipient pool. This is often done under the guise of "getting the cheaters off the rolls." Another even more common strategy has been to reduce benefit levels or, what amounts to the same thing, not to increase benefit levels at a rate commensurate with the increasing cost of living.

Rossi and his co-workers have calculated benefit levels for various programs in constant 1985 dollars, to show how the purchasing power of these benefits has eroded over time. Entitlement programs that have been indexed to the consumer price index (such as social security) have fared extremely well. In 1968, the average social security pension payment was worth $295 in 1985 dollars; the average payment in 1985 was $479 in 1985 dollars. Thus, the value of a social security pension has actually increased by 62% since 1968.

Social security, however, is for all practical purposes the *only* benefit program of which this is true. According to Rossi's calculations, the average SSI old-age payment value declined from $217 in 1968 to $164 in 1985; the average AFDC payment value declined from $520 to $325; the average Illinois general assistance payment value declined from $322 to $154, and so on. (It is useful to keep in mind while considering these figures that the 1985 dollar is only worth about one third of the 1968 dollar.) At one time not long ago, or so it would appear, many of these benefit payments would have been adequate to sustain a stable housing situation. The sharply declining real value of the average social welfare benefit, especially since 1980, is therefore no doubt one reason homelessness has been on the increase.

THE NATIONAL HCH EXPERIENCE[8]

As I have already mentioned, the National Health Care for the Homeless program had as one specific and well-defined goal the enrollment of as many homeless clients as possible in social welfare programs for which they were eligible. A recounting of the HCH program experience in this respect will therefore show just how firm the barriers noted above are.

The data collection instrument used in the HCH research project had a series of prompts asking whether the client was enrolled, at the time of contact, in any of the most common entitlement programs specifically: medicare, medicaid, Veteran's Administration programs (all sorts), SSI/SSDI, food stamps, social security, welfare (including AFDC), or other. This, to be sure, is not a complete list of programs in which homeless people might participate, but it covers the major ones. To avoid any possible confusion, here is a short summary of what each of these programs is:

- *Medicare* is a federally administered health insurance program for the elderly; eligibility is automatic for anyone eligible to receive social security benefits.
- *Medicaid* is a joint federal-state program of medical coverage for the indigent. Medicaid eligibility varies considerably from state to state; in

all states, persons on Aid to Families with Dependent Children (AFDC) are automatically medicaid-eligible, but other eligibility criteria differ between states.

- *Veteran's Administration* programs consist of all benefit programs administered by the federal Veteran's Administration, including veteran's pensions and medical benefits.
- *SSI* (supplemental security income) and *SSDI* (social security disability insurance) are income-transfer programs for the physically and mentally disabled, the latter restricted to those with work histories, the former not.
- The *food stamp* program is run through the U.S. Department of Agriculture and is based on a coupon system; persons receive food stamps and use them in lieu of cash to make food purchases.
- *Social security* includes all income transfer programs administered through the U.S. Social Security Administration, chief among them old age and survivors insurance (OASI).
- *Welfare* covers a wide range of state and local income transfer and related benefit programs, including AFDC (which is a national program administered through the states) and various others (known locally as general assistance, public relief, and so on).

How many homeless people receive some sort of assistance from one or more of these social welfare programs? Setting aside approximately one quarter of the clients whose benefit status was never determined, the split among the remainder was very nearly 50–50 between no benefits and any benefits. About half the HCH clients, in other words, were enrolled in some sort of entitlement program, and the other half were not. This summary figure, of course, averages over a range of extreme variability; project-to-project, the proportion of adult clients enrolled in any entitlement program varied from less than one quarter to more than 80%. Still, as an approximate national average over all participating cities, we can conclude that not more than about half of the homeless receive any form of social welfare assistance, despite the extreme poverty and inordinately high levels of disability characteristic of the group. Similar findings have been reported in many other studies.

The longer a client was active in the HCH health-care system, the higher the odds that he or she would be receiving some assistance. To illustrate, 43% of the clients seen once and only once were enrolled in at least one benefit, whereas 52% of the clients seen more than once were enrolled. This fact points to *some* underutilization of existing programs and underscores the need for fuller program participation among the homeless. Still, the relatively high proportion of one-time contacts known to be enrolled in an entitlement program

(43%) illustrates an important point; namely, that most of the HCH clients destined ever to be enrolled in benefit programs were already enrolled when they first made contact with the HCH system.

Among those not enrolled at the point of first contact, many would simply not have been eligible; some who were otherwise eligible will have refused to participate for their own reasons; still others would have been too disordered, intoxicated, or otherwise debilitated to make the effort to enroll them worthwhile. The point is that the number of homeless persons who are eligible to participate, willing and able to participate, and not already participating is likely to be fairly small, and this in turn sets strict limits on what advocates and case-workers for the homeless can accomplish through their own direct efforts.[9] These data suggest, in other words, that the underutilization problem, while nontrivial, may not be as widespread as many have argued.

Among the HCH clients receiving any benefits, relatively large fractions participated in more than one entitlement program. Among adult clients receiving welfare, for example, some 47% also participated in medicaid and 41% also received food stamps. Overall, about half of those receiving any benefit received more than one.

As would be expected, benefit statuses of HCH clients varied across background characteristics. The proportion receiving any benefit increased regularly and sharply with age, was higher among blacks than among other ethnic groups, and was somewhat although not sharply higher among women than men. Also of interest is the fact that those with chronic physical disorders were more likely to be receiving benefits than others.

To repeat, the proportion of clients receiving any benefits was highly variable across the HCH projects, ranging from a low of 22% to a high of 82%. Since a leading program goal was to enroll as many clients as possible in programs for which they were eligible, the project-to-project variation in the proportion of clients receiving any benefits was analyzed in great detail. Omitting the technical details and complexities of the analysis, the findings are summarized below:

First, it was obvious that the major—indeed, the overwhelming—factor was the relative leniency of each state's eligibility criteria for the major entitlement programs. Most of the explanation for the project-to-project variation in the proportion of clients receiving any benefits is simply that some projects were located in states where it is relatively easy to get people enrolled.

A second factor was compositional differences in the projects' client bases. For example, the proportion of women clients varied considerably across projects (from 22 to 49%); there were similar although smaller differences in the proportion of clients over age 65. Since women and the elderly are more likely to receive benefits than nonelderly men, it was thought that these compositional differences might turn out to be important. However, they were not. The effect in the statistical analysis for this variable, although positive, was small and not statistically significant.

A final factor in the analysis was the relative effort invested by each project in doing benefit work for their clients. The reasoning was that projects investing the most effort would have the most success and would therefore be the ones with the highest proportions of clients receiving benefits. But here too, the facts were somewhat different: the effect of project effort was again small and only marginally significant statistically.

Thus the conclusion was reached that compositional differences in client bases across projects were not significantly related to clients' benefit statuses; direct efforts by the projects to enroll clients in benefit programs were marginally significant; state-level differences in the leniency of eligibility criteria were overwhelmingly significant. Indeed, to indicate something of the relative power of these factors, the three variables in the analysis (effort, compositional differences, and leniency of eligibility criteria) together were found to explain 78% of the variation in the proportion of clients receiving benefits state-to-state. Of the 78% of variation explained, 3% was explained by composition of the client base, 6% by project efforts, and 69% by state-level differences in leniency. Thus, the latter is overwhelmingly the most important factor.

The implications of these results are significant. Whatever the level of effort on behalf of homeless clients, however long and hard social service caseworkers strive to enroll them in appropriate benefit programs, whatever the characteristics of the homeless population being served, in the end nothing counts for as much as state-to-state differences in the leniency of eligibility criteria. The problem, in short, is apparently not that homeless persons seriously underutilize the programs available to them, or that deficiencies of effort by the social service system result in many homeless persons not receiving the benefits they are due. The problem is that many states make it virtually impossible for homeless persons to receive any benefits through the exclusionary nature of their eligibility determination.

Thus the solution to the problem of inadequate welfare benefits for the homeless is to be found not in more diligent effort and not in cracking the intransigence of local welfare and other social service offices; relief must be sought at the level of state legislatures, where the criteria for participation and the benefit levels are set.

In order to confirm the point more directly, HCH clients were divided into four benefit status groups. For each of the seven major categories of entitlement programs, clients were sorted as follows:

GROUP I: Clients not known to be enrolled in the program in question, and with no evidence that the project was trying to get them enrolled. Roughly, it can be assumed that most of the clients in Group I either did not need or were simply not eligible for the program. This assumes, of course, that if there were any reason to think that the client had a need or might be enrollable, there would be some evidence of effort toward this end, consonant with the program goals.

GROUP II: Clients not known to be enrolled in the program in question, but with evidence that there was some work in progress to this end. In these cases, the project has made documented efforts to get the client enrolled, but without any indication of success. Group II can be assumed to consist of potentially enrollable clients, since the evidence of work in progress is, ipso facto, evidence of a judgment on someone's part that the client may be qualified for the program.

GROUP III: Clients known to be enrolled in the program in question, but with no evidence that the client's participation resulted from the direct efforts of the project itself. In most cases, Group III clients were already participating in the program at their point of first contact with HCH.

GROUP IV: Clients known to be enrolled in the program in question, and with evidence that the client's participation did result from the direct efforts of the project itself.

Adding together Groups III + IV reveals the proportional enrollments according to type of program. The most common benefits received by HCH clients were welfare/AFDC and medicaid (about 20% in each case), followed by food stamps (about 15%), then SSI/SSDI (10%), then social security, VA benefits, and medicare, in that order (each with about 5%). It is obvious that the large majority of clients were not enrolled and, so far as can be ascertained, probably not enrollable in each of the seven specific programs listed.[10] The fraction *enrolled* or *potentially enrollable* (Groups II + III + IV) was highest for welfare/AFDC (26.3%) and medicaid (24.2%), and lowest (not surprisingly) for medicare, social security, and VA benefits (5 to 6% in each case).

Thus we come to another important conclusion: Of all the benefit programs potentially available to the poor, the indigent, and the homeless, local and state general assistance (welfare) tends by far to be the most widely accessible; as the GAO report noted, general assistance will often be the *only* form of assistance available to the nondisabled and nonaged unless there are dependent children involved. Based on the above results, the fraction of the urban homeless either receiving welfare assistance or potentially eligible to receive welfare assistance is concluded to be on the order of 25% (specifically, 26.3% in these data).[11] Some three quarters, therefore, are found not to be eligible for or participating in even the one program of assistance that has the least strict eligibility criteria. This is perhaps the single best answer to the question of why the existing social welfare system does not already contain a solution to the problem of homelessness.

Of those who were in fact enrolled in each program (Groups III + IV), the percentages enrolled through the direct efforts of the projects were all less than 10%. About 6% of the clients receiving food stamps did so through direct project efforts; this was also true of about 5% of the clients receiving welfare/AFDC or SSI/SSDI and of about 3% of the clients receiving medicaid. Keep in mind that these are the results achieved in a program with a specific and definite goal to enroll as many homeless people as possible in all programs of assistance for which they are eligible.

We must therefore stress again that most of the homeless people seen in the HCH program were already receiving all the entitlements due them when they first made contact with HCH. The initial assumption, that there would be large fractions of eligible but nonparticipating clients whose lives could be improved simply by "plugging" them into the existing system, was wrong.

At the same time, the process of enrolling clients in social welfare programs is typically a time-consuming one. It is important to note that these data showed a considerable amount of "work in progress" for clients not currently enrolled. If all clients with an indication of work in progress eventually received the benefit in question, then the proportions ultimately receiving each benefit through the direct efforts of the HCH projects would increase substantially. In the case of welfare/AFDC, for example, the ultimate percentage (of those enrolled) who would have been enrolled through direct project efforts [(II + IV)/(II + III + IV)] could go as high as 25%; in the case of SSI/SSDI, as high as 28%; in the case of food stamps, as high as 20%. But in no case would the figure have gone beyond one third of the total.

In fairness to the HCH program, it must also be stressed that the process of getting clients enrolled in appropriate benefit programs is not the whole of the struggle. Once a client is or has been enrolled there is a second process of *keeping* them enrolled that can ofter consume as much or more of the total effort. In some cases, progran enrollments must be renewed every month; in all cases, they must be renewed periodically. New income certifications must be filed, pro gram participation forms must be updated, payees must be arranged, and so on. I suspect, in the end, that as much of the total HCH project effort in the entitlements areas was spent in keeping clients enrolled and in otherwise attending to the management of clients' benefits as in getting them enrolled in the first place.

SOME TENTATIVE CONCLUSIONS

Contrary to at least one popular stereotype, only about half of all homeless people receive any form of social welfare benefit; the other half survive on their own resources, without assistance from the wel- fare safety net. Most homeless people are already receiving most of the benefits to which they are entitled; the half who do not partici- pate in any assistance program are, for the most part, simply not eli- gible to do so. This too contradicts the stereotypical view that large fractions of the homeless are not participating in programs for which they are eligible. The problem is not so much one of underutilization but one of ineligibility, despite the obvious and in many cases press- ing level of need.

The extreme poverty of the homeless population has already been described. The average homeless person in America survives on something between 25 and 40% of the poverty-level income. Given this fact, even small levels of assistance can make a substantially large difference in a person's day-to-day living situation. To someone ac- customed to living on two or three dollars a day, an additional two or three dollars constitutes a major improvement. For this reason, the effort to expand program eligibility criteria to encompass larger frac- tions of the homeless is doubtlessly worthwhile. It is likewise worth- while to assure that homeless people do receive all the assistance due them; here the only proviso is that this will already be true of most homeless people.

At the same time, the ultimate goal of social service on behalf of the homeless is *not* to enroll them in benefit programs. This is one means to a larger end, that of getting people off the streets or out of the shelters and into some reasonably stable housing and social situation. It must be further added that the benefit levels typical of most social welfare programs are so low as to make only a marginal contribution to this larger end.

The state of Massachusetts, to illustrate, has one of the most generous AFDC programs to be found anywhere in the country.[12] Twice in the past few years, the state has been ordered by the state courts to increase AFDC benefits, because even the relatively generous Massachusetts benefits are not adequate to sustain a minimally decent standard of living. In the first order, the court compared the average costs of rental housing in the state with the average AFDC benefit and concluded that the benefit level could only be adding to the problem of homelessness.[13]

The point is that even if all homeless persons were successfully enrolled (and kept enrolled) in every existing benefit program for which they are eligible, the total benefit being received by most would still not be sufficient to solve their housing and related problems. The benefit work to be done on behalf of homeless people is best seen as crisis intervention only. Even in the best of circumstances, it does not and cannot represent an adequate solution to the more basic problem.

The vast expansion of social welfare programs in this country in the postwar period has already been granted. The amounts now being spent by the federal government—and by state and local governments—on social and human services are literally staggering, easily dwarfing any other category of expenditure. Under the Reagan administration, the various social and human services programs were continually on the block in an effort to control federal spending and rein in the deficit. Largely through congressional intervention, many of the proposed cuts were thwarted, and in the end, the great bulk of the welfare system was left more or less intact.

Yet there remain large fractions of the neediest and most destitute who receive no welfare benefits at all. Equally troubling, many who do receive benefits find that stable, secure housing for themselves and their families remains well beyond their means. As I have tried to emphasize, many homeless people would *still* be homeless even if they were full participants in the welfare system.

What, then, is to be done? Massive cuts in social welfare spending, such as Reagan tried to engineer, proved not to be politically popular, at least not in Congress. But there is probably not much sentiment, even in a Democratic Congress, for massive increases either. In thinking about possible solutions, political and economic realities must be kept in mind.

NOTES

1.   In 1984, the estimated total federal budget amounted to $854 billion
Of that sum, $238 billion was spent on national defense (28%) and $438 bil
lion was spent on human resources (51%). The outlay for social security an
medicare alone ($240 billion) exceeded the outlay for defense.
The domination of the federal budget by social and human services outlay
is a relatively recent development; as late as 1970, the defense outlay ($82
billion in that year) exceeded the human services outlay ($75 billion). One
critical factor involved in the progressively increasing share spent on social
and human services is that a 1975 Act of Congress tied social security benefits to the Consumer Price Index; benefit levels for social security recipients,
that is, are now adjusted annually to account for any increase in the cost of
living. (Data from *The Statistical Abstract of the United States,* 1975, p. 309.)

2.   It has come to light, for example, that there are people running shelters for homeless women with children who are not aware of the WIC program. WIC is an acronym for Women with Infants and Children and is
designed to provide adequate nutrition and medical care to infants and children who would otherwise not receive it. Virtually any impoverished and
homeless mother with dependent children would be eligible for WIC benefits, but only if she or her care providers and caseworkers were aware that
the program exists.

3.   Indeed, the criterion is that the person must be physically or mentally
incapable of performing *any* kind of "substantial gainful work" for which he
or she is qualified, *whether or not* such work is available in the local area.

4.   Healthcare for the Homeless Coalition of Greater St. Louis, *Program
Description,* 1986, (mimeo'd).

5.   See E. Bassuk, "The Homeless Problem." *Scientific American,* 251 (1),
pp. 40–45 (1984). The SSDI material appears on p. 41.

6.   See Julie Lam, *Homeless Women in America: Their Social and Health
Characteristics* (unpublished Ph.D. dissertation, Department of Sociology,
University of Massachusetts, Amherst, 1987) for data on the rate of AFDC par-
ticipation among homeless women with children.

7.   *The Condition of the Homeless in Chicago* (op. cit.), pp. 97–101.

8.   The following material is adapted from J. Wright and E. Weber, "Determinants of Benefit-Program Participation among the Urban Homeless: Results from a 16 City Study." *Evaluation Review,* 12:4 (August, 1988), pp. 376–
395, and is used here with permission of the publisher.

9.   It should *not* be inferred from this point that there is no work needed
to be done in the entitlements area for a homeless person who is found to
be receiving some benefit at the point of first contact. For example, such
persons may be eligible for additional benefits for which they are not currently enrolled. And even when people are already receiving all the benefits
for which they are eligible, there is the further problem of keeping them
enrolled in programs and ensuring that they make the best use of the benefits available to them.

10. Overall, as reported earlier, about half of all HCH clients were enrolled in at least *one* benefit program; it is also the case that the majority were not enrolled in any one *specific* benefit program. The proportion of adult clients who were enrolled in any specific benefit program is always less than 25%.

11. Keep in mind that the category "welfare" in these results *includes* AFDC. Most persons receiving SSDI, SSI or social security pensions would not also be eligible for welfare. Still, including the figures for these three benefits programs, the proportion of the homeless participating or apparently eligible to participate is still well under half.

12. In 1983, the average monthly AFDC payment per family varied across states from a low of $89 (Mississippi) to a high of $516 (Alaska). The Massachusetts average, $422, ranked as the fourth highest benefit, level among the 50 states, exceeded only by Alaska, California ($447), and Minnesota ($425). See *Statistical Abstract of the United States, 1985,* p. 381.

13. See "State says it can't afford to comply with welfare ruling," Daily Hampshire Gazette (Northampton, MA), 6 January 1987, p. 14. The latest ruling would boost the basic benefit for a family of three from the current $476 to "as much as $926 a month."

Who Can Be Helped, and How?

The only sensible way to begin this discussion is to admit that there are many among the homeless who cannot and will not be helped. Some will resist or refuse assistance; some are so profoundly destroyed already that they are, for all practical purposes, beyond help. Many of the chronically homeless alcoholics such as Radar (whose story was recounted at the opening of this book) have not been cured or rehabilitated despite literally hundreds of well-meaning attempts. Indeed, one is tempted to conclude that Radar and others like him are destined to die in much the same circumstances as they now live—homeless, besotted, broke, useless to any collective social purpose, dependent for survival on the largesse of society.

The point granted, I hasten to add that the existence of such elements within the homeless population is no excuse for diminished, mean-spirited or coldhearted efforts on behalf of the remainder. The solution is not indifference, but careful marshaling of available resources to help those that can be helped and those most in need.

HOMELESSNESS AS A POVERTY PROBLEM

I have argued throughout this book that homelessness is basically a poverty problem; it is created by a large group of extremely poor and socially marginal people who cannot compete successfully in an ever-dwindling low-income housing market. Viewed in this light, the solution to homelessness is ultimately easy: Do away with poverty and you will simultaneously do away with most homelessness as well.

This is a very attractive, elegantly simple position, most of all because by eliminating poverty, a considerable dent would be made in a wide range of other problems: crime, drugs, illegitimacy, disease, hunger, and a stunning assortment of other social ills. The hitch, of course, is that despite many decades of effort, no one has yet figured out just how to do away with poverty at an acceptable cost to society.

Why not just wipe out poverty in the nation? It is easy to see that the barrier is *not* primarily an economic one. How much money would it take to raise the income of every person in this country over the official poverty line? There are, as stated earlier, about 35 million people living below the poverty line. Some of them are only a little below the line, others are far below it. For purposes of a crude cal-culation, I have used the 1980 U.S. census data, the most recent dat reported that have sufficient detail on the incomes of the poor t allow a calculation.

The calculation proceeds as follows: in the 1980 U.S. census ther were 6,860,582 single individuals (i.e., one-person households) below the poverty line. The poverty level in that year for a single-person household was $4180. In contrast, the median income of those 6,860,582 single individuals below the poverty line was $2192. Thus the median income of the group was $1998 dollars below the poverty line, which is in turn the amount of additional income the average person in the group would need to be above poverty. Simple multi-plication will show that it would cost about $13.7 billion to raise all the single individuals above poverty level.

There were likewise 1,901,450 two-person households below pov-erty in 1980. The poverty line for a two-person household was $5363; the median income for the households in question, $3038; the aver-age income shortfall was $2325. Another $4.4 billion would be needed to raise all of these households out of poverty.

Continuing across all the household size groupings, we end up with a bottom line figure: $34.5 billion to bring everyone in the United States above the poverty line in 1980. Allowing for inflation in the years subsequent to 1980 and increases in the proportions and numbers of persons living below the poverty line since that time, we might guess that today it would take about $40 billion, about $1000 or so for every man, woman, and child now living below poverty.

It is useful to point out that $40 billion is not, at least theoretically, an unattainably large sum. Paper losses in the Black Monday stock market crash of October 1987 were said to amount to more than $500 billion, more than ten times what it would take to eradicate eco-nomic poverty in the country for one year. If the nation can sustain a capital loss on that scale and continue despite it, then we could cer-tainly sustain a "capital loss" of $40 billion to wipe out poverty.

Likewise, $40 billion would amount to a little less than a 10% in-crease in the 1984 federal human services budget ($40 billion/$438 bil-lion = 9.1%), and to a bit less than a 5% increase in the 1984 federal budget *in toto* ($40 billion/$854 billion = 4.7% increase). In fact, be-tween medicaid, AFDC, food stamps, general assistance, and the like, there is little doubt that we already spend $40 billion a year or more on the poverty problem. Certainly, one tenth or more of the existing human services budget must be spent in providing social welfare assistance to the nation's poverty families. Why not just give them the cash and be done with it?

The above suggests that the fundamental barrier to the eradication of poverty in this nation is *not* economic, but social and political. We lack not the funds, but the collective will to do it.

We do not seem to mind giving billions of dollars to doctors and health-care facilities to provide health services to the poor (that, after all, is what medicaid does), but we do seem to mind giving the same money to poor people themselves so they can purchase their own health care. Likewise, via Section 8, we give several additional billions to landlords to provide housing for the poor, rather than give them the money directly so they can purchase their own housing. We want to increase the food purchasing power of the poor so that they need not go hungry. But rather than give them money, we give them food stamps that can only be used for food.

The common denominator in all these examples (and in dozens of additional examples that could easily be appended) is that *we don't trust the poor with our money*. The operant mentality seems to be that if we just gave them the money, they would spend it on frivolous things. So we provide them with free services or subsidized services instead. In the process, we make a lot of doctors and landlords rich and we create a vast cadre of middle-class bureaucrats, welfare workers, case managers, and the like to administer our service programs. This approach may well ameliorate the problem of poverty, but it certainly is not going to solve it.

The above examples are instructive as we begin to think about what can be done with the homelessness problem in America today. The poverty example makes it obvious that we have to keep social and political constraints, as well as economic feasibility, in mind. Utopian fantasy about a "national right to housing law," although fun to contemplate, falls into the same category as "eliminate poverty." Both are out of the question in the current political environment. This is a sad unfortunate truth.

Assistance programs to ameliorate the more degrading aspects of a homeless existence are potentially in the cards. Some important legislation to this end has already been enacted. But a radical restructuring of the nation's political economy to eliminate homelessness (or poverty) once and for all probably is not in the offing.

The difference between amelioration and solution is the same as the difference between aspirin and penicillin. Aspirin lessens the severity of the symptoms of an infection; penicillin cures the infection itself. In the case of homelessness, the penicillin would be tough medicine to swallow: a direct and massive intervention of the federal government into the private housing economy to halt the continuing destruction of low-income housing and to provide vastly increase housing subsidies to the poverty population—all that just as the first step.

In an era when cutting the federal budget by many billions is doxology of Political Faith, agreed to as an imminent necessity by persons of nearly all political persuasions, no one can be expected to look kindly on a suggestion that we need to raise the federal expenditure on poverty or any other social problem by some $40 billion annually. To the contrary, it is the blood of the human services budget that is being spilled on the budget-cutting altar.

WHAT DOES HOMELESSNESS COST SOCIETY?

On the other hand, there is little doubt that homelessness already costs a lot of money. Until recently, most of the money spent in this area has been by the state and local governments, and private money—not federal funds. Indeed, as late as 1985, the General Accounting Office was able to describe the federal role in homelessness as largely "supplemental" to various state, local, and private efforts. Being dispersed across 50 state jurisdictions and tens of thousands of local jurisdictions, we have no firm collective sense of just how expensive the problem of homelessness has become. But consider the following:

The Human Services Administration of the city of New York operates a large number of shelters and other facilities for the homeless. One set of facilities is comprised of some 50 or so welfare hotels that are used at least in part to house homeless women with children once their time in the transitional shelters has been used up. Yvette Diaz and her family live in one of the larger and better known of these hotels.

It is not unusual for the city of New York to pay as much as $1500 to $1800 *per month* to rent one of these hotel rooms. This works out to $20,000 or more per year. The same sum, used as a direct housing subsidy to the Diaz family, might well allow them to rent that "clean apartment in a safe neighborhood" of which Yvette so fondly dreams. Instead, they live in a rundown, ramshackle, roach-infested old hotel, the three R's of Yvette's existence.

While New York City is no doubt an extreme example, the point that we as a society are already spending large sums of money each year to deal with the homelessness problem is valid. That being the case, it is therefore appropriate to ask whether the money is being spent in the most appropriate, useful, or effective possible ways.

The current costs of homelessness are not only dispersed across a large number of jurisdictions, they are also often indirect and hard to calculate. For example, research has shown that the rate of tuberculosis among the homeless is perhaps a hundred times the rate in the general population. There is no serious doubt that homelessness increases the number of persons at risk from this disease. What, then, does it cost local departments of public health across the nation to detect and treat the additional cases of tuberculosis that rising homelessness has caused? No one knows exactly, but we can be certain that it is not cheap.

Let me pose a series of rhetorical questions in the same vein: How many urbanites around the nation now customarily avoid certain downtown areas because of the large numbers of homeless people who gather there? And what is the dollar value of the trade and commerce that is thereby lost to businesses operating in those areas? How much lost tourism has there been in New York now that there are, by some estimates, 30,000 homeless people strewn around the city?

What does it cost us collectively to operate the many tens of thousands of temporary shelters, soup kitchens, missions, drop-in centers, and such that have sprung up to address the needs of the nation's homeless? How much needless overutilization of public hospital emergency rooms could be avoided if the homeless were given adequate primary health care? What is the dollar value to society of the wasted human capital represented by the "tattered bundles of humanity" that now litter our streets and consciences?

What would society be willing to pay to break the hold of extreme poverty on a bright young girl like Yvette Diaz, or an honest, hardworking family like the McMullans? What is it worth to us economically when we enable the otherwise destitute and downtrodden to live productive, independent lives?

What price do we pay in the court of world opinion when our major newspapers run almost daily stories about America's homeless on their front pages? What do we give up in negotiations with the Soviets over human rights when it is manifestly obvious to anyone that many of our own citizens do not enjoy decent housing, adequate nutrition, or suitable health care?

Again, my point is only to stress, first, that the problem of homelessness already costs a lot of money, and second, that it is very difficult to state in precise terms just what the costs have been.

Whether it would be cost-beneficial to spend X billions now to eradicate homelessness and thereby to avoid Y billions in costs in the fu
ture cannot be answered with the information at hand. But at th
very least, the total costs of homelessness to the nation are hig
enough by any reckoning to justify at least some new policy initi
tives. If we can afford the social and economic expense of living wit
homelessness, then we can also afford to do something about it.
What, then, should we do?

PREVENTION: RENT INSURANCE

One obvious problem in trying to figure out what can be done
about homelessness is that there are so many different kinds of
homeless people, each with their own unique problems and needs.
The needs of a homeless family with two or three children are very
different from the needs of an unattached homeless alcoholic. That
homelessness is "not one problem but many" also implies that there
is no one solution or approach that would work for all, but that many
different things need to be done.

One important fact that surfaces in the research studies reviewed
in this book, with many implications for this discussion, is that most
homeless people are *not* chronically homeless, but are *episodically*
homeless (or in a substantial fraction of cases, recently homeless for
the first time). A reasonable guess is that not more than one quarter
to one third of those homeless at any given time are chronically without housing. The most common pattern, instead, is one of occasional
periods or episodes of homelessness punctuating stretches of more
or less stable housing circumstances.

Among the substantial majority who are not chronically homeless,
but become temporarily homeless now and again through the vicis-
situdes of personal or economic misfortune, we can and should begin to think of *prevention*; that is, of measures that could be used to
stave off the periodic onset of homelessness in the first place. Remember, we are talking about half or more of the persons homeless
on any given evening.

What, then, is the pattern of existence that leads to episodic
homelessness, and where in that pattern might we fruitfully intervene? The essential problem is one to which I have alluded on many
previous occasions: many poor and near-poor families and individuals live dangerously close to the economic edge, especially those
whose housing costs consume half or more of their monthly income.

These households typically have few if any savings that provide the margin of security in the event of short-term problems or needs. In any given month, a single unexpected expense will often leave them with too little money to pay the rent. An unanticipated medical expense, or needed but unbudgeted repairs to the family car, or the unplanned but suddenly necessary replacement of some household good, or a layoff or a strike—any of these can easily leave an economically marginal family or person with insufficient resources to cover other equally necessary living expenses. Most people who found themselves in such a situation would, of course, have someone to whom they could turn for the needed short-term assistance, but the homeless are those of whom this generally is not so.

To say that a person or household lives "dangerously close to the edge" is to imply that people fall over the edge now and again, and that is exactly what is meant by episodic homelessness. Living close to the economic edge is like playing Russian roulette: pull the trigger often enough and sooner or later the gun fires. In other words, with a sufficiently large number of persons living sufficiently close to the edge, some of them will be over the edge at any given time and thus homeless.

In the analysis of the HCH data, I was able to distinguish between short-term (episodic) and long-term (chronic) homeless people. The assessed "reasons for homelessness" among the former group tended to revolve around housing, jobs, and related economic issues—eviction for nonpayment of rent, loss of job, general money problems, troubles with roommate or family, and the like. Among the latter, alcohol, drug, and mental-health problems were far more commonly cited. We could therefore go far toward preventing occasional homelessness if we could somehow create a pool of resources on which the episodically homeless could draw in times of economic misfortune.

The idea here is something along the lines of rent insurance, where, for a nominal sum, a family or a single individual could protect against the short-term loss of income that, by living too close to the edge, can cause a consequent loss of housing.

There is already a federal analogue to the sort of program I have in mind: the national flood insurance program (which has been on the books for about 15 years). In this case, the government determines the households and other properties that are at risk for flooding and then requires them to purchase flood insurance at a federally subsidized rate. The general idea is that in the long run it will prove cheaper to subsidize flood insurance on high-risk properties than to offer relief and rehabilitation assistance in the aftermath of a flood disaster.

Might the same not be true for families or persons at high risk for homelessness? Why not a national rent insurance program—available say, to any person or household living within 150% of the poverty line and spending more than 40% of its income on housing?

There would be many practical details to work out in such a pro gram, and this is not the place to address them all. How many times a year could a participating household or individual file a claim? How big could the claims be? How large a subsidy would the government have to provide to make such a program attractive to the insurance industry? What rates would have to be set? Would participation be mandatory for those in the highest risk categories? Satisfactory solutions to an equally wide range of practical issues were, however, worked out for the national flood insurance program, and I am confident the same could be accomplished here.

For want of access to a few hundred dollars once or twice a year, many persons and households suffer periodic episodes of a homeless existence. Insuring against this will not solve the larger problem, but it might well forestall or prevent the periodic homelessness of large numbers of economically marginal persons and families. It would at least give these persons and families somewhere to turn in the event of economic misfortune.

In some respects, poverty-level families with dependent children already have a version of rent insurance in place, i.e., the Aid to Families with Dependent Children (AFDC) program. Many homeless families consist of mothers with dependent children whose homelessness typically endures only while their AFDC paperwork is pending.

The existing range of benefits available to AFDC mothers in some states is laudable: a monthly cash payment, medicaid eligibility, often a Section 8 housing certificate, and in some states eligibility for subsidized day care as well. Some national standardization of the AFDC benefit package along these lines would be exceptionally useful although costly.

A more expeditious processing of AFDC paperwork would be adequate to prevent homelessness in many of these situations (especially when the homelessness of the mother and her children results from some marital disruption or similar loss of a breadwinner's income). One might also consider a national version of the emergency cash grants now given in some of the more generous states; these are quick-turnaround emergency funds given to AFDC-eligible families to sustain them in a stable situation while the AFDC paperwork clears.

Mothers, fathers, and intact parent pairs who are responsible for the care of dependent children should not be forced into a condition of homelessness for any period or reason. The ensuing devastation to the children, now described and documented in a number of studies, is too high a price to pay. The further and grossest inequity is that the children who suffer the most, bear no direct responsibility for their unfortunate fate.

To be sure, not all of the episodically homeless are families. Many single individuals suffer the same uncertain economic circumstances, and, to make matters worse, are rarely eligible for programs of assistance, excepting possibly general relief. In these cases, unsteady employment or no employment at all will often lie at the heart of the matter; they are stably housed when they are stably employed, and unhoused when they are not.

As discussed earlier, many people of this general description apparently avoid literal homelessness through the generosity of family and friends, and become homeless only once the patience or resources of these benefactors is exhausted. Perhaps what is needed in such cases is a program of cash subsidies to offset the burdens incurred by the households involved. Call it Aid to Families with Dependent Adults. At minimum, the federal government could recognize the added burdens assumed by household units attempting to maintain their adult members through periods of unemployment or other economic misfortune and give these households some break at income tax time (perhaps by the simple expedient of a more liberal and inclusive definition of "dependent").

One can think of many additional and more or less costly preventive measures that might be taken to thwart episodic homelessness. Among these would be the following:

1. To expand the range of workers covered by Unemployment Compensation. I mentioned earlier that nearly three quarters of those unemployed in any given month receive no unemployment benefits. Many of the extremely poor work in marginal or secondary sectors of the economy where fringe benefits such as health insurance or unemployment compensation are rare. Extending joblessness benefits to the unemployed in these sectors would forestall the short-term loss of housing in many cases.

2. To increase the length of time that unemployment compensation is paid. Unemployment benefits now end after 27 weeks without work. There is already a federal provision dating to 1981 that provides

13 extra weeks of benefits for the unemployed in states with high unemployment rates, but no state currently qualifies for these extended
benefits. On average, general assistance recipients in Chicago have
been unemployed for 18 or 19 months, and the homeless more than
40 months, both far in excess of even the expanded period (roughly
10 months). But there are still many for whom an additional 2 or 3
months of assistance would make an important difference.

3. To make employers aware of, if not responsible for, the often
severe economic hardship and dislocation attending large-scale lay-
offs, firings, and plant closings. The social and economic effects of
"capital mobility" are only beginning to be researched. One study
reports that 30% of the plants in existence in the United States in
1969 had been closed by 1976; the estimates are that plant closings
now eliminate nearly one million jobs a year.[1] No one knows how
many of the workers who are displaced by capital mobility eventually
become homeless, but certainly some must. At present, there is no
national policy that delineates the responsibilities of capital to its displaced labor force.

4. To create a program of low-interest bridge loans that would be
available to persons and families faced with impending homelessness. This is a variant on rent insurance. Obviously, most families
who are at the very edge of homelessness would be exceptionally
poor credit risks and could not rely on credit through private sector
lending institutions to sustain them over a rough period. Since we
often find that, sooner or later, we have to *give* these people and
families money anyway—directly through welfare, AFDC, and the
like, or indirectly through the provision of services for the homeless—perhaps it makes economic sense to *loan* them money in the
early period to sustain them in a stable housing situation. Why
should it not be possible for an economically marginal family to go to
the local welfare office and ask for a loan if they prefer it to direct
cash assistance? How much ultimate welfare dependency might such
a provision forestall?

5. To enact more stringent regulations governing the eviction of
persons and families caught in a short-term economic bind. Much
progress has been made in many localities in addressing tenants'
rights, and certainly the landlord's right to receive rent has to be re-
spected. After a sufficiently long period of nonpayment, eviction is
often unavoidable. The only serious issues are how long that period
should be and whether landlords ought not to be required to take
extenuating economic circumstances into account.

6. To establish a program of emergency "work relief" whereby dislocated workers would be offered short-term publicly subsidized employment to help them through an unsteady period. Public employment (sometimes called "workfare") is a contentious issue on many grounds. The unions rightly object to public employment when it takes away the jobs of their members; civil libertarians often object when public employment is suggested as a condition for assistance or relief. But the fact remains, even in the face of chronically high levels of unemployment among central city youth, that there is no shortage of work that needs to be done, including work for which those of modest or marginal skills and training are qualified. I am not talking here about "makework," but about things like clean streets, freshly painted park benches, mowed schoolyard lawns, and the like. Based on the HCH data, more than half of the unemployed but employable homeless are indeed looking for jobs. With no shortage of work that needs to be done, why is it not possible to find something productive and useful for them to do?

The employment situation in many of the central cities often makes it literally impossible for a young man of marginal training or skill to lead a productive, independent, self-supporting adult existence. Consequently, many turn to crime; some become homeless; a wide range of other social problems is created or abetted. Publicly subsidized work as the "employment of last resort" certainly represents a preferable alternative.

It would be foolhardy to suggest that any one of these measures would eliminate homelessness, even episodic homelessness; some people will continue to fall through the safety net no matter how tightly it is knit. At the same time, it is unquestionably true that there exists a large stratum of episodically homeless people whose periods of homelessness are triggered by short-term economic misfortune, and whose homelessness could therefore be prevented by measures that would sustain them through tough times.

These measures could be tied to various work provisions: only those available to work are eligible. Make clear that we are talking about short-term relief only. If you are still in trouble next month, we won't be able to help you. Couple all such measures to existing job counseling, job placement, and retraining programs; do whatever can be done to prevent a similar need from arising again later. But above all, at least make it possible for a family or individual at or near poverty to get through a tough stretch without the loss of their home.

HOMELESSNESS AS A HOUSING PROBLEM

As stated in Chapters 2 and 3, while homelessness is certainly a complex and multifaceted problem, the *ultimate* cause is the severe and widening shortage of low-income housing units. This is a prob-lem that all homeless people must confront. If low-income housing continues to disappear, and the poverty rate stabilizes or, worse, continues to increase, then the problem of homelessness will also increase, no matter what other kinds of measures are enacted.

The basic housing problem is a simple one: there is much more money to be made in supplying housing to the affluent than to the poor. Land and construction costs being what they are, it is very dif-ficult for the private sector to break even on the construction of low-rent units, much less to make a reasonable profit. The progressive gentrification of many cities has also meant that the customary flow of older housing from more to less affluent hands has been arrested. The near-total disappearance of the flops and rooming houses has left many cities without "housing of last resort" for the most mar-ginal segments of the population, making the temporary shelters for the homeless the only alternative to sleeping in the streets.

Unfortunately, there is no economical solution to the housing di-lemma. To talk housing is to talk big bucks. Moreover, additional housing subsidies for the poor, along the lines of Section 8, will be largely pointless unless the actual *supply* of affordable units is in-creased. Section 8, to be sure, was enacted on the optimistic assump-tion that the resulting increase in low-income housing demand and in the housing "purchasing power" of the poor would stimulate the private sector to increase the housing supply, but that has not hap-pened. There may be some alternative in this matter to a renewed federal commitment to the subsidized construction of low-income units, but frankly, I fail to see what it might be.

In some of the more progressive jurisdictions these days, develop-ers are required to include at least some moderately priced housing in their development plans, as a condition for the issuance of zoning and building permits. Given the sums of money being made on real-estate development, this does not seem an untoward or onerous re-striction. Perhaps some federal matching money could be targeted for large-scale development projects, to increase the numbers of low-rent units to be built. Certainly something along these lines could be considered at least for development projects that will displace, or un-house, large numbers of low-income people.

In an earlier era of downtown revitalization—the era of urban renewal—the persons and households displaced through renewal were often relocated, for better or worse, in public housing projects. Widely derided as "high-rise ghettos" or as "instant slums," there is little doubt that the public housing projects, while solving at least some problems, created many others. This is not the place to recount their dismal history. The era of public housing projects ended, at least symbolically, with the much-publicized dynamiting of the Pruitt-Igoe complex in St. Louis. Still, it is reasonable to wonder whether something like the public housing projects is not the only realistic alternative to the homelessness that now confronts us. Perhaps, with the benefit of hindsight, we could avoid many of the earlier mistakes.

In thinking about the housing nexus, we must also keep in mind that most homeless people are single, unattached, unaffiliated persons whose housing needs are therefore distinctive. If we cannot summon the political courage to build publicly subsidized apartment complexes, perhaps we can at least underwrite the construction and operation of rooming or boardinghouses, perhaps with on-site social, medical, mental health, and alcohol services as part of the basic package.

Some efforts along these lines are already being expended in several cities in California. With a combination of public and private money, old hotels are being purchased, refurbished, and outfitted as "aftercare" housing for recovering homeless alcoholics. While rooming houses of the sort I have in mind would be more expensive than shelters, they may not prove to be prohibitively more expensive. And they would at least provide the minimal dignity of some private space for each person.

Unlike shelters, the operating costs of these rooming houses could also be recovered, at least partially, via rents charged to the tenants. It would, of course, be essential to set up the fee schedule on a sliding scale, with the actual rent pegged to the tenant's ability to pay. Those with no ability to pay anything might trade labor for rent—for example, by working in the kitchen or as part of the custodial staff.

None of the housing options that confront us is cheap, and all of them have strongly negative symbolism. There is no doubt that many of the public housing projects were blights on the urban landscape—but so is homelessness. The subsidized rooming and boarding homes for the unattached homeless that I propose have struck at least one critic as "federally sponsored flophouses," which, of course, is precisely what they would be. Still, it is obvious that the nation is not going to eliminate poverty anytime soon, and the poor—even the desperately poor—have to live in *something*. Whatever that something turns out to be, we, society at large, will have to pay for it. If there is a cheaper, more attractive alternative than public housing projects and subsidized flophouses, it has escaped my attention.

SHORT-TERM AMELIORATION

We cannot expect any one of the above suggested measures, or all of them taken together, to prevent all cases of homelessness in all times, places, and circumstances. There has never been a time in this or any other society when there weren't at least some homeless people, and there never will be. No matter how much prevention we do, ameliorative measures—temporary shelter, food lines, and the like—will still be necessary for those who have fallen through the net.

Whatever stand one wishes to take on the "how many homeless" question, no one I know doubts that there are more homeless people than there are shelter spaces. Most shelters for the homeless report being filled to capacity most of the time, having to turn some people away or refer them elsewhere. It is thus easy to recommend that the existing short-term shelter capacity be expanded. In many cities, a *doubling* of capacity would be the minimum necessary to handle the short-term need.

There are many problems revolving around the shelters other than sheer capacity that should be addressed. First, with perhaps one or two exceptions, I have never been to a shelter that struck me as even a marginally nice or comfortable or attractive place to stay, even for a night. The adjectives that would be used to describe even the better homeless shelters include crowded, dirty, run-down, stark, and depersonalizing. For the worse shelters, roach-infested, hellish, dangerous, and degrading spring quickly to mind. I think it is a fair bet that many cities provide better accommodations for their stray animals than for their stray people, perhaps on the assumption that minimally decent accommodations do not encourage strayness among dogs.

In discussions of this issue with policymakers at the city level, I have often sensed a subtle, certainly unspoken feeling that if the shelters are made *too* nice, it will only encourage homelessness. Perhaps it would. At the same time, we are talking here about minimal standards of decency (and, not incidentally, about standards of fire safety and public health as well). We could easily stand not only to increase the shelter capacity in place but to greatly improve the existing stock as well.

The shelters tend not only to be run-down and shabby, but often dangerous, and many homeless people avoid them for just that reason. They are dangerous in two senses: first, because they often provide housing to dangerous people; and second, because their nature is such as to encourage the spread of infectious and communicable diseases. Many of the injuries treated in the national HCH projects were injuries sustained by shelter residents in altercations with other residents. This is a particular problem when the debilitated, disoriented, and defenseless are indiscriminately mixed with tough, aggressive, young men.

Having large groups of often enfeebled people sleeping close together in dormitory-style accommodations, sharing communal bathing, toilets, and dining facilities, must certainly abet the transmission of infectious and communicable diseases, ranging from minor although annoying upper respiratory infections at one extreme to serious and potentially fatal disorders such as tuberculosis at the other. When designing shelters for the homeless, the safety and physical well-being of the residents require more consideration than they normally are given.

Another problem is that many shelters operate with formal or informal exclusionary rules that reduce access among certain groups of homeless people. Barring people from shelters because they are intoxicated or actively hallucinating or otherwise disruptive is obviously justifiable on many grounds, but it renders highly problematic the securing of overnight shelter among the chronically alcoholic and the mentally ill.

Intact homeless families have posed special problems, in that there are very few shelters set up to satisfy their specialized needs. Providing even temporary shelter will often require that the family unit be broken up, the husband going off in one direction, the wife and dependent children in another, the adolescents, if any, in still a third. One temporary solution employed in many cities is to put these families up in hotel or motel rooms, but this is relatively costly and can only work on a very short term basis. In the long term, of course, the only morally defensible solution is to assist these families in every way possible to secure permanent and stable housing. There is thus an evident need for transitional shelters where whole families can be kept together for the weeks or months necessary to find acceptable housing.

Next to, or perhaps ahead of, the need for temporary shelter is the need for adequate nutrition. There are places where destitute people can get a free meal in almost every city of any appreciable size; indeed, the breadlines have returned on a scale unlike anything witnessed in this country since the Great Depression. The adequacy of the diet to be obtained in such outlets is open to question; the few studies that have been done suggest that the typical soup kitchen diet is more or less acceptable in terms of most of the basic nutrients but is exceptionally high in salt, starch, sugar, and fats.[2]

The New York City standard for meals served in its shelters for the homeless is that the menu provide at least one third of the recommended daily requirements for all known nutrients. (Where the remaining two thirds are to come from is a mystery.) Analysis of the actual meals served shows that they usually meet this standard, but the foodstuffs used to accomplish the purpose often are not ideal: lots of eggs (a cheap source of protein but very high in cholesterol and saturated fat), cheese (available free from the federal government but very high in salt), and processed foods such as lunch meats, hot dogs, sauerkraut, pickles, and so on.

One complicating factor is that many homeless people have chronic physical health problems whose proper management requires an appropriate and specialized diet of the sort not likely to be available in many, if any, soup kitchens or breadlines: the low-sodium diet essential for the management of hypertension, or the glucose-restricted diet necessary for the proper management of diabetes, for example. It is surely true that the nutrition to be obtained in free food outlets is preferable in all ways to that obtained by scavenging food items from street sources. Still, it is worth remembering that even homeless people sometimes have specialized dietary needs that are not met by current practice.

Next to food and shelter is the need for health care. Homelessness is an existential condition that is strongly destructive of physical well-being; as such, homeless people are often much more ill, on the average, than people in general or even poverty persons in general. Being poor, the homeless will rarely have health insurance to draw on when they need medical attention. A number of studies have shown that many homeless people utilize hospital emergency rooms as their primary health care facility, a needlessly expensive option.

Recent national legislation has begun to address the health care needs of the homeless population. The Stuart B. McKinney Homeless Assistance Act, enacted by Congress and signed by the President in the summer of 1987, provides for a wide range of support services on behalf of the homeless population, including specifically the provision of primary health care services. The experiences of the HCH projects demonstrated conclusively that it is indeed possible to engage the nation's homeless population in a professional system of health care.

It is useful to stress that before the existence of the HCH program, this was *not at all obvious*. The homeless, it was frequently said, were too hostile toward institutions, too suspicious and disaffiliated, too hard to locate, and too noncompliant to help very much. This, to be sure, is no doubt true of a sizable fraction, but it is not true of them all. What the HCH program demonstrated, first and foremost, was that *something* could indeed be done to alleviate the health problems of many homeless people. What Congress has decided is that it is time to get on with the task.

It remains to be seen how long the federal commitment to homelessness, as embodied in the McKinney Act, will endure. Currently, the Act is only funded for 2 years; the hope is that many local health-care projects and facilities, once "seeded" with federal money, will find other ways to stay in business once the federal commitment expires. An alternative that can be justified on many grounds ranging from the moral to the sheerly administrative is a permanent federal commitment to basic health care for all needy, indigent, and medically underserved elements of the American population, whether they happen to be homeless or not.

COORDINATION OF SERVICES

One especially commendable stipulation in the McKinney Act is that local health programs for the homeless coordinate service delivery with independent mental health, alcoholism, and drug abuse programs. As we have seen, as many as two thirds of the homeless population may suffer one or more of these disorders, and perhaps one quarter suffer two or more; thus there is an evident need for coordination, communication, and resource sharing between health-care programs on the one hand and mental health, alcoholism, and drug programs on the other.

Historically, the multiply disabled homeless have tended to fall between the cracks of the existing service delivery system. One consequence of improved coordination of services among these various components should be integrated treatment programs designed specifically for those who are both alcohol abusive and mentally ill (the most common pattern of co-occurrence). The need for such programs is a very pressing and, to date, largely unaddressed one.

An equivalent need exists for better coordination of the *health-care* system (including physical and mental health as well as alcohol and drug programs) with the larger *social service* system. The McKinney Act requires local applicants to be eligible to receive payments under medicaid and medicare, the obvious intent being to reclaim as much of the cost as possible under the provisions of existing programs. This will ensure at least some degree of coordination between health-care facilities, on the one hand, and local medicaid and social security offices, on the other.

Other social service systems of particular importance to the homeless population, as we have seen, include food stamps, general assistance, the various disability programs, Veteran's Administration benefits, and, for the families with dependent children, AFDC. Because of the inherently fragmented nature of these and other social services, the most (and perhaps only) effective means of coordination is aggressive case management and advocacy for the unique needs of homeless people.

THE SOCIAL WELFARE SYSTEM

I have argued that the existing social welfare system, even if fully exploited, does not and cannot represent a complete solution to the problems of the homeless, many of whom are not eligible to receive services under the provisions of the existing system. This tends to be especially true of young single males, the largest demographic subgroup within the homeless population. There are, to be sure, some homeless persons eligible to receive services who are in fact not receiving them; one essential component of effective case management is to insure that homeless persons receive all the benefits, services, and entitlements for which they are eligible. But the preceding analysis showed that most homeless persons are already enrolled in most programs for which they are eligible.

Perhaps the single greatest problem currently inherent in the social welfare system is the steady erosion in the value of program benefits over the past decade or two. There is no cheap solution to this problem either; sharp increase in benefit levels is needed, in order to return them to their former real value. As in the Massachusetts case discussed at the end of Chapter 7, the average benefit levels now characteristic of most social welfare programs are so low in purchasing power that they can only be contributing to the rise of the homelessness problem. (Social Security is the major exception.) If a destitute family or individual is unable even to maintain a stable housing situation on the average assistance payment, then perhaps we should cease the delusion that we even *have* a social welfare system.

Somewhere between one fifth and one quarter of the homeless in fact are employed, even if only sporadically; somewhere between three quarters and four fifths, therefore, are not. Among those not employed, more than half (some 60% or so) are assessed by their care providers as definitely or probably not employable. (Interestingly, a number who were assessed as definitely or probably not employable were also reported as "looking for work.") Many are unemployable because of their addiction to alcohol, many because of their poor mental health, some because they are physically unable to work. And yet the proportion of homeless receiving any sort of disability payment (such as SSDI, SSI, or veteran's disability) is not more than about one fifth. While no one wishes to encourage alcoholism among the homeless by defining it as a disabling condition that qualifies a person to receive SSDI, we should recognize that mental disorders are often no less disabling than physical disorders and accordingly liberalize the eligibility criteria for persons with such conditions.

ALCOHOLISM

It should be recognized that chronic alcoholics comprise a large share of the chronically homeless, and a proportionally much smaller share of the episodically homeless. Indeed, only chronic psychiatric difficulties rival alcohol abuse as the precipitating condition for a chronically homeless existence, especially among chronically homeless men.

The existing alcohol treatment system is not well suited to the unique needs of homeless alcoholics. The best treatment and rehabilitation facilities imaginable can have but modest effects if, at the end of treatment, the patient returns to a life on the streets, which has been the typical case. There is an evident need for aftercare facilities for recovering homeless alcoholics where the maintenance of sobriety is encouraged and rewarded.

One promising (although relatively expensive) avenue is the so-called alcohol-free hotel (mentioned earlier in this chapter) that provides housing and social services to recovering homeless alcoholics who have finished a detoxification or alcohol rehabilitation program. Although no quantitative evaluations of these programs have been conducted, the impressionistic evidence suggests a considerable degree of success in maintaining sobriety. Certainly the chances for success are better if one can provide an environment where sobriety is valued than if the patient is released to the streets, where drunkenness is often a way of life.

Many homeless people encounter long delays while awaiting placement in a detoxification or rehabilitation program. Regardless of aftercare provisions, the sheer number of alcohol (and drug) treatment slots available needs to be increased. It is difficult enough to persuade many homeless alcoholics to accept treatment. A delay of days, weeks, or months in finding an open treatment slot is therefore a particular frustration; in the interim, the motivation to accept treatment may and often does abate.

MENTAL ILLNESS

Next to alcohol abuse, mental illness is the second leading problem within the homeless population, especially among the chronically homeless, and particularly among chronically homeless women. The existence of large numbers of mentally ill persons among the homeless may or may not be proof that deinstitutionalization has failed as a social policy, but it is certainly evidence of some unanticipated problems in the implementation of that policy.

One obvious problem is that the initial promise of a wide range of community-based mental health services, including "halfway housing" for those otherwise not reintegrated with family or community, has never been kept. Many communities proved unexpectedly resistant to the location of such facilities in their midst. This has been called the NIMBY problem—not in my back yard. That is, everyone seems to agree that such facilities are needed, even desperately needed, but no one seems to want them nearby. It is an unfortunate, if understandable, attitude.

As stated in Chapter 6, the elimination of all institutions is not the only alternative to large, impersonal, and degrading establishments; smaller, more humane, and more effective institutions are another option. I do not think we do the homeless mentally ill any service in our continued insistence that institutionalization is to be avoided at all costs. Many of the homeless mentally ill clearly need some sort of 24-hour-a-day total care living environment; to provide anything less is little short of cruel.

Part of the problem is that many people have been seduced by the so-called labeling theory of mental illness: the theory that if you label people mentally ill, or treat them as though they are mentally ill, then they will come to exhibit the symptoms of mental illness and eventually *become* mentally ill. There is no doubt some value in such a viewpoint. At the same time, no serious researcher doubts that much mental illness is organic, biochemical, and/or neurophysiological in character, and likewise, no serious researcher believes that people with problems of this sort will show dramatic improvement in their mental health simply because others no longer treat them as though they are mentally ill.

Certainly much good was accomplished in unchaining the gates of the mental institutions, but some evident harm was also done in the process, harm that must now be redressed. There are some among the mentally ill homeless who have not been and will never be successfully reintegrated into the larger society. It is appropriate to be concerned about the civil liberties and rights of these people, but not if it leads to a complete disregard for their safety, comfort, and physical well-being.

CONCLUSION

In the end, the dynamics of homelessness derive from large-scale trends in the nation's political economy. Homelessness is the unforeseen and, one hopes, unwanted residuum of larger social changes that cannot and will not be rolled back.

Changes in the national and world economies have led to a progressively increasing demand for highly skilled, technically trained labor; there has been a corresponding and irreversible decline in the demand for unskilled, untrained labor. The result is a perpetual employment problem for those of low or marginal skills—and with it, a large pool of persons living at the economic margin, at high risk of homelessness.

The urban social system that formerly encapsulated this segment of the population—the skid row areas, complete with their missions, cheap boardinghouses, soup kitchens and day-labor outlets—has largely disappeared, its housing function now assumed by the shelters for the homeless, its employment (or income) function taken over, fitfully and only in part, by the social welfare system.

In conjunction with all this has come the virtual decimation of the low-income housing supply. The high incomes and personal affluence that have accrued to many as a result of economic and technical change have also altered the character of urban housing demand, demand that leaves progressively less and less room (or economic incentive) for housing the poor. Obviously making matters worse are the recent large-scale changes in our treatment of the mentally ill, the progressive devaluation of the social welfare dollar, the decriminalization of public drunkenness, rising rates of drug abuse, and all the many other factors touched on in this book.

The rise of the new homeless thus provides a case study in what Robert K. Merton described as the "unanticipated consequences of purposive social action." The "revitalization of downtown" was intended to arrest the process of urban decay that had become endemic in many cities. And yet the result—as palpable as it was unintended—has been a sharp increase in the numbers of permanently displaced homeless people living in our cities. Likewise, the intent of deinstitutionalization was to return the mentally ill to their families and communities, to environments less degrading and probably more therapeutic than the large mental hospitals were. The result, however, has been to consign a segment of the mentally ill population to a street existence.

Much the same can be said for all the various trends and developments that I and many others have identified as contributing to the homelessness problem. No one really *wanted* homelessness on the scale that we now experience it; no one in their right mind actually *likes* the idea of hundreds of thousands of destitute and homeless people wandering aimlessly and hopelessly over the urban landscape. Even the coldest of hearts would prefer that homelessness not exist.

If the creation of the problem was largely inadvertent, the solution assuredly cannot be. There is no ongoing trend or development anywhere in this society, as far as I can tell, that will somehow automatically solve the homelessness problem given enough time. The large numbers of homeless children now being seen almost everywhere imply that the homelessness of the next generation is already well underway.

Thus, we can either ignore the problem, letting it run its own course, growing or abating as it will; or we can intervene along one, several, or all of the lines I have suggested in the previous pages. Solutions to or, minimally, ameliorations of the problems of homelessness are assuredly within our means. Homelessness on the present scale is something that should never have been allowed to happen in the first place. Compassion, mercy, and social justice dictate that we do all we can to end it, if not in this decade, certainly in the next, so we can march upright into the twenty-first century, unfettered by this national disgrace.

NOTES

1. See C. Perrucci, R. Perrucci, D. Targ, and H. Targ, *Plant Closings: International Context and Social Costs* (Hawthorne, NY: Aldine de Gruyter, 1988), pp. 20–24.

2. M. Winick, "Nutritional and Vitamin Deficiency States." Ch. 7 in P. W. Brickner *et al.* (eds.), *Health Care of Homeless People* (New York: Springer, 1985).

BIBLIOGRAPHY

Alcohol, Drug Abuse, and Mental Health Administration, (1983). *Alcohol, Drug Abuse, and Mental Health Problems of the Homeless: Proceedings of a Roundtable.* U.S. Department of Health and Human Services, Public Health Service, Rockville, MD (31 March and 1 April).

Alstrom, C. J., Lindelius, R., and Salum, I. (1975). "Mortality among homeless men." *British Journal of Addictions,* 70: 245–252.

Archard, P. (1979). *Vagrancy, Alcoholism and Social Control.* London: Macmillan Press Ltd.

Atlas, J. and Dreier, P. (1980). "The housing crisis and the tenant's revolt." *Social Policy,* 10:4.

Bachrach, L. (1984). *The Homeless Mentally Ill & Mental Health Services: An Analytical Review of the Literature.* Report prepared for the Alcohol, Drug Abuse and Mental Health Administration, U.S. Department of Health and Human Services, April.

Bachrach, L. (1984). "Interpreting research on the homeless mentally ill, some caveats." *Hospital and Community Psychiatry,* 35 (9): 914–916. (a)

Bachrach, L. (1984). "Conference report: Research on services for the homeless mentally ill." *Hospital and Community Psychiatry,* 35 (9): 910–913. (b)

Bahr, H. and Caplow, T. (1974). *Old Men Drunk and Sober.* New York: NYU Press.

Ball, J. F. and Havassy, B. E. (1984). "A survey of the problems and needs of homeless consumers of acute psychiatric services." *Hospital and Community Psychiatry,* 35:9 (September, 1984), pp. 917–921.

Bassuk, E. (1984). "The homeless problem." *Scientific American,* 251 (1): 40–45.

Bassuk, E., Rubin, L., and Lauriat, A. (1986). "Characteristics of sheltered homeless families." *American Journal of Public Health,* 76: 1097–1101.

Beeghley, L. (1984). "Illusion and reality in the measurement of poverty." *Social Problems,* 31 (3): 322–333.

Bogue, D. J. (1963). *Skid Row in American Cities.* Chicago: Community and Family Study Center, University of Chicago Press.

159

Brady, J. (1983). "Arson, urban economy, and organized crime: the case of Boston." *Social Problems,* 31 (1): 1–27.

Brickner, P. W. *et al.* (1985). *Health Care of Homeless People.* New York: Springer.

Brown, C., McFarlane, S. *et al.* (1983). *The Homeless in Phoenix: Who Are They and What Should Be Done?* Report prepared for the Consortium for the Homeless by the Phoenix South Community Mental Health Center.

Carliner, M. (1987). "Homelessness: A housing problem?" In R. Bingham, R. Green, and S. White (eds.), *The Homeless in Contemporary Society.* Beverly Hills: Sage Publications, pp. 119–128.

Cohen, N., Putnam, J., and Sullivan, A. (1984). "The mentally ill homeless: Isolation and adaptation." *Hospital and Community Psychiatry,* 35 (9): 922–924.

Community Emergency Shelter Organization and Jewish Council on Urban Affairs. (1985). *SROs: An Endangered Species.* Chicago.

Downs, A. (1983). *Rental Housing in the 1980's.* Washington, DC: The Brookings Institution.

Erikson, J. and Wilheim, C. (eds.). (1986). *Housing the Homeless.* Rutgers University: Center for Urban Policy research.

Farr, R. K., Koegel, P., and Burnam, A. (1986). *A Study of Homelessness and Mental Illness in the Skid Row Area of Los Angeles.* Los Angeles: Los Angeles County Department of Mental Health, March.

Fingarette, H. (1988). "Alcoholism: The mythical disease." *The Public Interest,* 91: 3–22.

Fisk, N. (1984). "Epidemiology of alcohol abuse and alcoholism." *Alcohol Health and Research World,* 9 (1): 4–7.

Fodor, T. "Toward Housing the Homeless: The Single Room Occupancy Alternative." Unpublished paper.

Freeman, R. and Hall, B. (1986). "Permanent Homelessness in America." Washington, DC: National Bureau of Economic Research, August.

Harrington, M. (1963). *The Other America.* Baltimore: Penguin Books.

Hartman, C. (1983). *America's Housing Crisis.* Boston: Routledge and Kegan Paul.

Health and Welfare Council of Central Maryland. (1986). *Where Do You Go from Nowhere? Homelessness in Maryland.* Baltimore, MD: Department of Human Resources, August.

Healthcare for the Homeless Coalition of Greater St. Louis. (1986). *Program Description,* (mimeo'd).

Hope, M. and Young, J. (1986). *The Faces of Homelessness*. Lexington, MA: Heath and Company.

Hopper, K. and Hamburg, J. (1984). *The Making of America's Homeless: From Skid Row to New Poor, 1945–1984*. Report prepared for the Institute of Social Welfare Research. New York City: Community Service Society.

Institute for Research on Poverty. (1987–1988). "Tracking the homeless." *Focus*, 10 (4): 20–24.

Jones, D. L. (1974). "The strolling poor: Transiency in eighteenth century Massachusetts." *Journal of Social History*, 8: 28–54.

Jones, R. E. (1983). "Street people and psychiatry: An introduction." *Hospital and Community Psychiatry*, 34 (9): 807–811.

Kasinitz, P. (1984). "Gentrification and homelessness: The SRO occupant and the inner city revival." *Urban and Social Change Review*, 17: 9–14.

Kelly, J. (1985). "Trauma: with the example of San Francisco's shelter programs." In P. W. Brickner *et al.*, *Health Care of Homeless People*. New York: Springer, Ch. 5, pp. 77–92.

Knight, J. (1987). *Alcohol Abuse Among the Homeless*. Unpublished doctoral dissertation, University of Massachusetts, Amherst.

Knight, J. and Lam, J. A. (1986). *Homelessness and Health: A Review of the Literature*. Unpublished manuscript. Amherst, MA: Social and Demographic Research Institute.

Koegel, P. and Burnham, M. (1987). "Traditional and nontraditional alcoholics." *Alcohol Health and Research World*, 11 (3): 28–33.

Lam, J. (1987). *Homeless Women in America: Their Social and Health Characteristics*. Unpublished Ph.D. dissertation, Department of Sociology, University of Massachusetts, Amherst.

Lam, J. and Wright, J. (1987). *The Homeless Family: A Contradiction in Terms*. Unpublished paper. Amherst, MA: Social and Demographic Research Institute.

Lamb, H. R. (1984). "Deinstitutionalization and the homeless mentally ill." *Hospital and Community Psychiatry*, 35 (9): 899–907.

Lipton, F. R., Sabatini, A., and Katz, S. (1983). "Down and out in the city: The homeless mentally ill." *Hospital and Community Psychiatry*, 34 (9): 817–821.

Massachusetts Committee for Children and Youth. (1986). *No Place Like Home: A Report on the Tragedy of Homeless Children and their Families in Massachusetts*. Boston: MCCY.

Monkkonen, E. H. (1984). *Walking to Work: Tramps in America, 1790–1935*. Lincoln, NE: University of Nebraska Press.

Moore, R. and Malitz, F. (1986). "Underdiagnosis of alcoholism by residents in an ambulatory medical practice." *Journal of Medical Education,* 61: 46–52.

Mowbray, C. T. (1985). "Homelessness in America: Myths and realities." *American Journal of Orthopsychiatry,* 55 (1): 4–8.

Mulkern, V. and Spence, R. (1984). *Alcohol Abuse/Alcoholism among Homeless Persons: A Review of the Literature.* National Institute of Alcohol Abuse and Alcoholism, Rockville, MD, November.

Nashville Coalition for the Homeless. (1986). *Newsletter.* Nashville, TN.

Newman, S. and Owen, M. (1982). *Residential Displacement in the US: 1970–1977.* Ann Arbor, MI: Institute for Social Research.

Norman, C. (1986). "Sex and needles, not insects and pigs, spread AIDS in Florida town." *Science,* 234: 415–417.

Perrucci, C., Perrucci, R., Targ, D., and Targ, H. (1988). *Plant Closings: International Context and Social Costs.* NY: Aldine de Gruyter.

Redburn, F. S. and Buss, T. F. (1986). *Responding to America's Homeless: Public Policy Alternatives.* New York: Praeger.

Robertson, M. (1987). "Homeless veterans: An emerging problem?" In R. Bingham, R. Green, and S. White (eds.), *The Homeless in Contemporary Society.* Beverly Hills, CA: Sage Publications, Ch. 4 pp. 64–81.

Robinson, F. G. (1985). *Homeless People in the Nation's Capitol.* Washington, D.C.: University of The District of Columbia, Center for Applied Research and Urban Policy.

Rossi, P. (1987). "The New Homeless and the Old: Lessons from Recent Social History and Social Research." The Jenson Lecture on Sociology and Public Policy, Duke University, November.

Rossi, P. (1988). *Homelessness in America: Social Research and Public Policy.* New York: The Twentieth Century Fund.

Rossi, P. and Wright, J. "The determinants of homelessness." *Health Affairs,* 6:1 (Spring, 1987): 19–32.

Rossi, P., Wright, J., Weber, E., and Pereira, J. (1983). *Victims of the Environment: Loss From Natural Hazards in the United States.* New York: Plenum Press.

Rossi, P., Fisher, G., and Willis, G. (1986). *The Condition of the Homeless in Chicago.* Amherst, MA: Social and Demographic Research Institute.

Rossi, P., Wright, J., Fisher, G., and Willis, G. (1987). "The urban homeless: Estimating composition and size." *Science,* 235: 1336–1341.

Roth, D. and Bean, G. J. (1985). "Alcohol Problems and Homelessness: Findings from the Ohio Study." Ohio Department of Mental Health, Office of Program Evaluation and Research, July, 1985.

Roth, D., and Bean, G. J. (1986). "New perspectives on Homelessness: findings from a statewide epidemiological study." *Hospital and Community Psychiatry,* 37(7): 712–719.

R. W. Johnson Foundation. (1983). *Special Report,* 1. Princeton, NJ: Robert Wood Johnson Foundation.

Segal, S. P., Baumohl, J., and Johnson, E. (1977). "Falling through the cracks: Mental disorders and social margin in a young vagrant population." *Social Problems,* 24 (3): 387–400.

Shepherd, M. *et al.* (1966). *Psychiatric Illness in General Practice.* London: Oxford University Press.

Smith, N. (1985). "Homelessness: Not one problem but many." *The Journal of the Institute for Socioeconomic Studies,* 10 (3): pp. 53–67.

Snow, D. A. *et al.* (1986). "The myth of pervasive mental illness among the homeless." *Social Problems,* 33:5 (June, 1986), pp. 407–423.

Special Committee on Aging. (1978). *Single Room Occupancy: A Need for National Concern.* An information paper prepared for the U.S. Senate Special Committee on Aging. Washington, DC: U.S. Government Printing Office.

Stagner, M. and Richman, H. (1985). *General Assistance Families.* Chicago: National Opinion Research Center.

Stone, M. (1972). "The politics of housing: mortgage bankers." *Society,* 9:9 (July–August, 1972), pp. 31–37.

Tessler, R. and Dennis, D. (1988). *A Synthesis of NIMH–Funded Research Concerning Persons Who Are Homeless and Mentally Ill.* Amherst, MA: Social and Demographic Research Institute, August, 1988.

U.S. Bureau of the Census. (1985). *Statistical Abstract of the United States.* Washington, DC: U.S. Government Printing Office, 1985.

U.S. Department of Agriculture, Human Nutrition Information Service. (1979–1980). *Food Consumption and Dietary Levels of Low-Income Households, November 1979–March 1980.* Nationwide Food Consumption Survey, Preliminary Report No. 10.

U.S. General Accounting Office. (1985). *Homelessness: A Complex Problem and the Federal Response.* Washington, DC General Accounting Office.

U.S. House of Representatives, Select Committee on Children, Youth and Families. (1987). *The Crisis in Homelessness: Effects on Children and Families.* Hearings before the Select Committee, 24 February 1987. Washington, DC: U.S. Government Printing Office.

Vernez, G., Burnham, M., McGlynn, E., Trude, S., and Mittman, B.

(1988). *Review of California's Program for the Homeless Mentally Disabled*. Santa Monica, CA: The Rand Corporation.

Von Eckhardt, W. (1979). "New mood downtown." *Society*, 16 (6): 4–7

Winick, M. "Nutritional and Vitamin Deficiency States." In P. W Brickner *et al.* (eds.), *Health Care of Homeless People*. New York: Springer, 1985, Ch. 7, pp. 103–108.

Wright, J. (1987). *Selected Topics in the Health Status of America's Homeless*. Special Report to the Institute of Medicine, National Academy of Science, May.

Wright, J. (1988). "Homelessness is not healthy for children and other living things." *Journal of Child and Youth Services,* in press. (a)

Wright, J. (1988). "The mentally ill homeless: What is myth and what is fact?" *Social Problems,* 35 (2): 182–191. (b)

Wright, J. (1988). "The worthy and unworthy homeless." *Society,* 25 (5): 64–69. (c)

Wright, J. and Knight, J. (1987). *Alcohol Abuse in the National "Health Care for the Homeless" Client Population*. Washington, DC: National Institute of Alcohol Abuse and Alcoholism.

Wright, J. and Lam, J. (1987). "Homelessness and the low income housing supply." *Social Policy,* 17 (4): 48–53.

Wright, J. and Weber, E. (1987). *Homelessness and Health*. New York: McGraw Hill.

Wright, J. and Weber, E. (1988). "Determinants of benefit-program participation among the urban homeless." *Evaluation Review,* 14 (4): 376–395.

Wright, J. D., Rossi, P. H., Night, J. W., Weber-Burdin, E., Tessler, R. C., Steward, C. E., Geronimo, M., and Lam, J. (1985). *Health and Homelessness: An Analysis of the Health Status of a Sample of Homeless People Receiving Care through the Department of Community Medicine, St. Vincent's Hospital and Medical Center of New York City: 1969–1984*. Amherst, MA: Social and Demographic Research Institute.

Wright, J. *et al.* (1987). "Homelessness and health: Effects of life style on physical well being among homeless people in New York City." In M. Lewis and J. Miller (eds.), *Research in Social Problems and Public Policy,* Vol. 4. Greenwich, CT: JAI Press.

Name Index*

*Numbers in italics provide the page where a complete reference is given.

Subject Index